Palgrave Macmillan Studies in Banking and Financial Institutions

Series Editor: Professor **Philip Molyneux**

The Palgrave Macmillan Studies in Banking and Financial Institutions are international in orientation and include studies of banking within particular countries or regions, and studies of particular themes such as Corporate Banking, Risk Management, Mergers and Acquisition. The books' focus is on research and practice, and they include up-to-date and innovative studies on contemporary topics in banking that will have global impact and influence.

Titles include:

Elena Beccalli and Federica Poli (*editors*)
BANK RISK, GOVERNANCE AND REGULATION
LENDING, INVESTMENTS AND THE FINANCIAL CRISIS

Domenico Siclari (*editor*)
ITALIAN BANKING AND FINANCIAL LAW
Supervisory Authorities and Supervision
Intermediaries and Markets
Crisis Management Procedures, Sanctions, Alternative Dispute Resolution
Systems and Tax Rules

Fayaz Ahmad Lone
ISLAMIC FINANCE
Its Objectives and Achievements

Valerio Lemma
THE SHADOW BANKING SYSTEM
Creating Transparency in the Financial Markets

Imad A. Moosa
GOOD REGULATION, BAD REGULATION

Elisa Menicucci
FAIR VALUE ACCOUNTING
Key Issues Arising from the Financial Crisis

Palgrave Macmillan Studies in Banking and Financial Institutions
Series Standing Order ISBN: 978–1–403–94872–4
(*outside North America only*)

You can receive future titles in this series as they are published by placing a standing order. Please contact your bookseller or, in case of difficulty, write to us at the address below with your name and address, the title of the series and the ISBN quoted above.

Customer Services Department, Macmillan Distribution Ltd, Houndmills, Basingstoke, Hampshire RG21 6XS, England

---

Transforming Payment Systems in Europe

Edited by

Jakub Górka
University of Warsaw, Poland

First published 2016 by
PALGRAVE MACMILLAN

Palgrave Macmillan in the UK is an imprint of Macmillan Publishers Limited, registered in England, company number 785998, of Houndmills, Basingstoke, Hampshire RG21 6XS.

Palgrave Macmillan in the US is a division of St Martin's Press LLC, 175 Fifth Avenue, New York, NY 10010.

Palgrave Macmillan is the global academic imprint of the above companies and has companies and representatives throughout the world.

Palgrave® and Macmillan® are registered trademarks in the United States, the United Kingdom, Europe and other countries.

ISBN: 978–1–137–54120–8

This book is printed on paper suitable for recycling and made from fully managed and sustained forest sources. Logging, pulping and manufacturing processes are expected to conform to the environmental regulations of the country of origin.

A catalogue record for this book is available from the British Library.

Library of Congress Cataloging-in-Publication Data

Górka, Jakub, 1980– author.
   Transforming payment systems in Europe / Jakub Górka.
     pages cm
   Includes bibliographical references.
   ISBN 978–1–137–54120–8 (hardback)
   1. Electronic funds transfers – Europe. 2. Charge accounts – Europe.
   3. Consumer credit – Europe. 4. Point-of-sale systems – Europe. I. Title.
HG1710.G67 2015
332.1′78—dc23   2015033225

To all enthusiasts of monetary and payment systems

Contents

List of Figures

List of Tables

Preface and Acknowledgements

Mobile and electronic wallets, instant payments, cryptocurrencies, big data, cloud computing, wearables, contactless, one-click buy, social media, the Internet of Things are buzzwords we hear and read about daily. They are gradually passing into the vocabulary not only of people who are savvy about technology but also of ordinary people who are keen to find out about everything the new products and technologies have to offer. This is *signum temporis* – unprecedented and accelerating changes in consumer and business habits driven by ongoing innovation.

The European and global payments landscape is undergoing a process of continuous transformation. Although it is difficult to predict any developments over a longer time horizon, in this book an attempt is made to evaluate the trends and problems, which will, with great likelihood, define the future.

The volume covers selected topical issues regarding payment systems in Europe. It contains eight chapters. Some discuss fundamental problems such as substitution between cash and non-cash payment instruments, payment costs, demand for cash/deposits and payment culture, while others focus on new phenomena such as two-sided platforms, interoperability, private digital currencies, decentralised ledgers, blockchain, mobile payments, the problem of attaining critical mass, regulatory challenges and competition between bank and non-bank payment service providers.

In Chapter 1, Jürgen Bott and Udo Milkau show how the payment system has evolved from cash-based to interoperable current account networks, centralised business platforms and finally to decentralised virtual currency peer-to-peer systems such as Bitcoin. They emphasise the impact of digitalisation, which has triggered a tremendous growth in payment services, helping new intermediaries emerge on the market and build on a safe and trusted banking infrastructure where money transfers are executed with non-cash payment instruments that include credit transfers, direct debits, payment cards and, more recently, hybrid payment mechanisms. Digitalisation has produced disruptive innovation in a two-sided market of payers and payees. Its structure has become more complex and multilayered. Sustainable growth goes hand in hand with dynamic disruption. The Single Euro Payments Area (SEPA) project promotes integration and the necessary standardisation in Europe. It provides guidelines, rules and regulations for the traditional domain of competition between banks and non-banks (competition–cooperation nexus in retail payments) and for the competition between centralised payment platforms (traditional banking platforms, card payments platforms and alternative payment business platforms such as PayPal). Bott and Milkau detect a serious disruptive innovation gradually strengthening and gaining significance, i.e., decentralised payments in digital currencies with no need for bank intermediation and a central trusted authority (like the central bank). Such decentralised systems are based on a distributed, public and transparent ledger with the blockchain protocol. The authors assess the benefits and drawbacks.

In Chapter 2, Janina Harasim outlines general trends in the use of cash and non-cash payments instruments (e.g., credit transfers, direct debits, payments cards, cheques and e-money), describing changes in the payment mix both in Europe and globally. She includes useful and up-to-date statistics that are revealing about the demand for cash and cashless instruments in recent years. Harasim predicts a decline in cash usage and the development of cheaper and better alternatives, also in low-value transactions. She finds it important to address the problem of financial inclusion and financial education, which are the prerequisite for the development of non-cash payments. Furthermore, she sees a great potential in payment innovations such as contactless EMV cards, proximity and remote mobile payments, electronic wallets, e-credit transfers and e-direct debits. However, when it comes to ensuring the rapid diffusion of innovation, she highlights its key determinants, *inter alia*, addressing the problem of the critical mass, creating common technical standards, enhancing cooperation between payment stakeholders, and incentivising consumers and merchants. European regulations such as the revised Payment Services Directive (PSD2), the Interchange Fee Regulation (IF/MIF Reg) and national regulations on cash limits impact the retail payments market and its participants. As Harasim argues, the regulations' objectives are not always achieved, but their role cannot be underestimated. The crucial factor in driving cash out of circulation is consumers' willingness to change their payment habits.

In Chapter 3, Leo Van Hove verifies whether libertarian paternalism offers novel ways to discourage the use of cash by consumers. The interesting concept of libertarian paternalism or "nudging" originates from behavioural economics. It assumes that small changes to the choice context can impact consumer decisions, for example by steering consumers towards using particular payment instruments. Van Hove explains what is described as "nudging", i.e., the provision of soft incentives, and what is too strong or too intrusive to qualify as libertarian paternalism. When justifying the so-called war on cash (WOC), he refers to the central banks' studies on payment instruments' social costs, which show that cash is a pretty expensive means of payment compared to debit cards. Therefore, for policy reasons, its usage should be reduced. Further, Van Hove elaborates on the types of nudges that can be applied in the payments area by governments, central banks, commercial banks and merchants. There is little empirical evidence on nudging effects, however; four studies are discussed in this respect. He concludes by addressing the question of whether adopting the concept of libertarian paternalism in payments by making changes to the choice context is a promising avenue to explore.

In Chapter 4, Nikolaus Bartzsch and Franz Seitz empirically investigate whether cash is still the king, or whether card payments negatively influence demand for banknotes. They estimate the demand for euro banknotes issued in Germany using vector error correction models separately for small and high denomination banknotes and Dynamic OLS (DOLS) for medium denomination banknotes. Germany is the major issuer of euro banknotes to the Eurosystem, not only meeting the demand of its own country but also satisfying the demand from abroad. According to the data presented, over 70% of euro banknotes issued in Germany circulate outside its own territory, with the lion's share going outside the euro area. The growth in the cumulated net issuance of euro banknotes in Germany is almost entirely driven by foreign demand. Bartzsch and Seitz identify five reasons for holding cash: transaction, a store of wealth, availability of alternative means of payment (cards), size of the shadow economy and demand by non-residents. They test them econometrically by selecting adequate variables (sometimes proxies) in order to explain the demand for cash. The estimation results and conclusions are different depending on the category of banknotes (small, medium and high denominations). However, the study shows that cash is still an important payment instrument. The euro is held in high esteem outside of the euro area, as shown by the strong foreign demand for it. However, there are also other factors which, to a varying degree, determine the holding of banknotes. Seitz and Bartzsch, taking into account short- and long-term dynamics, estimate the impact of card payments in this respect compared to, among others, transaction and hoarding.

In Chapter 5, Nicole Jonker focuses on interchange fees in card payments or, more specifically, on their regulation in different countries. Interchange fees in four-party schemes are paid by acquirers to card issuers. They have long been blamed for inflating the costs of card acceptance for merchants and indirectly for consumers, causing higher retail prices (two-sided market). After years of lawsuits and investigations, public authorities in different countries have decided to intervene by capping these fees and introducing other regulations aimed at bringing more transparency and competition to the payments market. Jonker discusses regulatory measures taken in Australia, the United States, Spain, Poland and most recently in the European Union, where they took the form of the Interchange Fee Regulation that entered into force in June 2015. Regulations are compared, revealing both similarities and differences. Jonker assesses their pros and cons and attempts to determine their impact on the payments market and its participants, primarily consumers and merchants.

In Chapter 6, Jakub Górka discusses what should be done to make the competitive position of non-bank payment service providers – payment institutions (PIs) and electronic money institutions (EMIs) – equal to that of well-entrenched players: the banks. He argues that several intertwining issues are of paramount importance: (1) the right to assign account numbers compliant with the IBAN standard; (2) access to designated payment systems and to central banks' infrastructure and (3) access to bank accounts by Third Party Providers (TPPs). These issues are analysed in the light of international standards and current legislation, including the revised Payment Services Directive (PSD2). Górka refers to the results of a survey he conducted on International Bank Account Numbers (IBANs)/International Payment Account Numbers (IPANs) in which he sought to establish which authorities in the SEPA countries are responsible for assigning bank identifiers/sort codes and whether non-bank PSPs are allowed to issue IBANs/IPANs to users' payment accounts. A theoretical risk assessment of PIs' and EMIs' activity is included with the aim of showing how new entrants differ from banks. Górka presents his opinion that newcomers play a significant role in fostering competition and innovation in the payments market in Europe and that their services, including mobile wallets (which, in the future, should become fully-fledged payment accounts with an instant payment feature), will bring value-added to consumers and businesses.

In Chapter 7, Malte Krueger deals with mobile payments. As he shows, they are subject to boom-and-bust cycles. Two m-payments waves are described, the first occurring before the dotcom crash in 2000, and the second happening right now. The booms are separated by a decade of stagnation. Krueger examines what is crucial for the successful rollout of mobile payments in Europe. Reaching critical mass is not an easy task. He recognises impediments and mistakes of the past and diagnoses the current situation, starting with an analysis of new technologies such as Near Field Communication (NFC), Host Card Emulation (HCE) and tokenisation, all of which grow with the spread of smartphones and mobile internet. The success stories of m-Pesa, Apple and Square are presented, while attention is drawn to mobile P2P payments and real-time money transfers. Krueger also refers to the role of different payment service providers, including telcos, banks and shopping platforms. He explores the European policy, making critical remarks, and sums up by sharing his view on the future of mobile payments.

In Chapter 8, Harry Leinonen compares decentralised blockchain and common ledger-based payment systems, which are developing now, with the traditional centralised batch-based payment systems that have been in place for many years. Bitcoin, Litecoin, Peercoin and other virtual currencies are growing in number and are gaining popularity. They are thoroughly analysed in the chapter. Leinonen explains blockchain technology and makes clear that it could also be implemented elsewhere than in virtual currency systems, for example in traditional payment or securities clearing and settlement systems. He underlines the advantages of a decentralised blockchain ledger which could provide real-time payments with global reach in a cloud-based environment. Virtual currencies are methodically examined in terms of settlement medium, unit of account and financial instrument. Leinonen dispels some myths about Bitcoin concerning its cost, independence from third parties or the immediacy of transaction confirmation process. He also describes the Bitcoin system's shortcomings in the context of its value against national currencies and the attendant risks. What he sees as a challenge, but also an inevitable necessity, is bringing virtual currencies within the scope of regulation and supervision. Leinonen proposes licensing different types of activities performed in the virtual currency business with the aim to protect consumers and to ensure fair competition.

Each chapter has been written by academics and professionals from public and private institutions in five countries (Belgium, Finland, Germany, the Netherlands and Poland) with the aim of ensuring that the views presented are well balanced and show a variety of different perspectives. What is surprising and worth underlining is that all these perspectives smoothly complement each other. Payment systems in Europe are undergoing constant and multifaceted transformation. The many aspects of this process are analysed in this book.

I would like to thank my colleagues – the chapter authors. It was a pleasure to cooperate with all of them on this exciting project. I would also like to thank my editors at Palgrave Macmillan, who helped guide it towards publication.

Notes on Contributors

Nikolaus Bartzsch works at the Deutsche Bundesbank, where his responsibilities include forecasting, modelling and decomposition of cash demand and analysing the cash cycle in Germany. He has published several articles on these issues. After his academic education in Economics at the University of Bonn, he took part in a trainee programme at the Hamburgische Landesbank. In 2000, he switched to the Economics Department of the Deutsche Bundesbank where he worked in the money market liquidity section and in the financial accounts section.

Jürgen Bott is a professor at the University of Applied Sciences in Kaiserslautern, Germany and a visiting professor and guest lecturer at several universities and business schools. He holds a PhD from the University of Frankfurt. Before his academic career he gained working experience with JP Morgan, the Deutsche Bundesbank and McKinsey. He is an academic advisor to the European Commission and member of a number of supervisory boards. He is a consultant for banks, their customers and international organisations, including the International Monetary Fund.

Jakub Górka is an assistant professor at the Faculty of Management, University of Warsaw, Poland. Currently, he is a member of the Payment Systems Market Expert Group (PSMEG) helping the European Commission to prepare legislative acts or policy initiatives on payment issues. He is the author of two books on payments and money, as well as numerous research papers, reports and business articles. He has prepared expert opinions for the National Bank of Poland, the Polish Ministry of Finance and private non-profit and commercial companies engaged in the payments business.

Janina Harasim is a professor at the Faculty of Banking and Financial Markets and Vice-Rector for Science, Research and Academic Staff Development at the University of Economics in Katowice, Poland. She lectures on bank competition strategies, payment systems and retail payments market. She is a member of the Polish Academy of Science. Her recent research focuses on issues related to retail banking, alternative financial services and the transformation of the retail payments market. She is the author and co-author of more than 120 publications on these and other subjects. She is a member of supervisory boards and of The Coalition for Non-Cash Payments and Micropayments established by The Association of Polish Banks.

Nicole Jonker is a senior economist at the Nederlandsche Bank (Dutch central bank), Retail Payment Systems Policy Department. She has been involved in various empirical studies in retail payments. Her articles have appeared in *Applied Economics, De Economist, Journal of Banking and Finance, Journal of Economic Perspectives, Journal of Economic Behavior and Organization, Journal of Financial Market Infrastructures, Kyklos* and *Review of Network Economics*. She is also involved in policy work related to retail payment systems, including payment cards and interchange fees. She holds a PhD in Economics from the University of Amsterdam.

Malte Krueger is Professor of Economics at the University of Applied Sciences in Aschaffenburg, Germany and works as a consultant for PaySys Consultancy in Frankfurt. He holds a PhD in Economics from the University of Cologne. He has worked as a research fellow at the Bank of Spain, and at the universities of Western Ontario, Durham, Karlsruhe and Frankfurt as well as at the European Commission. His articles on payment issues have appeared in academic and industry journals.

Harry Leinonen is a financial counsellor in the Financial Markets Department at the Finnish Ministry of Finance, where his remit focuses on payment and settlement systems. He has, over the years, participated in several domestic and international committees and working groups on payments and securities settlement issues especially within the European Central Bank and Commission. He was attached to the Bank of Finland for several years in an advisory capacity, having previously worked in the Finnish banking industry for about twenty years in positions connected to payments system activities. He is the author of several articles and books on these issues.

Udo Milkau is the Head of Strategy and Market Development for Transaction Banking at DZ BANK, Germany. After graduating in Physics, he worked as a research scientist at CERN, CEA de Saclay and GSI. He holds a PhD from Goethe University, Frankfurt. Thereafter, he held management positions in the automotive industry and consulting firms before joining DZ BANK. He was also a part-time lecturer at Goethe University Frankfurt. He is a member of the Payments Services Working Group of the European Association of Co-operative Banks in Brussels and of the Operations Manager Contact Group (OMCG) of the European Central Bank (ECB).

Franz Seitz is Professor of Economics at Weiden Technical University of Applied Sciences, Germany. He holds a PhD from Regensburg University. Prior to joining academia, he worked at the Deutsche Bundesbank. He has published numerous articles in national and international journals, *inter alia*, on payment systems and cash topics. For many years he has been a consultant to the European Central Bank and the Deutsche Bundesbank.

Leo Van Hove is Professor of Economics at the Vrije Universiteit Brussel, where he teaches courses in monetary economics and the economics of information. His current research interests include payment instruments, network effects, e-commerce and access to finance. His articles on these and other subjects have appeared in the *Journal of Money, Credit, and Banking, International Journal of Electronic Commerce, Economic Modelling, The Service Industries Journal, Energy Economics, European Journal of Operational Research*, and *Journal of Media Economics*. He is invited regularly as a guest speaker by central banks and payment providers.

1
A Market for Payments – Payment Choice in the 21st Century Digital Economy

Jürgen Bott and Udo Milkau

1.1 Introduction

One approach to define what a 'market' is was given by Michel Callon, who suggested a difference between a market and a marketplace in English language (1998): *'While the market denotes the abstract mechanism whereby supply and demand confront each other and adjust in search of a compromise, the marketplace is far closer to the ordinary experience and refers to the place in which exchange occurs.'* The term 'marketplace' conjures organised transactions between buyers and sellers like a street market or a shopping mall. The object of those transactions – goods or services – has a price, and this price will be paid at the end of the transaction.

From this perspective, a payment is part of a transaction (to settle the price), but is there a market for payments itself? Looking back in history, a British gentleman paid tradesmen, such as a carpenter or a tailor, in pound sterling (silver) but an artist or a barrister in guineas (gold); and perhaps he paid with a bill of exchange (paper) or even with grandma's china (article of value) when he had run short of money. The payment itself had a price for one or both agents of the transaction, whether a monetary one or non-monetary such as delay, convenience, trade usances, image or trust. Today, customers perceive a variety of different options to pay: cash (banknotes), credit transfer, credit cards, PayPal, payments via iTunes accounts, iDEAL in the Netherlands, Faster Payments and Paym in UK, Swish in Sweden, Alipay or Tenpay in China, M-Pesa in Kenya, vouchers at the canteen, loyalty reward points at some merchants, Open Metaverse Cent (a system for payments in different virtual worlds), virtual currencies based on decentralised consensus systems (such as Bitcoin) and so on, depending on the situation.

This list is, obviously, a collection of different things: payment instruments, payments systems, payment providers and 'digital alternatives'. From banking point of view this list seems to be a strange mixture. But these are the payment options customers can select (as consumers) or offer (as merchants). Carl-Ludwig Thiele, a member of the board of Deutsche Bundesbank, described the future of payments as: *'colourful and manifold'* (Thiele, 2015, translation by the authors). This 'colourful and manifold' development is typical for an emergent phenomenon called a market, as Russell Roberts (2005) defined: *'We call these [emergent] phenomena "markets". Most of what we study in economics called markets are decentralized non-organized interactions between buyers and sellers.'*

To understand payments as a market for different, dynamically developing payment options is a new point of view compared to a centrally planned and regulated payment system. On the one hand, a payment systems landscape may be static for some decades, but show an evolution over time including leaps forward in development. For example, the current 'digitalisation', such as the Internet and smartphones, has provided technical solutions at marginal differential costs and literally in the hands of the consumers, which triggered a wave of new payment offerings. On the other hand, payments cover only a small part at the end of a whole commercial process. They are closely related to the specifics of those different processes depending on industry, situation, frequency of transactions and relationships between the agents: a onetime payment in a restaurant with a tip is a different process compared to a regular, but varying payment to a utility.

For a closer look at the market for payments and the development from cash to interoperable networks, centralised business platforms and decentralised consensus systems, it is worthwhile to start with a brief consideration of the transition from the cash-based ecosystem to the traditional four-party payments systems with a (salary) bank account, which emerged in the late 1950s/early 1960s in many European countries.

1.2 Industrialisation of payments

In many European countries, the days of the pay envelope ended in the late 1950s to early 1960s. This development illustrates the transition from a cash-based economy to electronic payment systems, which was initiated by innovative companies that recognised the benefits of electronic payments. As subject matter expert working in a medium-sized enterprise in Germany, Karl Weisser wrote about that development (1959, translation by the authors): *'It is surprising that in the age of electronics and automation, in payroll accounting and wage payments many companies still use methods that belong to the time of day labourers'*. Those innovators in the 'real economy' applied the industrial paradigm of electronics and automation to the banking sector and established the payment systems with the four parties: companies/merchants and their banks on one side and employees/consumers and their 'retail' banks on the other one. Before that point in time, the contribution of banks to connecting companies/merchants and employees/consumers was limited mainly to cash distribution and cash collection services. Banks' core services – term, scale and risk transformation in corporate banking (equity, bonds and loans) and retail banking (saving versus loans) – were more or less separated from payments. With the introduction of the salary account, banks started to become an integrated part in the economic system along process chains such as purchase-to-pay.

The introduction of the retail current account, together with payment settlement between the banking sectors, was an enormous innovation because it combined the strength of banks in running accounts in a trusted, secure and stable manner with the industrial paradigm of electrification and automation of processes. With this first industrialisation of payments (see Figure 1.1), account-based services for retail payments have become part of core banking services. Electronic payments were established in the – regulated – space of banking with fees typically paid be the initiator of payments.

By including cashless payments services almost seamlessly into core banking functions, banks have enriched the processes of their customers. They contributed significantly to economic prosperity with integrated operational and financial features. With the further development of payment standards, the cash-based landscape changed to a highly efficient payments ecosystem, as central component current accounts are the hub for nearly all electronic payments and settlement of liquidity between the banks. As current example, in Germany today, nearly 80% of all payment transactions are 'retail' payments between consumers and merchants (bill payments by credit transfer, direct debits and card payments; 'B2C') or between companies and employees (including pensions or social benefit payments) and only about 10% are peer-to-peer payments between private customers (Milkau, 2010). It has to be remarked that about 80% of all payment transactions at the point of sale in Germany are still in cash (Wörlen *et al.*, 2012), whereas much fewer point of sale transaction are made by cash in other European countries. Nevertheless, the introduction

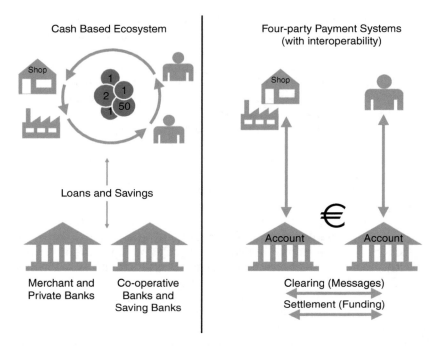

Figure 1.1 Schematic development from a cash-based economy (left) to the current 'four-party' payment system with interoperable bank (right)

of the salary account in Europe (and similar card accounts) was the origin of the typical four-party payment models we recognise as fundamental for payment industry today (see for example Kokkola, 2010),[1] and in reality there is a mixture between a cash-based part and an electronic payments part with a different ration from country to country.

1.3 Sustainable efficiency versus dynamic disruptions in payments

The account-based payments systems developed over decades and were continuously optimised by the payments industry. The European Central Bank (Martikainen *et al.*, 2012) reported empirical evidence that the electrification of the retail payments systems promotes economic growth. Enriching shopping and buying processes with the most adequate means of payment is of overall economic importance.

The culminating point of the development in Europe was the development of SEPA, the Single Euro Payments Area, as part of the political agenda to harmonise the European economy '*to become the most competitive and dynamic knowledge-based economy in the world*' (Lisbon Agenda, 2000). SEPA supported the 'Digital Agenda for Europe' (European Commission, 2010): '*Only in an integrated payment market will it be possible for enterprises and consumers to rely on safe and efficient payment methods.*' A recent study (PwC, 2014) requested by the European Commission DG Internal Market and Services reported that SEPA has: '*Potential yearly savings to all stakeholders of €21.9 billion – a recurring annual benefit resulting from price convergence and process efficiency*'.

The European banking community supported the long-term social benefits of SEPA from the beginning with a self-regulated approach between banks in Europe. The individual banks made significant investments in SEPA and the interoperability of retail payments in Europe because all partners adherent to the SEPA scheme are responsible for their individual payment systems. There is neither a 'general infrastructure' (for example a power grid or a telecommunication network) in payments, nor a 'public good' (like streets or railways).

Nevertheless, the development of sustainable efficiency and the success of the introduction of SEPA did not address a genuine flaw of the typical four-party payment model. As shown in Figure 1.1, this model comes with a decoupling of payments processing from the interaction between buyers and sellers. While information in the market for goods and services were exchanged 'non-electronically' for decades in the non-banking space, payment-related information travelled with the intra-banking processes of clearing of payment messages and settlement of funds between banks. The paradigm for the intra-banking space was interoperability.

As long as there was no technological innovation in the market, this model worked very well. But with the proliferation of 'digitalisation', disruptive innovations took place also in the payments industry.[2] The term 'disruptive innovation' was coined by Clayton M. Christensen (Christensen and Bower, 1995; Christensen, 1997). Although his approach was criticised by others for the lack of predictive power (for example Danneels, 2004) and for the lack of reaching beyond technological product innovations[3] (for example Markides, 2006), his model fit the changes in payments rather well. He proposed that (technological) innovations emerge in niches and take root initially in simple products, but then develop to disruptive competitors. Taking PayPal for example with its roots in two companies (Confinity and X.com founded in 1998/1999) for payments with Palm Pilot or, respectively, via e-mail, it had about 157 million active digital wallets at the end of 2014. Today, PayPal is a prototype for a 'business platform' with payment transaction within the PayPal ledger between different PayPal clients' accounts on a prepaid basis. In parallel and especially in European countries such as Germany, PayPal developed into a new type of payments clearing service, facilitating payments flow between bank accounts of the clients outside PayPal. In this case each transaction is directly settled by (SEPA) direct debit or credit card transaction against the payer's account and the payees usually transfer their funds at end of day or end of week to their bank accounts.

The result of this development since 2000 is an intermediation by new entrants in the payments landscape.[4] These intermediators entered into the traditional relationship between banks and payment institutes and clients (merchants or consumers). These new entrants can be described from two different perspectives. From the point of view of the client, they provide the 'colourful and manifold' portfolio of payment solutions for the clients' payment requirements. From the perspective of the payments landscape, they can be distinguished into three main groups:

• added-value providers on-top of interoperable payment systems,
• centralised business platforms, and
• decentralised consensus systems (or public ledger systems with block-chain protocol).

Added-value providers intermediating typically in card-based payments as acquirers (at the point of sale), as payment services providers (in e-commerce) or as 'supermerchants' (for example the Swedish company iZettle with a combination of cheap card readers coupled to smartphones plus handling of the card payments in the name of iZettle on behalf of the merchant) did not alter existing interoperable payment models fundamentally, but sit on top of the traditional payments landscape. In contrast, centralised business platforms and decentralised consensus systems have been changing the payments ecosystems[5] disruptively.

1.4 SEPA Reloaded

Before turning to those new developments, it is important to keep the opportunities in mind, which are based on the achievements of SEPA. Nearly one decade ago, the European Central Bank (ECB, 2006) pointed out that the major benefits of SEPA would materialise only if the project was future oriented:

> The major benefits of the SEPA, as emphasised in the Third Progress Report, will materialise only if the project is future-oriented. This is why the SEPA is not restricted to the translation of existing national

procedures, infrastructures and standards into European ones. Rather, **the SEPA anticipates how payment systems should look at the end of the decade, paying due attention to the new possibilities offered by progress in information technology.** This forces European actors to rethink what they have so far taken for granted. In this context, the SEPA project is contributing significantly to the Lisbon agenda, which, inter alia, aims to promote the competitiveness and dynamism of the European economy. Already today, European payment systems often have a leading position in the world in terms of automation. This competitive edge has to be preserved, and innovative solutions have to be found to meet the technological challenges in the European payment landscape. (ECB, 2006, p. 8, emphasis by the authors)

The European Commission's Directorate-General for Internal Market and Service (EC, 2006) estimated the whole financial benefits of SEPA at about €122 billion per year with the lion's share of some €100 billion per year generated from e-invoicing integrated in the end-to-end purchase-to-payments process, as calculated by Leinonen (2005). Unfortunately, this aspect of process integration diluted in the following discussion about the implementation of SEPA, leaving 'naked' e-invoicing without the integration aspect decoupled from SEPA payments.

Nevertheless, the original vision is still right. Looking at the taxonomy of payments in the end-to-end purchase-to-payments process in Table 1.1, both real-time and batch payments could be integrated on the same 'digital' basis that is the interoperable exchange of XML-based SEPA messages. SEPA still has the potential to make the original vision come true.

1.5   Digitalisation in payments

The proliferation of mobile-/Internet-based technologies (aka 'digitalization') has not been changing the fundamental laws of economics, but has triggered a lot of changes in how clients can access and also provide or contribute[6] to services. Milkau and Bott (2015) summarised some features of digitalisation with an impact on payments:

- open communication standards,
- consumerisation of technology putting smart devices – literally – in the hand of the consumer, and
- information transparency and marginalisation of transaction costs (in the sense of O.E. Williamson's work about transaction cost economics[7]).

Table 1.1 Taxonomy of current means of payments in the end-to-end purchase-to-payments process as seen from the payer's and payee's point of view at the moment of the check-out

Basic Layer	XML e.g. as in SEPA (with SCT, SDD, SCF)					
Speed	real-time for beneficiary (intermediate availability or final guarantee)			deferred availability on beneficiary account		
Payment Type	Instant payment* (real-time availability of funds for payee)	Online banking payments (i.e. SCT with real-time feedback)	Cards payment with immediate guarantee to the payee)	E-Invoice payments based on SCT	Direct debit with mandate (SDD)	Credit transfer (SCT)
Integration	via real-time interface	via PSP (payment service provider)	POS or PSP	E-Invoicing with integration to online banking account	SDD mandate	IBAN

Note: * see ERPB (2014).

With open communication, 'always-on' devices and marginalised costs for searching, purchasing, monitoring and so on, the consumer is able to select single services himself. That includes payment services in e-commerce, but more and more also at the point of sale.

In parallel, the same features of digitalisation set the stage for new intermediaries (between clients with their access technology and traditional producers of goods and providers of service). Traditional 'brick-and-mortar' intermediaries – like book shops – with asymmetric information advantage and (limited) access to product information were replaced by Amazon and other so-called centralised business platforms. Those centralised business platforms facilitate the exchange between buyer and seller, the agents representing the two sides of a market, whether they are companies like Amazon (books, consumer electronics and much more), Google and Facebook (individualised advertisement) or Apple (music via iTunes or app store). This is the background for the statement of Francisco Gonzáles (2013), CEO of BBVA, as he recently put it into a nutshell: '*Banks need to take on Amazon and Google or die*'.

Comparing these centralised business platforms and banks as 'interoperable' payment providers, the first ones facilitate general interactions between buyer and seller (advertisement, searching, order, monitoring and others), whilst the second ones facilitate one special type of interactions between buyer and seller: payments. Both target at the same focal point, the interaction of buyers and sellers, and both process electronic messages along a process chain (see Figure 1.2, left). Nevertheless, centralised business platforms and banks as parts of an 'interoperable' payment industry represent different competition modes for the payment market: competition for the market versus competition in the market as described by Kemppainen (2014).

The interoperability of the traditional bank-based payment industry is built upon mutually agreed rules and regulations, such as the SEPA formats. This resulted in a 'competition–cooperation nexus in retail payments' – a term coined by Kemppainen a decade ago (Kempainnen, 2003). Likewise, banks have been collaborating with their clients, for example along end-to-end purchase-to-pay or payroll-to-pay processes, and cooperating with providers such as dedicated payments or card processors for many years and continue to do so with new partners in a constantly changing economy. As Carl-Ludwig Thiele wrote recently (2014a, translation by the authors): '*The cooperation and coexistence of banks and non-banks in payments is not reversible any longer.*'

The 'competition for the market' model of the centralised business platforms is an antagonistic model and characterised for example by a statement of Peter Thiel, co-founder of PayPal (2014): *'If you want to create and capture lasting value, look to build a monopoly.'* As Minor *et al.* (2011) figured out in an experimental analysis, a competition of platforms shows a general tendency to develop into monopolistic structures ('winner takes it all') or, respectively, into oligopolies, if the platforms address different client groups (for example region, community, special interest, etc.). A dynamic development shows path-dependency and can yield a temporally meta-stable duopoly as already described by Hotelling (1929). All in all, intermediation by centralised business platforms can be illustrated as indicated in Figure 1.2 (left): platforms are shown at the top (trying to win the market as a whole) and banks at the bottom (as interoperable financial institutions).

For a very first estimation about the market shares of new 'digital' players, one can take the prediction of Pratz *et al.* (2013) as a starting

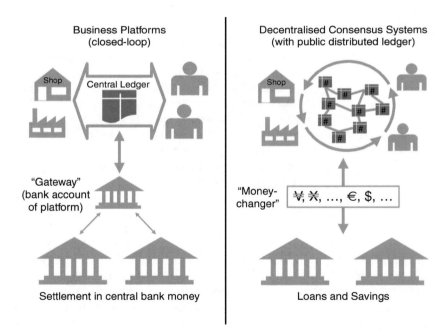

Figure 1.2   Comparison between 'business platforms' with a central ledger (left) with decentralised consensus systems (right) with either a 'gateway' or a 'money-changer' as interface to the world of bank accounts

point (see Figure 1.3 and Table 1.2). They forecast a tripartition of the European payment revenues between standard electronic payments (primarily banks), card payments (banks, card organisations plus new entrants) and alternative payment methods (primarily non-banks and especially business platforms). One can understand this development as stagnation for traditional banking revenues from payments, taking into account that interchange fees in Europe for issuing banks will be capped by European regulation, while non-bank players are expected to show exponential growth rates.

As indicated in Figure 1.2 (left), currently centralised business platforms need some gateway to the banking industry to achieve the final transfer of funds between bank accounts and the settlement within the banking system in central bank money. Therefore, centralised business platforms can be regarded as a new type of clearing systems linking bank accounts. For example, PayPal facilitates payments in e-commerce between Internet shops and consumers – but the transfer from the consumers and to the merchants' bank accounts are standard SEPA transactions in Europe. And if one does not want to keep one's money with PayPal all the time taking this credit risk, the money has to be transferred to the banking system. But what will happen in case companies indeed start to make salary payments directly to the employees' PayPal or iTunes accounts?

Table 1.2 Revenue developments in the European banking industry based on an approach described by Pratz *et al.* (2013)

Revenue source	Revenue growth	Main players
Alternative payment methods	Exponential	Non-banks including new 'digital' players such as centralised business platforms, but potentially open market for banks
Card payments	Organic and moderate	Mature Industry (card organisations, issuers, acquirers) plus new market entrants such as Apple Pay (using the existing basis)
Standard electronic payments (incl. SEPA)	Organic and moderate	Traditional banking industry (banks and payment institutes) with a unique and exclusive position for banks when it comes to the final settlement in central bank money

1.6   Decentralisation of payments?

In a Quarterly Bulletin of the Bank of England (Ali *et al.*, 2014), the authors argued that:

> '...the key innovation of digital currencies is the 'distributed ledger' which allows a payment system to operate in an entirely decentralised way, without intermediaries such as banks.' (p. 262, emphasis by the authors)

An international workshop, P2P Financial Systems 2015, organised by Deutsche Bundesbank, the University of Frankfurt's Sustainable Architecture for Finance in Europe (SAFE) research centre and University College London in January 2015 discussed the developments of those 'distributed ledgers' and the underlying advances in the theory of distributed (computer) systems, in game theory and in cryptography. All those concepts have, naturally, assumptions and limitations, and a practical implementation – such as the Bitcoin system – may deviate from the original concepts.

The basic concept of a digital currency payment transaction, such as Bitcoin transactions, consists of 'distributed ledgers' with 'consensus systems' and the 'blockchain' protocol. This concept is a rather sophisticated one as elaborated by Milkau and Bott (2015). It was developed to solve a number of scientific problems such as the Byzantine Generals Problem (how to handle secure message transfer in a decentralised system without any trust and without a central 'authority') and the Double Spending Problem (to avoid that a digital payment message is copied and sent more than once). This basic concept has to be distinguished from commercial applications such as exchanges for virtual currencies and from the use of Bitcoins as assets.

Many central banks and financial service authorities have investigated virtual currencies as currencies or assets in recent years: from the ECB (2012) to Hong Kong Monetary Authority (HKMA, 2015). The US Securities and Exchange Commission (SEC, 2013) discussed 'Ponzi Schemes Using Virtual Currencies', and the Dutch Central Bank (DNB, 2014) wrote 'Virtual Currencies Are Not a Viable Alternative'. All those central banks and financial services authorities do not see a risk for monetary policy and state control of the money supply for the time being, simply for the fact that the amount of Bitcoins in circulation is tiny compared to US dollar or euro. But there are risks for consumers associated with the use of virtual currencies today and the HKMA (2015) *'reminds the public to be aware of the risks associated with Bitcoin'.*

A general overview of the Bitcoin system is given in a recent book on *Mastering Bitcoin* by Antonopoulos (2014), and the reader is referred to this work for a detailed discussion about the whole Bitcoin ecosystem with different agents: nodes, miners, mining pools, exchanges, wallet providers, etc. Today, the structure of this ecosystem is not a uniformly peer-to-peer system, as this is usually the starting point in theory. Consumers with a simple payment transaction dislike running a computer note in the Bitcoin network. Eyal and Sirer (2014) pointed out '*Bitcoin is no longer decentralized*'[8]; and, as Ito (2015) wrote, '*there is currently centralization in the form of mining pools and core development, the protocol is fundamentally designed to need decentralization to function at all*'.

Although the current real-world implementation of Bitcoin seems blurred and the original concept jeopardised, one can still agree with the Bank of England that the 'distributed ledger' (with the implementation of a distributed consensus system) is a real innovation with new opportunities for payments. Figure 1.2 (right) illustrates an ideal world, in which all payment users (consumers or merchants and employers) are equal peers of a distributed consensus system and all run uniform nodes based on open source software implementation and consumerised[9] hardware such as mobile devices.

Such an ideal implementation of a distributed public ledger system as a truly peer-to-peer payment network requires more theoretical research and practical work. However, the result of such an exercise could be a homogeneously distributed payment system without any central technical hub comparable to the use of cash (as illustrated in Figure 1.1 left versus Figure 1.2 right). A system like this (ideal implementation) could provide benefit to all users, but would decouple banks from the payment ecosystem and reduce the role of banks to the (traditional) provider of savings and loans. In niches, such as remittance payments or, admittedly, payments in the so-called 'dark net' for illegal transaction such as the Silk Road case, users are already paying with Bitcoins and will continue as long as they – from their subjective point of view – see any benefits for them compared to a traditional bank payment.

1.7   A closer look at distributed public ledger technology

For distributed ledger technology there are three layers: (1) the unique distributed public ledger with its local replica on the nodes of the network, (2) a protocol for the exchange of transactions in the public ledger, and (3) a consensus system to achieve synchronisation across the distributed local replica, i.e. to keep the distributed legder consistent. This has to be compared to traditional payment systems with (a) different ledgers at each bank, (b) an interoperable protocol for the clearing of transactions between accounts in different ledgers, (c) a settlement in central bank money (or in commercial money in international payments) to achieve finality, and (d) typically reconciliations between different ledgers to guarantee the principles of accounting. Also, a significant difference is the question of 'trust', as decentralised systems start with the assumption that the nodes in the network cannot be trusted at all, whereas regulated banks act as custodians for the clients' accounts. The substitution of this "trust by regulation, legislation and auditing" is a consensus mechanism of distributed public ledgers. But, asynchronous decentralised consensus is always a compromise because Fischer, Lynch, and Paterson pointed out in their seminal paper 'Impossibility of Distributed Consensus with One Faulty Process' (Fischer *et al.*, 1985) that it is impossible to enforce consensus for all situations. Together with another problem that there can be so called 'forks' of the blockchain sequence in locally separated replica of the distributed ledger, distributed public ledgers operate at the cost of contradiction of the principles of accounting (or at least, of a very different point of view about finality and correctness of a ledger).

Finally, it is important to mention that in the meta-competition between interoperable banks (with 'competition in the market'), business platforms (with 'competition for the market') and distributed ledger systems (as egalitarian peer-to-peer networks with consenus) there are two developments. The different generic characteristics of the three antagonists are summarised in Table 1.3. Two remarks are important. First, there are different variants either for business platforms (commercial business platforms vs. platforms of central banks such as RTGS+/TARGET2), or for decentralised ledgers, for which either different consensus algorithms are in use in public distributed ledgers, or different 'agreement' mechanisms in private distributed ledgers(see Table 1.3). Second, there is a development from early theoretical conception to long-term real-world implementation as shown in Figure 1.3: for example, the development of the Bitcoin system for a real peer-to-peer network towards a hierarchy and – as seen from the point of view of users – further to a 'platform' with a separation between users on the outside and a 'central' structure on the inside.

Nevertheless, one can imagine a system in which the distributed ledger with the blockchain is really running 'in the hand of the consumer'in a preconfigured way (either on a dedicated mobile device or 'in the cloud'

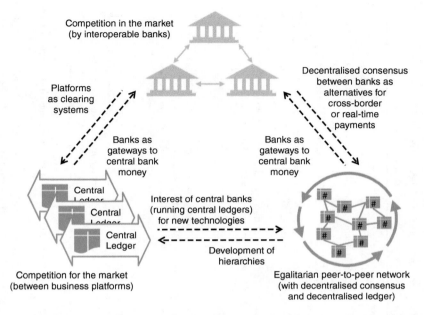

Figure 1.3 Comparison of possible developments or blending between the three generic types (i) interoperable banks with *'competition in the market'*, (ii) business platforms with *'competition for the market'* and (iii) distributed consensus systems, which are designed from first principle as decentralised, egalitarian peer-to-peer networks

Note: The double arrows indicate the development paths between the three different theoretical alternatives in reality.

with access by an app via mobile phone). In this configuration, there is no central black box anymore (provided by some non-transparent system of minors), but each and every user is part of the decentralised ledger in his roles as payer and payee.

Furthermore, some blending between the alternatives exist, as business platforms need banks as gateway to the world of central bank money and banks evaluate decentralised consensus systems (between banks) as alternatives for cross-border or real-time payments. For banks, such developments and potential cooperation are currently analysed, asking the question how to generate benefits for the (end) user: either as payer or, respectively, as payee.

Table 1.3 Comparison between (i) interoperable systems, (ii) centralised platforms and (iii) types of decentralised distributed ledger systems

Alternative	Advantages	Disadvantages
Interoperable Systems	• Efficiency due to 'competition in the market' with rather low costs for bulk payments • Commonly agreed rules books incl. return/reject transaction, etc. • Regulation with - Protection of client assets - Security of client data - AML/CFT • Settlement in central bank money (for example via RTGS+/TARGET2) • Management of systemic risk as part of regulation and oversight • Regulation, law and audits provide (a proxy for) trust for the system	• Slow development due to agreements to be achieved between participants • Bulk payments with delayed (D+1) booking on client accounts • Costs for multiple implementations in all banks (for example in case of SEPA migration) • Danger to be regarded as kind of 'public infrastructure' or 'social good', although paid by banks • Danger of an illusion of security • Reconciliations with significant costs especially between Nostro and Loro account in correspondent banking (for SWIFT payments)
Centralised Platforms	• Efficiency due to economies of scale • Real-time processing in central ledger (all transactions are 'on-us' transactions)	• Tendency to develop into monopoles ('competition for the market') • Counterparty risk (of platform providers) • Cost for redundancy and/or business continuity management • Systemic risk (all participants linked to the central ledger as a 'hub')
Distributed Ledgers: a) public distributed ledgers	• No need for trust within a network and for enforcement of trust by a central authority • Public ledger and open source development • Resilience against failure or fraud (as basic assumption of the concept!) • Blockchain as real innovation in the development of decentralised computer systems • Availability (24/7/365) of a fault-tolerant decentralised network • Community with innovations based on private entrepreneurship	• A priori, asynchronous distributed consensus systems are always a compromise due to theoretical limitations [a] • Difference between theory (with assumptions) and real-world developments: for example, development of networks from egalitarian peer-to-peer systems into a hierarchical structure, as not all users want to contribute (with active nodes) but just send or receive transactions • Limitation of efficiency due to consensus mechanism with 'proof-of-work – high cost for 'production' of a transaction of some Euro (as proof-of-work has to be costly by design) – limited speed because consensus (i.e. 'mining' of a new block) takes an average time of 10 minutes far away from being real-time

- Bitcoin as a first working implementation of a pragmatic compromise to get a distributed ledger system running in real world

  - 'finality' assumed by common consensus after six blocks (equal to one hour), but current examples of forks (see below) do not support any definition of finality
  - limited scalability because block size and mining frequency are a barrier for any high-volume transaction business
- Need of gateways to real-world to get a connection to central bank money (today)
- Public ledgers with traceable transactions (not anonymous!)
- Problem to 'update' open source software, as all users have be convinced, and to keep all nodes in synchrony (see for example the temporally fork within Bitcoin for six blocks at 4 July 2015 due to inconsistent software updates in the network)
- Alternative consensus mechanisms to Bitcoin/Proof-of-Work such as Proof-of-Stake approaches with coin owners = coin guards have the 'nothing at stake' problem, that the individual nodes of the network have no 'positive' incentive [b]

Distributed Ledgers: b) private distributed ledger

- Solutions for 'private' networks with known participants, i.e. with a 'whitelist' of nodes in the network
- No need for inefficient consensus mechanisms such as proof-of-work, which are replaced by efficient agreement or majority voting mechanisms between known participants
- Speed of validation of transactions (few seconds)
- Additional features such as so call 'smart contracts' to trigger further actions in the network

- Various implementations including Ripple Consensus Protocol (RCP), Interledger Protocol (ILP), Hyperledger's protocol etc.
- Protocols with (majority) voting in sub-sets of nodes, in which each server maintains a unique node list that is 'trusted' by this server [c] with an opaque situation after the so called 'Stellar Fork' of Dec. 2014 [d, e] and with limited empirical experiences about the existing implementations
- Other Byzantine agreement protocols and especially 'federated Byzantine agreement' (FBA) as published in a draft paper in May 2015 [f] to be reviewed and tested in real-world implementation
- Fragmentation of current development with many different virtual currencies and with different approaches for alternative mechanism to consensus

Sources: References: [a] Fischer *et al.* (1985); [b] Poelstra (2015), [c] Cohen *et al.* (2015), [d] Higgin (2014), [e] Craig (2015), and [f] Mazières (2015).

1.8   A market for payments far from equilibrium with a meta-competition

After about four decades of stability in the payments landscape following the introduction of salary and card accounts, mobile-/Internet-based technology has created 'digital disruptions' and a change of paradigm since the year 2000. In the last century, the set of payment instruments was limited and standardised: the user had a choice among cash, cards, credit transfer and direct debits, which were typically not substitutional, but linked to specific payment processes. The focus was on efficiency (for the system) and interoperability (between banks) – an approach reaching the climax with SEPA on the European level.

At the beginning of this century, research started to take a closer look at the two-sided payment market facilitating interactions between agents of different types (consumers and merchants) and trying to 'on board' them by charging or incentivising each side. One milestone in the research was the conference on Two-Sided Markets in Toulouse, 23–24 January 2004, and results were compiled by Rochet and Tirole (2006).[10] Nevertheless, two-sided markets were described as markets with consumers and merchants, but with some 'neutral' instrument in between (usually a card). In parallel, banks invested over decades in the continuous improvement of efficiency and optimised the traditional structure of the four-party model with payment instruments (initiation or authentication), clearing of payment messages and settlement (transfer of funds).

This development can be seen as an 'efficiency trap' in the sense of Clayton M. Christensen. Especially in electronic and mobile commerce, banks relinquish it to non-bank innovators to create new payment products as seen from the consumers' perspective. Similar to the trigger by employers in the 1950s/1960s with the introduction of salary accounts and electronic salary payments, the 'digitalisation' has been changing the payment market fundamentally and has generated a dynamic development far from equilibrium in a multilayered ecosystem.

The first layer consists of the traditional payment industry with the paradigm of interoperability and a 'competition in the market' between regulated financial institutions with mutually interchangeable payment products based on common specifications (such as SEPA credit transfer or SEPA direct debit). The second layer includes the current digital disruptors with their 'competition for the market', the paradigm to intermediate in the relationship with clients and the objective to look-in clients on their business platforms. Although there is some kind of 'cold' coexistence today, the dominance of AliPay in China can be seen as an example for further development. The third layer is represented by the future potential of truly decentralised peer-to-peer payment systems based on the model of 'consumers = producers'.[11] People could 'share' payments in decentralised ledgers and run blockchain protocols as they share selfies or produce comments about the new restaurant across the street. All three layers together establish an ecosystem with meta-competition between interoperability (with competition in the market), centrality (with competition for the market) and decentrality (peer-to-peer system without traditional competition).

Additionally to this meta-competition, there is a growing public discussion defining parts of this ecosystem as some kind of 'public good'. Three statements from 2014, which are of course not statistically significant, might illustrate the current development:

- *'a social planner will therefore want to support the use of cards relative to cash. As the model predicts card usage to be a decreasing function of the interchange fee, the optimal response is to set a low or even negative fee.'* (Korsgaard, 2014)
- *'Member States shall ensure that the services referred to in Article 17 [payment account with basic features] are offered by credit institutions free of charge or for a reasonable fee.'* (EU, 2014)
- And a recent paper of the Euro Retail Payments Board (ERPB, 2014) explained: *'The debate seems to have moved beyond the discussion on the existence of a business case, to the acknowledgement of the "social good" nature of instant payments and the users' expectation that relevant solution should be available.'* (emphasis by the authors)

Taking these solitary statements, the first layer of an interoperable payments industry with SEPA credit transfer and direct debits seems to be regarded as some kind of 'public infrastructure', although individual banks made significant investments to achieve this implementation of SEPA.

Such interference in the complex payments ecosystem has an imminent danger to jeopardise the efficiency, stability and security of the payment system. The problem of innovation without interoperability was addressed by the Chicago Payments Symposium held on 22 and 23 October, 2012 at the Federal Reserve Bank of Chicago: *'Participants noted during the consumer payments market discussion that today's disconnected innovation is proliferating multiple, incompatible, closed-loop solutions. Many expressed concern that this "balkanization" will weaken consumer experience and confidence and limit adoption of payment innovations'* (Federal Reserve Bank, 2012). The future development of a market with meta-competition plus potential external interference needs further theoretical research and analysis of empirical data. A recent paper of Roth and Milkau (2015) illustrated the hesitant migration of clients to SEPA with data, which can be fit by an exponential function. If (at least a majority of) clients do not recognise an individual 'measurable' benefit from new payment instruments such as SEPA credit transfer and SEPA direct debit, they will wait as long as possible to achieve the migration. Clients chose from the point of view of the – sometimes rather subjective – mental accounting of the benefit (see Thaler, 1985). But the 'consumer choice' can also be a starting point to describe the payments ecosystem from a different perspective.

1.9   The choice of the customers – from payment instruments to payment 'buttons'

Nobody is actually keen on making a payment; would anybody agree that payment is 'sexy'? People want to buy a book on the Internet, have a pizza, book a trip or check-out of a hotel. There is a lot of in-depth analysis about consumer payment choice, typically comparing traditional means of retail payments: cash, checks, card, electronic payments etc. (see for example Rysman, 2010; Cohen and Rysman, 2013; Schwartz and Ramage, 2014; Bennett *et al.*, 2014; Hasan *et al.*, 2014; Bundesbank, 2015).

However, if one studies a 'digitalised' payment situation, a consumer in e-commerce may have the choice at the check-out for example among PayPal, iDEAL, VISA, MasterCard, SOFORT, invoice payment, cash-on-delivery and other options. Obviously, this is not the list of means of payments typically analysed in consumer payment choice studies. Digitalisation shifted the consumers' choice from means of payments (with competition in the market between banks offering current account with more or less identical payment offerings) to 'payment brands'. In e-commerce, people do not pay with 'SEPA' but with a trusted brand. In an extreme situation, they do not even select an option, but simply pay with Amazon's '1-Click button'. This is a highly efficient and rather convenient process for a consumer to finalise a purchase and check-out with a payment process running in the background based on the consumer's profile with a preselected/preferred payment solution.

Digitalisation is going to achieve results for the clients, which were demanded from the traditional payments industry for example in Heidi Miller's well known speech at SIBOS 2004 with her call for simplicity, efficiency for the clients, innovations and cost reduction by digitalisation:

Customers tell us they need to achieve substantial improvements in their own efficiency and productivity. They want us to help them re-engineer their supply chains, speed their order-to-pay cycles, free working capital, and integrate seamlessly with their internal transaction and information systems. They want it in real time, across all borders. And of course, they want more value at lower cost. [...] customers cannot understand why an overnight delivery service can tell them exactly where a package is from the second it leaves their premises to the moment it arrives at its destination, but banks cannot tell them exactly where a cross-border payment is as it moves through the process. (Miller qtd in Bott, 2009)

The more these e-commerce payment options proliferate the point-of-sale, the more the choice shifts from means of payments provided by the traditional supply side to strong brands competing for the market. If in ten years, we would – in a gedankenexperiment – ask of consumers and merchants how they would pay or accept payments in different buying/selling situations they might answer, for example, with cash, with ApplePay, with AribaPay, with Amazon One-Click, with VISA or MasterCard, with PayPal One Touch, with a loyalty reward program, with 'Snel en Simpel Betalen' in the canteen,[12] with iDEAL, with Faster Payments and so on. Of course, some will say that they pay with credit transfer or with direct debits. But how many will answer 'with a SEPA payment instrument cleared by an ACH and settled to my bank account'? In the context of the different payment situations, customers will select different payment option, which they identify by name or brand. Criteria for the selection of those names or brands can be price including rebates, convenience, loyalty rewards or special offers, speed of delivery and similar benchmarks. Vice versa, the merchants may select their payment options with an evaluation of conversion rate (e-commerce), speed at check-out (point-of-sale), optimised integration in the whole buying/selling-process or integration into the ecosystem of producer–merchant–service provider and total cost calculation. This seems to be the market for payments in the future.

1.10 Conclusion – a market far from equilibrium

All in all, the payments ecosystem is a multilayered, two-sided market far from equilibrium – something we understand in parts only for the time being. Further research is needed to decipher the interdependencies between the different players and layers. Any interference in such complex market structures could potentially cause unexpected consequences. Even if only a part of this market structure is in scope, a stable regulatory framework is needed for the payments industry to develop, as recently Thiele (Thiele, 2014b) pointed out, elaborating on the example of 'MONNET'. Some economic predictability would have been needed for any entrepreneurial approach – especially as it is known since the work of Chamberlin (1933) that a (meta-stable) equilibrium of a duopoly in one-dimensional competition will turn unstable when a third firm is added to this market. However, the current market for payments is in a tremendous transition triggered by the disruptive power of digitalisation. This is an exciting 'real world' experiment about the dynamic development of markets far from equilibrium.

Notes

1. Some unofficial money transfer systems – typically 'Hawala' systems (El-Qorchi, 2002; and Passas, 2006) – work similarly, with a clearing of information messages between agents in different countries ('hawaladar') and an underlying settlement.
2. Although this discussion is focused on domestic retail payments including payments in the SEPA area, 'digitalisation' also wipes out the difference between 'domestic' and 'cross-border'. If somebody buys in the Internet and pays for example with PayPal, it is simply a payment between buyer and seller – independent from 'real world' borders and different payment systems.
3. It would be beyond the scope of this paper to discuss differences between product innovations and business model innovations as discussed for example by Casadesus-Masanell and Ricart (2010) or Amit and Zott (2012). For the payments industry the phase of innovation was triggered by Internet technology, then this technology was wrapped in payment products, and later those first entrepreneurs changed the whole business of the payments industry.
4. A new wave of innovation may come with the development of the 'Internet of Things' for example presented at the 2015 Consumer Electronics Show (CES) in Las Vegas. Everything with a 'smart' before – such as smarter activity tracker (such as fitness trackers), smart home (heating and electricity meters) and smart cars (such as Google's self-driving car project) – is hype currently. Even as it remains rather opaque what the real benefits for the consumers will be, this technology provides great opportunities for analysis of consumers' behaviour, and consequently for predictive and prescriptive analysis, which in turn can be monetised for example for individualised real-time advertisements.
5. Although a primary focus in this discussion is on retail payments between merchants/industry and consumers, there are similar effects in business-to-business payments.
6. For example by 'sharing' self-produced texts, songs, photos, videos, etc.
7. see Williamson, 1981; Williamson, 2009; and Gibbons, 2010.
8. For a detailed discussion see, for example, Eyal and Sirer (2013) and Eyal (2014).

9. To be compared to the situation today with the requirement of dedicated hardware (application-specific integrated circuit (ASIC) chips) for Bitcoin 'miners'.
10. Another review article is Rysman (2009).
11. This model comes with the danger of the 'Tragedy of the Commons' to retain an incentive mechanism for a (large) number of participants playing a repeated game without trying to achieve individual advantages at the expense of the other ones. This was the title of an article written by Hardin (1968). A deeper analysis was made by Elinor Ostrom *et al.* (1999) in their seminal work 'Revisiting the Commons: Local Lessons, Global Challenges'.
12. See Equens (2012) about the development of 'Quick and Easy Payments' as biometric payment with fingertips for caterers.

References

R. Ali, J. Barrdear, R. Clews, and J. Southgate (2014) 'Innovations in payment technologies and the emergence of digital currencies', Bank of England, *Quarterly Bulletin*, Volume 54 No. 3, 3Q2014.

R. Amit and C. Zott (2012) 'Creating value through business model innovation', *Sloan Management Review*, 53 (3), 41–49.

A. M. Antonopoulos (2014) *Mastering Bitcoin – Unlocking digital cryptocurrencies*, O'Reilly Media, Sebastopol, CA, USA, December 2014.

B. Bennett, D. Conover, S. O'Brien, and R. Advincula (2014) 'Cash continues to play a key role in consumer spending: Evidence from the diary of consumer payment choice', Federal Reserve System's Cash Product Office (CPO), April 2014.

J. Bott (2009) 'The Single Euro Payments Area – New alliances required to tip the market', ECRI Research Report No. 10, aei.pitt.edu/11454/1/1871, accessed Feb 1, 2015.

Bundesbank (2015) 'Zahlungsverhalten in Deutschland 2014', Deutsche Bundesbank, 2015.

M. Callon (1998) 'Introduction: The embeddedness of economic markets in economics', *The Sociological Review/Special Issue: Sociological Review Monograph Series: The Laws of the Markets*, Edited by Michel Callon, Volume 46, Issue S1, pp. 1–57.

R. Casadesus-Masanell and J.E. Ricart (2010) 'From strategy to business models and onto tactics', *Long Range Planning*, 43 (2), pp. 195–215.

E.H. Chamberlin (1933) *The theory of monopolistic competition: A re-orientation of the theory of value*, Harvard University Press, Cambridge, MA.

C.M. Christensen (1997) *The innovator's dilemma: When new technologies cause great firms to fail*, Harvard Business School Press, Boston, MA.

C.M. Christensen and J.L. Bower (1995) 'Disruptive technologies: Catching the wave', *Harvard Business Review*, January–February 1995.

D. Cohen, D. Schwartz and A. Britto (2015) 'The Ripple ledger consensus process', ripple.com, 20 February 2015; https://ripple.com/knowledge_center/the-ripple-ledger-consensus-process/ (accessed 21 May 2015).

M. Cohen and M. Rysman (2013) 'Payment choice with consumer panel data', Federal Reserve Bank of Boston, *Working Paper* No. 13–16.

M. Craig (2015) 'The race to replace Bitcoin', Observer, 5 February .2015; http:// observer.com/2015/02/the-race-to-replace-bitcoin/#ixzz3aySVvO4Z (accessed on 23 May 2015).

E. Danneels (2004) 'Disruptive technology reconsidered: A critique and research agenda', *Journal of Product Innovation Management*, 21 (4), pp. 246–258.

De Nederlandsche Bank (DNB) (2014) 'Virtual currencies are not a viable alternative', *DNBulletin*, 8 May 2014.

European Commission (EC) (2006) 'Consultative paper on SEPA incentives', European Commission, Internal Market and Services DG, 13 February 2006, p. 41f, http://ec.europa.eu/internal_market/payments/docs/sepa/sepa-2006_ 02_13_en.pdf (accessed 28 January 2015).

European Central Bank (ECB) (2006) 'Towards a Single Euro Payments Area – Objectives and deadlines fourth progress report', February 2006.

European Central Bank (ECB) (2012) 'Virtual currency schemes', October 2012.

M. El-Qorchi (2002) 'The Hawala system', *Finance and Development*, A quarterly magazine of the IMF, 39 (4).

Equens (2012) 'Albron selects Equens for "Quick and Easy Payments"', Equens press release, 15 May 2012.

Euro Retail Payments Board (ERPB) (2014) 'Pan-European instant payments in euro: Definition, vision and way forward', ECB, 12 November 2014, https:// www.ecb.europa.eu/paym/retpaym/shared/pdf/2nd_eprb_meeting_item6.pdf (date accessed 4 January 2015).

European Union (EU) (2014) 'Directive 2014/92/EU of the European Parliament and of the Council of 23 July 2014 on the comparability of fees related to payment accounts, payment account switching and access to payment accounts with basic features', *Official Journal of the European Union*, L 257, Volume 57, Art. 18, 28 August 2014.

European Commission (2010) 'A digital agenda for Europe', COM(2010) 245, Brussels, 19 May 2010.

M.J. Fischer, N.A. Lynch and M.S. Paterson (1985) 'Impossibility of distributed consensus with one faulty process', *Journal of the ACM*, 32(2), pp. 374–382.

I. Eyal (2014) 'The miner's dilemma', ArXiv 1411.7099, November 2014, http:// arxiv.org/abs/1411.7099 (accessed 1 February 2015).

I. Eyal and E.G. Sirer (2013) 'Majority is not enough: Bitcoin mining is vulnerable', 15 November 2013, http://arxiv.org/pdf/1311.0243v5 (accessed 1 February 2015).

I. Eyal and E.G. Sirer (2014) 'It's time for a hard Bitcoin fork', hackingdistributed. com, 13 June 2014, http://hackingdistributed.com/p/2014/06/13/in-ghash-bitcoin-trusts/ (accessed 1 February 2015).

Federal Reserve Bank (2012) 'Fed and industry leaders discuss the future of payments at the Chicago Payments Symposium', Federal Reserve Financial Services, *FedFocus* December 2012, https://www.frbservices.org/fedfocus/ archive_general/general_1212_01.html (accessed 30 March 2014).

R. Gibbons (2010) 'Transaction cost economics: Past, present, and future?', *Scandinavian Journal of Economics*, 112(2), pp 263–288.

F. Gonzáles (2013) 'Banks need to take on Amazon and Google or die', *Financial Times* (Europe), 3 December 2013.

G. Hardin (1968) 'The tragedy of the commons', *Science*, 162 (3859), pp. 1243–1248.

I. Hasan, E. Martikainen and T. Takalo (2014) 'Promoting efficient retail payments in Europe', *Journal of Payments Strategy & Systems*, 8 (4), pp. 395–406.

S. Higgin (2014) 'Stellar network fork prompts concerns over Ripple consensus protocol', Coinbase, 9 December 2014, http://www.coindesk.com/stability-questions-dog-ripple-protocol-stellar-fork/ (accessed 10 March 2015).

Hong Kong Monetary Authority (HKMA) (2015) 'The HKMA reminds the public to be aware of the risks associated with Bitcoin', 11 February 2015, http://www.hkma.gov.hk/eng/key-information/press-releases/2015/20150211-3.shtml (accessed 13 February 2015).

H. Hotelling (1929) 'Stability in competition', *The Economic Journal*, 39 (153), pp. 41–57.

J. Ito (2015) 'Why Bitcoin is and isn't like the Internet', 18 January 2015, https://www.linkedin.com/pulse/why-bitcoin-isnt-like-internet-joichi-ito (accessed 30 January 2015).

K. Kemppainen (2003) 'Competition and regulation in European retail payment systems', Bank of Finland Discussion Paper No. 16/2003, 9 June 2003.

K. Kemppainen (2014) 'Competition–cooperation nexus in the European retail payments market: Views from a network industry perspective', *Journal of Payments Strategy & Systems*, 8 (4), pp. 386–394.

T. Kokkola (ed., 2010) 'The payment system: Payments, securities and derivatives, and the role of the Eurosystem'. European Central Bank.

S. Korsgaard (2014) 'Paying for payments – Free payments and optimal interchange fees', ECB Working Paper 1682, June 2014.

H. Leinonen (2005) 'Bank provided e-invoicing structures and benefits', Memorandum Suomen Pankki – Financial Markets and Statistics, 9 December 2005.

Lisbon Agenda (2000) 'Presidency conclusions', Lisbon European Council, 23 and 24 March 2000.

C. Markides (2006) 'Disruptive innovation: In need of better theory', *The Journal of Product Innovation Management*, 23, pp. 19–25.

E. Martikainen, H. Schmiedel, and T. Takalo (2012) 'Convergence in European retail payments', ECB Occasional Paper Series, No. 147.

D. Mazières (2015) 'The stellar consensus protocol – A federated model for Internet-level consensus', Draft, Stellar Development Foundation, 15 May 2015; https://www.stellar.org/papers/stellar-consensus-protocol.pdf (accessed 23 May 2015).

U. Milkau (2010) 'A new paradigm in payments: The strengths of networks', *Journal of Payments Strategy & Systems*, 4 (3), pp. 277–288.

U. Milkau and J. Bott (2015) 'Digitalisation in payments: From interoperability to centralised models?', *Journal of Payments Strategy & Systems*, Vol. 9, No. 3., pp. 321–340

D. Minor, T. Hossain and J. Morgan (2011) 'Competing match makers: An experimental analysis', *Management Science*, 57(11).

E. Ostrom, J. Burger, C.B. Field, R.B. Norgaard and D. Policansky (1999), 'Revisiting the commons: Local lessons, global challenges', *Science*, 284, pp. 278–282.

N. Passas (2006) 'Demystifying Hawala: A look into its social organization and mechanics', *Journal of Scandinavian Studies in Criminology and Crime Prevention*, 7, pp. 46–62.

A. Poelstra (2015) 'On stake and consensus', 22 March 2015; https://download.wpsoftware.net/bitcoin/pos.pdf (accessed 23 May 2015).

A. Pratz, J.W. Bloos, O. Engebretsen and M. Gawinecki (2013) 'European payments strategy report – Winning the growth challenge in payments', A.T. Kearney, Inc.

PricewaterhouseCoopers (PwC) (2014) 'Economic analysis of SEPA – Benefits and opportunities ready to be unlocked by stakeholders', high-level analysis by PwC's Corporate Treasury Services as requested by the European Commission DG Internal Market and Services, European Union, 16 January 2014.

R. Roberts (2005) 'The reality of markets', Library of Economics and Liberty, 5 September 2005.

J.C. Rochet and J. Tirole (2006) 'Two-sided markets: A progress report', *The RAND Journal of Economics*, 37 (3), pp. 645–667.

G. Roth and U. Milkau (2015) 'Payments from a cooperative bank's perspective: SEPA and beyond', *Journal of Payments Strategy & Systems*, 9(1).

M. Rysman (2009) 'The economics of two-sided markets', *Journal of Economic Perspectives*, 23 (3), pp. 125–143.

M. Rysman (2010) 'Consumer payment choice: Measurement topics', in: The Changing Retail Payments Landscape: What Role for Central Banks?, An International Payment Policy Conference Sponsored by the Federal Reserve Bank of Kansas City (pp. 61–81).

S. Schwartz and A. Ramage (2014) 'From mail to mobile – A new generation in payments', Payments Studies Group, The Federal Reserve Bank of Richmond, 31 March 2014.

Securities and Exchange Commission (SEC) (2013) 'Ponzi schemes using virtual currencies', SEC Pub. No. 153, 7(13).

R. Thaler (1985) 'Mental accounting and consumer choice', *Marketing Science*, 4(3), pp. 199–214.

P. Thiel (2014) 'Competition is for losers', *Wall Street Journal*, 12 September 2014.

C.L. Thiele (2014a) 'Trends und Perspektiven im Zahlungsverkehr', Die Bank, N. 4/2014, p. 19: 'Das Mit- und Nebeneinander von Banken und Nichtbanken im Zahlungsverkehr ist nicht mehr umkehrbar.'

C.L. Thiele (2014b), 'SEPA – Der Wegbereiter für den Zahlungsverkehr von morgen', Keynote Speech auf der Payments Konferenz der Euro Finance Week, Frankfurt, 19 November 2014 ('aber das Scheitern der inzwischen schon fast in Vergessenheit geratenen Initiative für ein europäisches Kartensystem ("MONNET") hat uns gezeigt, dass stabile Rahmenbedingungen in diesem komplizierten Geschäft entscheidend sind. Und der bis dahin von der EU-Kommission verfolgte einzelwirtschaftliche Ansatz war in dieser Hinsicht eher abträglich. Denn der Aufbau von Infrastrukturen im Zahlungsverkehr macht hohe Investitionen notwendig.')

C.L. Thiele (2015) 'Die Zukunft des Bezahlens', Speach, Deutsche Bundesbank, 5 May 2015, Wie sieht die Zukunft des Bezahlens aus? Meiner Meinung nach bunt und vielfältig.

K. Weisser (1959) 'Bargeldlose Lohn- und Gehaltszahlung: ihre Durchführung in der Praxis', Betriebswirtschaftlicher Verlag Dr. Tb. Gabler GmbH, Wiesbaden.

O.E. Williamson (1981) 'The economics of organization: The transaction cost approach', *The American Journal of Sociology*, 87 (3), pp. 548–577.

O.E. Williamson (2009) 'Transaction cost economics: The natural progression', The Sveriges Riksbank Prize in Economic Sciences in Memory of Alfred Nobel

2009, Prize Lecture, 8 December 2009, http://www.nobelprize.org/nobel_prizes/economic-sciences/laureates/2009/williamson-lecture.html, (date accessed 8 August 2014).

H. Wörlen, M. Altmann, H. Winter, J. Klocke, J. Novotny, and R. Uhlitzsch (2012) 'Payment behaviour in Germany in 2011 – An empirical study of the utilisation of cash and cashless payment instruments', Deutsche Bundesbank, 17 October 2012.

2
Europe: The Shift from Cash to Non-Cash Transactions
Janina Harasim

2.1 Cash and non-cash transactions in European countries – general trends

2.1.1 Use of cash and non-cash payments: areas of predominance

Traditional payment systems were built around cash. Non-cash payment instruments, including payment cards, used most often besides cash in retail payments, occurred quite recently, as it was in 1940–1950s. Innovative payment instruments that may become an alternative for cash have even a shorter history.

Currently, cash and non-cash payments are perceived as equivalent even though the spheres and scopes of their circulation are different. Generally, supply of cash and non-cash payments as well as the scale and range of their use depend on many factors such as regulatory framework, interests of parties involved in payment execution (payment services providers – PSPs, acquirers, clearing and settlements agents, as well as end users of payment services, including consumers and merchants), economic and social determinants (for example, the level of economic wealth or diversity in incomes), cultural factors (for example, the importance of personal relationships) or technological ones (access to the Internet and mobile devices).

Non-cash payments are predominant in transactions concluded between legal persons. Payments between public institutions (G2G) or between enterprises (B2B) are conducted largely in non-cash form which results first of all from the fact that non-cash transactions are safer, more comfortable and cheaper. They enable to reduce huge costs (cash involves several social costs to individuals – especially the poor – as well as business and the government) and the size of the shadow economy. In transactions between a legal person and a natural person, the use of non-cash instruments is not so common. This is because, even if B2C and G2C payments (for example payment of salary or social benefits) take the non-cash form, transfers in the reverse direction, for example payments for purchase of goods and services or regular payments (like bill payments, credit instalment repayment and payment of insurance premiums) are still often executed using the cash – see Table. 2.1.

Therefore, payments made with the participation of consumers are the area where cash is used most frequently. Moreover, P2P (person-to-person or peer-to-peer) transactions are the sphere of largest cash predominance. Cash is also relatively often used in C2B (consumer-to-business) transactions executed face-to-face at a physical point of sale or in remote way, most often on the Internet. This type of transactions will be further referred to as retail payments. They will be approached as low-value payments made by consumers, so they will not include low-value payments made between enterprises (B2B), between enterprises and public institutions (B2G) or between public institutions (G2G).

Table 2.1   Usage of cash and non-cash instruments by type of the settlement

Details		Creditors*		
		Consumers (C or P)	Enterprises (B)	Public institutions (G)
Debtors*	Consumers (C or P)	P2P Mainly cash Rarely CT	C2B Cash, Cards DD (paying bills) rarely CT	C2G Cash or CT
	Enterprises (B)	B2C Mainly CT, rarely cash	B2B Mainly CT Possible legal limits on cash usage	B2G Mainly CT
	Public institutions (G)	G2C Mainly CT Rarely cash	G2B Mainly CT	G2G Mainly CT

*C – Consumer or P – Person/Peer, B – Business, G – Government
CT – Credit Transfer
DD – Direct Debit
Source: Own work.

Retail payments have a lot of specific features. They are:

- typically made in large numbers by large numbers of transactors and typically relate to purchases of goods and services in both the consumer and business sectors;
- made using a range of payment instruments much wider than large-value payments and in more varied contexts, including, for example, payments made in person at a point of sale as well as for remote consumer and commercial transactions; and
- characterised by extensive use of private sector systems for the transaction process and for clearing (Bank for International Settlements, 2002, p. 6).

2.1.2 Pace of development of non-cash transactions and changes in payment mix

Recent years have been a period of almost continuous increase in the number of non-cash transactions all over the world. However, the growth is quite diversified and reaches significantly higher levels in regions clustering developing countries (CEMEA – Central Europe, Middle East and Africa, Latin America and developing countries of Asia), in comparison with regions gathering mostly developed countries – see Table 2.2. In the latter group double-digit paces of increase in the volume of non-cash transactions were reported only in developed countries of the Asia-Pacific region. In Europe and Northern America the pace of growth in non-cash transactions was relatively low, which can be partly explained

Table 2.2 Non-cash transactions by region – number and growth, 2008–2012

Regions	Number of Worldwide Non-Cash Transactions by Region (Billion)					CAGR (%) 2008–2012
	2008	2009	2010	2011	2012	
Emerging Asia	11.8	13.6	16.4	19.5	23.9	19.3
CEMEA	11.7	15.3	19.4	23.3	28.8	25.2
Latin America	18.9	23.8	25.6	29.3	32.5	14.6
Mature Asia-Pacific	22.0	26.3	27.2	30.1	33.5	11.0
Europe (including Eurozone)	74.2	77.2	80.8	84.2	87.6	4.3
North America (US and Canada)	111.2	113.1	116.6	124.0	127.9	3.6
Global	249.8	269.4	286.0	310.4	334.3	7.6

Sources: Capgemini and RBS (2013, p. 7), Capgemini and RBS (2014, p. 7).

by the fact that non-cash turnover is already significantly developed there.

After the financial and economic crisis of 2008 to 2009 in the majority of world regions, a clear slowdown of the pace of growth in non-cash transactions was reported (Capgemini *et al.*, 2011, p. 9). In the years that followed, this pace started to grow again, however, mainly in developing countries. In the USA, in 2011 it reached as much as 6.4% (in comparison with the previous year), but in 2012 it was already by half lower (only 3.2%). This was caused, among others, by impact of new interchange fee regulations which limit the maximum permissible interchange fee that a covered issuer can collect from merchants for a debit card transaction.[1] In the same period in Europe a smaller decline was reported in the pace of increase in non-cash transactions – from 4.3% in 2011 to 4.0% in 2012. However, the situation in Europe was really diversified. The rate of growth of non-cash transactions was in 2011 (in comparison with the previous year) definitely lower in the countries of the Euro Area than in other EU countries. In the first group Spain and Ireland reported even the fall in the volume of non-cash transactions in comparison with 2010 (respectively by 1% and 0.8%), whereas the highest growth in number of these transactions occurred in Finland (10%) while the average rate in Europe was on 4.2%. In the countries outside the Euro Area the volume of non-cash transactions was growing the fastest in Poland (14.6%), as well as in Great Britain and Denmark (7.6% each) (Capgemini *et al.*, 2013, p. 8). In 2012 the pace of growth of non-cash transactions in Europe was influenced, among others, by actions taken by governments and banks aiming at discouraging the use of cash for low-value transactions (for example the Netherlands or Sweden).

A diversified level of development of non-cash transactions in particular regions is accompanied by huge differences in application of particular payment instruments – see Figure 2.1. Basic non-cash payment instruments include credit transfer, direct debit, payment cards and cheques. Differences in the range of their use are mainly the result of diversity of payment cultures, which were shaped for years under the influence of historical, economic, social, psychological and technological, etc., factors.

Increase in payment cards use and decline in the share of cheques are a common feature of changes that have been occurring over recent years. As a result, payment cards became a fundamental instrument used in non-cash payments across the globe. However, their share in the total number of non-cash transactions was very diversified – the largest in

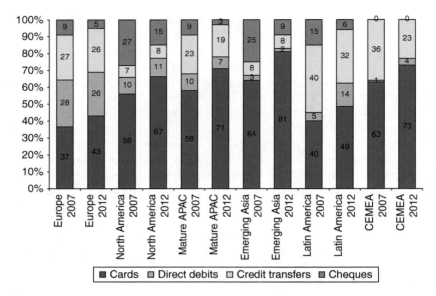

Figure 2.1   Change in payment mix by region, %

Note: APAC – Asia and Pacific .

Sources: Capgemini and RBS (2013, p. 11), Capgemini and RBS (2014, p. 9).

the countries of Emerging Asia (over 80%) whereas the lowest, which is quite surprising, in European countries, where it reached 43% in 2012.

However, there are no more similarities between regions. And if in Northern America and in the countries of Emerging Asia, cheques are the second payment instrument with respect to importance, in the regions of Latin America, CEMEA and Mature APAC, between 19 and 32% of non-cash payments is made via credit transfer. The use of direct debit was in these regions relatively small (the largest in Latin America where it reached 14% in 2012) similarly to cheque usage.

In Europe the payment mix is totally different. Although also here payment cards are the basic instrument of non-cash payments, their predominance is not as evident as in other regions. A relatively high share of direct debit and credit transfers that reach a similar level (26% of the total number of non-cash payments in 2012) is a typical feature of the payment mix in Europe. Cheque usage appears to have declined, and in 2012 it reached 5%. The volume of transactions made by particular payment instruments is shown in Figure 2.2.

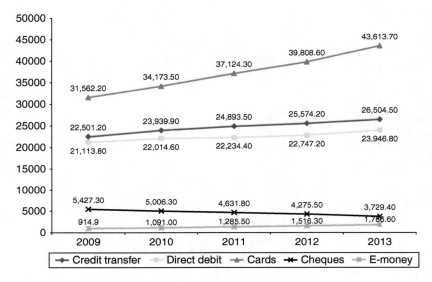

Figure 2.2 Use of non-cash payment instruments within the EU, number of transactions

Source: EBC Statistical Data Warehouse (ECB, 2015).

Nevertheless, European countries differ significantly with respect to the scope of use of particular non-cash payment instruments. Generally payment cards and direct debit are much more often used in the EU-15 countries, and credit transfer is more popular in the new EU countries – see Table 2.3.

Further growth in non-cash turnover seems to be an irreversible trend. A.T. Kearney predicts (A.T. Kearney, 2013, p. 3) that in the nearest future in Europe, which represents a third of the total number of non-cash transactions in the world, the volume of non-cash payments will grow faster than in recent years. This should result, among others, in the decline of the share of cash in retail payments from around 70% in 2015 to 60% in 2020 – see Figure 2.3.

2.1.3 The share of cash in performed payments and major areas of its use

However, it ought to be stated that rapid growth of non-cash transactions does not necessarily mean cash displacement in money circulation (Górka, 2009, p. 53). In contemporary monetary systems, the size

Table 2.3 Countries of the largest share of particular payment instruments in the number of non-cash transactions, 2013

Payment instrument	1st position		2nd position		3rd position		EU	Euro area
	Country	Share (%)	Country	Share (%)	Country	Share (%)	Share (%)	Share (%)
Credit transfer	Bulgaria	80.1	Hungary	57.5	Croatia	55.8	26.5	25.9
Direct debit	Germany	49.8	Spain	41.1	Austria	36.2	23.9	29.0
Card payments	Denmark	71.8	Portugal	67.6	Estonia	66.9	43.6	37.5
Cheques	Malta	26.3	Cyprus	16.4	France	13.6	3.7	4.4
E-money	Luxemburg	87.7	Italy	5.4	Greece	2.2	1.8	2.3
Others	Italy	6.5	Hungary	1.2	Austria	0.9	0.4	0.6

Source: Own work based on European Central Bank (2015).

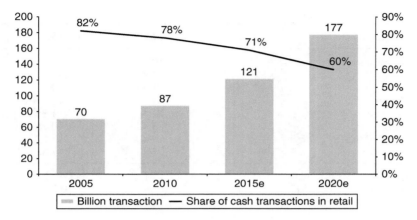

Figure 2.3 Growth of non-cash transactions in Europe and share of cash, 2005–2020e

Source: Based on A.T. Kearney (2013, p. 3).

of money supply and the share of cash in circulation are the result of a specific game between central bank (increasing or decreasing the amount of money in the banking system and influencing the money supply by e.g. modifying reserve requirements), commercial banks (creating money through giving loans in cash and non-cash form) and non-banking entities (deciding about storing of their resources in cash or non-cash form). Among the latter, there are consumers who have a decisive impact on the share of cash in circulation.

This thesis seems to be confirmed by the data of the Bank for International Settlements. It shows that rapid growth of non-cash transactions in recent years has been accompanied by an increase in the value of banknotes and coins in circulation in relation to GDP, particularly in the countries that have relatively high levels of this rate – see Table 2.4. It occurred in almost all countries or regions included in the table except for India. Apart from India, the fall in the value of this rate was reported in Sweden and the Republic of South Africa, among others: a slight growth was reported in Korea, Mexico and Turkey, whereas in Canada, Australia and Great Britain its level was relatively stable in the analysed period (Bank for International Settlements, 2014, p. 443).

Cash still remains a basic payment instrument in many regions – it is almost exclusively used by inhabitants of Latin America, Asian countries (except for developed countries of the Asia-Pacific region) and Africa. According to McKinsey, in 2007, 98–99% of payments in

Table 2.4   Banknotes and coins in circulation: value as a percentage of GDP

Region	2008	2013	Change (%)
Euro Area	8.50	10.23	+1.73
Hong Kong SAR	10.88	14.29*	+3.91
India	12.27	11.49	−0.78
Japan	17.17	19.74	+2.57
Russia	10.61	12.46	+1.85
Singapore	7.74	8.49	+0.75
Switzerland	9.13	11.40	+2.27
United States	6.05	7.40	+1.35

Note: * data for 2012
Source: Bank for International Settlements (2013, p. 439) and (2014, p. 443).

Indonesia, India, Columbia, Russia, China and Mexico were made in cash (Denecker *et al.*, 2009, p. 10). Until recently, also the BRIC countries were the region characterised by definite predominance of cash. However, in recent years the development of non-cash transactions in the majority of the BRIC countries resulted in the fact that Brazil, China and Russia were among the top ten countries with the largest volume of non-cash payments (Capgemini *et al.*, 2012, p. 6). Europe and developed countries of the Asia-Pacific region are the areas where cash usage is relatively small, similarly to the USA.

The share of cash within the M1 money supply is one of the basic measures of cash turnover. In the European Union for several recent years the level of this rate has been quite stable and fluctuated within the range of 17.1–19.7%, whereas in the Euro Area its evident growth from 10.5% in 2001 to 17–18% between 2008 and 2009 was observed – see Figure 2.4. Increase in the share of cash in M1 particularly observed in 2008 confirms the thesis that financial crises and economic break-downs are accompanied by the loss of trust in non-cash payments and growth of trust in cash, or at least growth in demand for cash. The relatively high share of cash in M1 remaining after 2008 can therefore be considered to be a sign proving the lack of conviction that the economic situation was stabilised, but it can also be a result of low interest rates persisting in Europe.

European countries are characterised by significant differences with respect to the share of cash in narrow money. The countries of very high, over 30%, share of cash in 2013 included Romania, Hungary and Bulgaria, whereas on the other side in Sweden and Great Britain this rate was below 5% – see Figure 2.5.

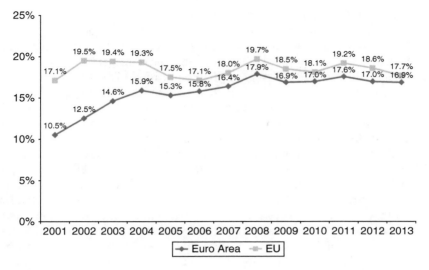

Figure 2.4 Cash value as a percentage of narrow money (M1), 2001–2013
Source: EBC Statistical Data Warehouse (ECB, 2015).

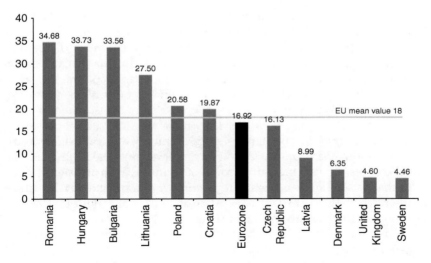

Figure 2.5 Cash value as a percentage of narrow money (M1): cross-country comparison, 2013
Source: EBC Statistical Data Warehouse (ECB, 2015).

It should be emphasised that the countries characterised by high share of cash in narrow money are at the same time the countries of relatively high rate of financial exclusion (measured by the number of bank accounts and the number of non-cash transactions per inhabitant).

Nevertheless, the still very strong commitment of societies in many European countries to cash is first of all proved by significant share of cash payments in the total number of payments (its share in the value of payments is much lower). According to McKinsey, in 2007 the share of cash in retail payments in European countries was relatively high, yet significantly diversified. The highest level of this rate, even higher than 90% was reported in the countries of Central and Eastern Europe (for example, it was 94% for Poland), but Germans also paid in cash quite frequently (75%). The lowest rates of cash usage were reported in Finland, Sweden and France where its share in retail payments reached respectively 47%, 54% and 55% (Denecker *et. al.*, 2009, p. 10). In the following years this rate was falling, but the decline was rather slow. According to the European Central Bank, in 2012 the average rate for the EU countries reached 59.7%, while for the countries of the EU-15, it reached 54.5%, and for the remaining countries, 75.8%. The gap between the country with highest share of cash in retail payments, that is, Greece (96.6%) and Luxembourg with the lowest share (29.1%), reached 67.5 percentage points. On the basis of ECB data, it can be stated that the countries in which cash is still of major importance in payments include mainly the countries of Southern Europe, such as Greece, Italy, Malta, Cyprus and Spain, and the countries of the new Member States, including Bulgaria, Romania, Lithuania, Poland, Czech Republic and Slovakia. In the first group, apart from cultural factors, it can result from the fact that they are countries of developed tourism, and in the second from a relatively short period of development of non-cash transactions. On the other side, there are small developed countries of Western Europe (Luxembourg, Denmark and the Netherlands) and Scandinavian countries (Finland and Sweden) – see Figure 2.6. The differences between indicated groups of countries are really significant – in the first, the share of cash in total number of transactions falls within the range between 75 and 97%, whereas in the countries of developed non-cash transactions this rate reaches 29–38%.

Cash is a preferred form of payment, particularly in low-value transactions made at the point of sale. Its share is the highest in the case of the so-called micropayments.[2] They are transactions of very low value, in case of which the use of a payment card is uneconomical. Propensity to pay in cash is inversely proportional to the amount of payment. As

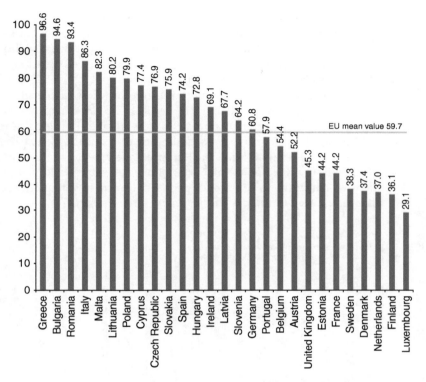

Figure 2.6 Share of cash in retail payments in EU countries (%), 2012
Source: Based on (Schmiedel *et al.*, 2012, p. 22).

research shows, cash is used mainly in cafes, snack bars, fast food restaurants and in P2P payments, while doing shopping in small shops, in urban transport, vending machines and while making payments for services (for example leisure activities) (Deutsche Bundesbank, 2012, p. 40 and pp. 52–57; Koźliński, 2013, pp. 121–143 and pp.165–169; Sveriges Riksbank, 2015).

Such a high share of cash transactions is unfavourable from the macroeconomic point of view, due to high costs and difficulties in reducing the shadow economy. In 2006, the European Payment Council (EPC) assessed the costs of cash in EU at more than EUR 50 billion per year, that is 0.4–0.6% of GDP (European Payment Council, 2006, p. 7). Similar conclusions were formed by European Central Bank that, on the grounds of results of research conducted in thirteen EU countries,[3] assessed that in 2012 these costs amounted to EUR 45 billion. This made

0.96% of GDP in the countries participating in the study. The costs of cash transactions are incurred by central banks and commercial banks. They are associated with the issuing of banknotes and coins, distribution, maintenance of cash transaction infrastructure as well as destruction of banknotes and coins and so on.

A little hope for changing consumers' attitudes towards cash is given by research conducted in April 2015 by ING Group, in which half of the Europeans declared that they used cash less frequently than a year before. The hope is even greater because, among the countries where the rate of such people is higher than the European average, there are countries of high cash usage, including Turkey, Poland, Spain and Romania. On the other hand, the lowest rate of people declaring less frequent use of cash was reported in Austria and Germany – see Figure 2.7.

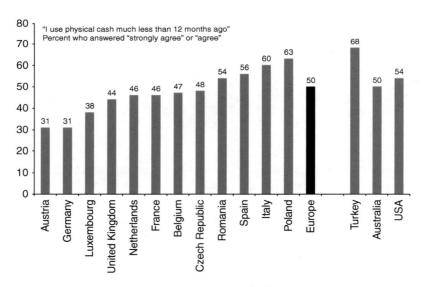

Figure 2.7   Share of people declaring less frequent use of physical cash, %
Source: ING (2015, p. 21).

2.2   Challenges to overcome in order to reduce cash usage

2.2.1   Why we pay in cash and how this can be changed

There are many reasons for frequent use of cash in retail payments; however, apart from habit, the most important of them are associated with the features of cash that are highly valued by consumers such as anonymity and comfort as well as low cost of making payments.

Anonymity is one of specific features of cash because in comparison with other payment instruments, cash does not leave any traces of conducted transactions. So for people willing to stay anonymous, cash remains the best method of making payment. Paying in cash is also comfortable; while comfort is perceived first of all as ease of use, however, it is also often associated with the speed of payment. The awareness of actual possession and the possibility to access cash at any time is an additional factor that is very important for many people and contributes to the use of cash.

Costs associated with use of cash are diversified, and the method of their assessment and perception significantly depends on what position the assessing person occupies in cash circulation. Consumers perceive cash as free, which results from the absence of additional payments related to cash payments that non-cash payments are often charged with. However, this way of thinking is wrong. It is a consequence of the same level of prices of purchased goods and services, which is irrespective of the payment instrument used. This is because some payment costs (for example *interchange fee*) are hidden in the price of goods and services, while this mostly concerns non-cash payments. Therefore, the customer who pays cash indirectly is bearing the costs of payment infrastructure necessary for non-cash payments that they do not use. Cash also seems to be free of charge for the majority of merchants who do not include the costs associated with internal cash transactions within the company in the structure of costs. Due to the aforementioned reasons, using price stimuli (that usually prove to be efficient in influencing the change of users' behaviours) for reducing cash payments may be really difficult.

Thus, reducing cash transactions will not be easy and will create many challenges to overcome – see Figure 2.8.

It demands firstly providing the access to basic financial services including a payment account to the largest possible part of society. However, it ought to be stated that it does not need to be a standard bank account. This is because the increasingly growing number of non-bank PSPs offer the possibility to make payments with the use of innovative forms of payment with no use of a bank account, or with the use of this account, but only as a source of liquidity. Therefore, it is about providing the consumers with the right of access to basic accounts allowing for non-cash payments which can also be offered by non-banking financial institutions including payment institutions.

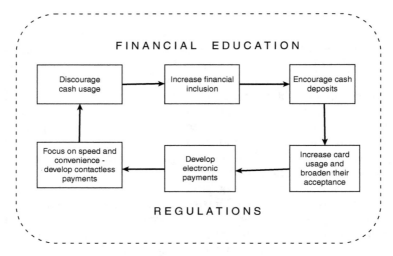

Figure 2.8   Challenges to overcome in order to reduce cash usage
Source: Own work.

Decreasing use of cash is also favoured by:

- shift from paper-based payments (cheques or 'paper' credit transfer and direct debit) towards electronic payments (payment cards and credit transfer as well as direct debit made in electronic way, also referred to as ACH payments); and
- development of payment innovations, particularly those that may become a substitute for cash in face-to-face transactions.

Government-led initiatives including regulations fostering non-cash payments will also be very helpful. They should be supported be general measures promoting the convenience, speed and safety of non-cash payments and educational actions aiming at encourage electronic payments. Major types of actions favouring reduction of cash transactions, and thus development of non-cash transactions, are presented in Section 2.2.2 –2.2.6 of the chapter.

2.2.2   Increasing financial inclusion

Paying cash may be a question of choice, but sometimes it is the consequence of the lack of access to a bank account, and so it is a derivative of financial exclusion. The European Commission defined financial exclusion as 'a process whereby people encounter difficulties accessing and/

or using financial services and products in the mainstream market that are appropriate to their needs and enable them to lead a normal social life in the society in which they belong' (European Commission, 2008, p. 9). Numerous studies prove that the lack of access to financial services can lead to poverty traps and inequality (Banerjee and Newman, 1993; Aghion and Bolton, 1997; Beck *et al.*, 2007). Therefore, financial exclusion generally leads to social exclusion, although this relationship also happens to be reverse. Thus, providing all interested parties with access to basic financial services, including an account that allows for execution of non-cash payments, is the initial condition for reducing cash transactions; this is described with the notion of financial inclusion. In developed countries financial inclusion is usually defined very generally as the ability of an individual, household or group to access appropriate financial services or products (The UK Cards Association, 2015). On the other hand, in developing countries it is emphasised that it is about providing, first of all, the weakest and the poorest with accessibility to basic financial services while noticing that they should be simple, convenient, transparent and cheap. In this way financial inclusion is defined by the Reserve Bank of India and The Banking Association South Africa[4] – among others. A growing body of research shows that financial inclusion can have significant beneficial effects for individuals, providing both an economic and a political rationale for policies that promote financial inclusion. A formal account makes it easier to transfer wages, remittances and government payments. It can also encourage saving and open access to credit.

Despite growing interest in the subject of financial inclusion, the methodology of its measurement is still quite poorly developed. At the beginning, the number of bank accounts per inhabitant was considered the main measure of the rate of financial inclusion, but this measure had many limitations (Allen *et. al.*, 2012, p. 3). The World Bank developed more perfect measures of financial inclusion, taking into consideration also non-banking institutions that can keep accounts enabling non-cash payments. The access to an account at a formal financial institution – a bank, credit union, cooperative, post office or microfinance institution is the basic measure of financial inclusion applied by the World Bank. For most people, having such an account is perceived as an entry point into the formal financial sector.

It might seem that the problem of lack of access to financial services does not concern Europe, but in reality it turns out that even the highly developed countries are not free of it. According to the World Bank in 2011 account penetration differed enormously between high-income and developing economies: while it was nearly universal in high-income economies, with 89% of adults reporting that they have an account at a formal financial institution, it was only 41% in developing economies. Among regions, the Middle East and North Africa had the lowest account penetration, with only 18% of adults reporting a formal account. Account penetration in the region varied sharply across groups with different individual characteristics – the rate of owners of accounts was growing together with the level of affluence and education; it was also higher among city inhabitants than among village inhabitants; furthermore, it was possessed more often by men than women (Demirguc-Kunt *et al.*, 2013, p. 2).

According to data published three years later, the scale of financial inclusion improved in all groups of countries, although not to the same extent. In 2014 in highly developed countries 94% of adult citizens had an account at a formal financial institution, whereas in developing countries the figure was 54%. However, in the latter group there are enormous differences between particular regions – account penetration ranges from 14% in the Middle East to 69% in East Asia and the Pacific. The category of mobile money account, which is rare on the world scale, was distinguished for the first time in the report. Having it as the only account was declared by only 1% of the respondents; 1% also had a mobile money account and an account at a formal financial institution. However, there are regions in which mobile money accounts are much more popular, like for example in Sub-Saharan Africa, where 12% of adults and as much as a third of account owners have just the mobile money account. In thirteen African countries penetration of mobile money accounts is 10% or more, and this rate is the highest in Kenya (58%). This is the result of the development of the M-Pesa mobile payments system. Outside Sub-Saharan Africa ownership of mobile money accounts remains limited. In South Asia the share of adults with a mobile money account is 3%, in Latin America and the Caribbean 2%, and in all other regions less than 1% (Demirguc-Kunt *et al.*, 2015, pp. 11–13).

In Europe the share of people who have a formal account amounted in 2011 to 86% (at world average of 50%) (Demirguc-Kunt and Klapper, 2012, p. 11). This means that around fifty-eight million European consumers aged over 15 did not have a bank account at that time. Out of this number approximately twenty-five million people wanted to open such an account. The share of EU citizens who did not have a bank account was significantly diversified and ranged between 1% in Netherlands and Sweden (in Denmark and Finland this rate was close to zero) and 55% in Romania. On average, in the European Union 14% of the population did not have a bank account.

A lot of people having no payment account say they do not need or want one. This was stated by 56% of people who did not have an account; elderly people (aged 55 and more) and retired people were predominant in this group. This response was also more common among people of lower levels of education. Sharing another's payment account is a further common reason why 9% of consumers have no account, 7% occurred to be too young to open it and 5% were refused to open the account due to various reasons, including lack of regular income, bad credit history, inadequate documentation or with no explicit reason (European Commission, 2012b, p. 25).

In 2014 the scale of financial inclusion in European countries increased significantly both in the countries of the EU-15 and in the remaining countries – see Figure 2.9.

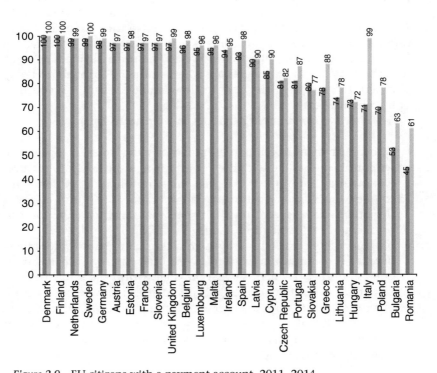

Figure 2.9   EU citizens with a payment account, 2011, 2014

Sources: Demirguc-Kunt and Klapper (2012, pp. 50–52), Demirguc-Kunt *et al.* (2015, pp. 83–84).

At the same time, the largest improvement was reported in Italy, Romania, Bulgaria and Poland in which, three years before, the rate of people having an account at a formal institution was relatively low.

The lack of access to a bank account has negative consequences both for PSPs and for consumers. PSPs have fewer incentives to offer their services on the internal market or to enter new markets, which limits competition, and consequently influences increase in prices and decrease in the quality of services offered to consumers. The lack of access to a basic payment account in turn makes it impossible for consumers to make a full use of the internal market while hampering, for example, cross-border and remote transactions. Therefore, the European Commission developed a project of a directive regulating the problem of access to the payment account with basic features, payment account switching and comparability of fees related to payment accounts. The Payment Account Directive (PAD) was accepted in April 2014 by the European Parliament and published in July 2014. Member States will have two years (until 18 September 2016) to implement the Directive into national legislations, after which the rules become effective. The aim of this Directive is to enable consumers who want to open and use a payment account to access basic payment services anywhere in the EU for their everyday payment transactions. This ought to allow, among others, for reduction of the financial exclusion.

The Directive on Payment Accounts concerns three areas:

- access to payment accounts: these provisions provide all EU consumers, without being residents of the country where the credit institution is located and irrespective of their financial situation, with a right to open a payment account that allows them to perform essential operations, such as receiving their salary, pensions and allowances or payment of utility bills and so on;
- payment account switching: by establishing a simple and quick procedure for consumers who wish to switch their payment account from one to another payment service provider within the same Member State and to assist consumers who hold a payment account with a bank and want to open another account in a different country; and
- comparability of payment account fees: by making it easier for consumers to compare the fees charged for payment accounts by payment service providers in the EU.

Member States are obliged to ensure that bank accounts with basic features are not offered only by credit institutions keeping current accounts only with the use of Internet tools. The same principles, associated with the access to the account, also ought to be applied towards consumers who, while not being the citizens of a particular Member State, do not have a permanent residential address but stay in its territory legally. These people many times had a limited possibility to open an account with basic features by means of which they could make any payments.

However, it ought to be stressed that consultations regarding current account with basic features showed significant differences concerning the issue of what institutions and on what rules payment accounts with basic features should be offered. The consent concerned only the issue that EU citizens ought to have the right (but not be obliged) to open such an account; however, if it is about possible measures to improve access to such an account and increase transparency of fees related to payment account, the attitudes were rather diversified. The discussion also concerned features of such an account while the availability of borrowing facilities (overdraft) was especially criticised.

Finally, it was accepted that payment accounts with basic features would be offered by credit institutions and other PSPs and that the PAD would concern ten to twenty payment services that are most commonly used by consumers and generate the highest costs for them. Services within the account ought to be executed free, or the fees applied should be reasonable (their amount ought to correspond to the national level of income and consider averaged fees collected by credit institutions in a particular Member State).

However, efficiency of the PAD in increasing the scale of financial inclusion will mainly depend on detailed solutions, including price policy of the institution offering such accounts. This is because already nowadays there are cheap, most often free, Internet accounts that still have not solved the problem of the lack of access to financial services. This results from the fact that using them requires having the access to a computer and the Internet and also elementary skills related to using them. Yet, the majority of people who do not have bank accounts are elderly people and/or less-educated, who usually do not have such possibilities and skills. Because of the same reasons, these people will not be able to make use of, among others, price comparison websites being an elementary tool also allowing for comparison of fees related to payment accounts.

However, finally it should be mentioned that analyses conducted in many countries, especially those with a large share of cash in their money supply (including Poland) prove that in the long term an increase in the use of banking services translates into an increase in the share of non-cash in M1 (and thereby decline in the share of cash), yet it does not need to bring decrease in the amount of cash money (Gumuła, 2013, p. 47). This happens, among others, when opening an account is a result of for example a legal obligation. The use of banking services favours increase in non-cash turnover when deposits are accumulated on the account and when it is used to make payments. This is because the fact of having an account does not change payment habits and preferences.

2.2.3 Development of electronic payments

Developing electronic payments is another way to reduce cash usage. Rapid growth of electronic payments is a result of a series of many factors among which the most important include dynamic development of communication and information technologies and expansion of e-commerce and social and cultural changes, particularly changes in the lifestyle and behaviours of contemporary consumers among them.

Development of technology cannot be stopped. Furthermore, for more than a hundred years, the rate of adoption of new technologies has been getting shorter. And if in the case of the airplane it took sixty-eight years to gain fifty million users, and it the case of the radio it was thirty-eight years, the Internet reached this number of users in seven years, and contactless cards in four years, and in the case of mobile applications in banking, predictions indicate it will take only two years – see Figure 2.10.

Modern technologies significantly influence the way of doing shopping and using financial services – they lead to us buying them in a remote way more frequently, mostly on the Internet (EFMA and McKinsey & Company, 2012, p. 5). However, the development of modern communication and information technologies has had the largest impact on the way payments are made. It is associated with a specific feature of payment service that is not a separate financial service, but a final element of transactions consisting most often in the purchase of goods or services. And if it is so, its form ought to be extremely adjusted to the nature and method of a 'basic' transaction – because then its value and usability for the selling party and the buyer are achieving the maximum.

We can distinguish two groups among them: electronic payments based on traditional payment instruments (card payments and ACH payments, that is, e-credit transfer and e-direct debit), and electronic payments that are a result of payment innovations (for example

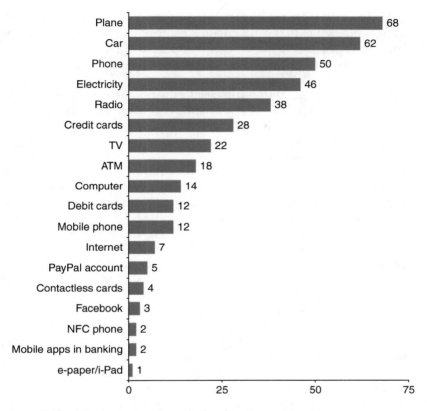

Figure 2.10   Adoption rate* of new technology innovations
Note: * Years needed to gain 50 million users.
Source: Own work based on King (2013, p. 299).

contactless cards, mobile payments or online payments). It needs to be emphasised that ACH payments can replace cash in face-to-face transactions only in a limited degree. Much larger possibilities in this field are offered by payment innovations, including particularly contactless payments. A slightly different situation is observed in the case of remote transactions. In e-commerce, relatively seldom is payment made in cash; however, development of innovations allowing for replacement of existing forms of payment is also progressing slowly. It seems obvious that in the case of transactions conducted online also the process of payment ought to take place online. It is understood by such companies as PayPal or Google that offer their customers the forms of payment taking into account the transaction context that is adjusted to the purchasing process. The largest possibilities are provided in this respect by mobile payments because a mobile phone (usually smartphone) can be used not only for payment, but also to immediately gather information that can be useful in relation with the purchase we want to make (information about the account balance, debt level, dates of repayment of credit instalment falling in the nearest future or information about competitive prices of goods/ services).

Despite fast development of online payments, as it is shown by research conducted by A.T. Kearney, in European e-commerce payments are still mostly made by payment cards. The largest group of countries – called 'card markets' where online buyers prefer paying with cards includes Denmark, the United Kingdom, France, Norway, Spain and Switzerland, i.e., countries of high card penetration. Germany is the country in which ACH payments are predominant – its online market is dominated by credit transfer (both prepayments and by invoice) and direct debit. According to A.T. Kearney, it does not result from consumers' or merchants' preferences, but rather from the absence of targeted, convenient solutions. The most modern forms of payments are applied in the so-called ObeP (online banking e-payment) markets: the Netherlands, Sweden, Finland and Poland where banks have provided convenient ways to pay online from bank accounts (A.T. Kearney, 2013, pp. 9–10).

The need to popularise online payments that enable consumers to complete transaction in a safe, fast and convenient way is increasingly more urgent because e-commerce is dynamically growing in the world – for the last five years average annual growth of the rate of e-commerce sales in the B2C segment has been higher than 20%. According to the E-commerce Foundation, global e-commerce sales, that in 2010 reached USD 820 billion, should grow to USD 2.25 billion in 2015 (E-commerce Foundation, 2014b, p. 18). In 2013, Europe – in which 565 million (69.2%) inhabitants use the Internet, and nearly one third do shopping online – was the market located in the second position in the world with respect to the size of turnover (USD 361.1 billion), after the Asia-Pacific region, and before the USA – see Figure 2.11. Great Britain, Germany and France are the three largest e-commerce markets in Europe – in 2013 they represented nearly 61% of total e-commerce turnover in Europe (E-commerce Foundation, 2014a, p. 19). At the same time, the European e-commerce market has a large development potential that allows for forecasting equally dynamic development of electronic payments in their most innovative way.

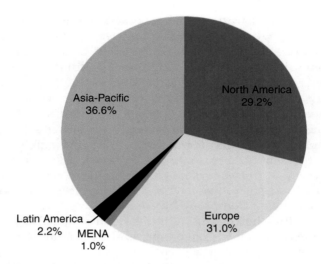

Figure 2.11 Share of regions in global B2G e-commerce, 2013

Note: * MENA – the Middle East and North Africa region.

Source: E-commerce Foundation (2014b, p. 14).

Evolution of consumers' payment habits, which is a result of deep social and cultural changes, is the third factor favouring replacement of cash and payments based on paper documents with electronic payments. Significantly easier access to information among consumers makes them become more aware and demanding; they have the skill to acquire, process and then use knowledge which results in the fact that they want more and more to be co-creators of products and services they make use of. The greatest turning point in consumer behaviours takes place under the influence of mobile technologies. Mobile devices such as tablets and smartphones, initially intended for a small group of people fascinated with technological innovations, became mass consumer products. They are used not only for communication, but also constitute a source of information, entertainment and education, or a way to access location or financial services.

The hierarchy of consumer values is also changing – for an increasingly larger group their own needs are becoming most important. This feature is the most evident among the youngest, a very promising group of consumers, often referred to as Generation Y, Millennials, Peter Pan or Boomerang Generation, whose habits (including payment habits) are just currently being shaped. The term Millennials generally refers to the generation of people born between the early 1980s and the early 2000s. They are distinctive – connected, practical, tech-savvy and socially aware. The Generation Y opportunity is imminent and vital – their annual spending is expected to be $2.45 trillion by 2015. As the affluence, influence and financial appetite of this demographic group grow, financial institutions need to attract its members and win them as customers for the long term. Generation Y, similarly to their forerunners, the Generation X, prefer financial services offered at low cost; they value convenience, ability to perform more activities online and quicker service (Deloitte, 2008, p. 5). Convenience perceived as ease of use of the payment instrument is becoming for contemporary consumers one of the fundamental features they expect also in the field of payments. In face-to-face transactions, convenience means accepting many payment solutions with a short processing time. In online transactions, consumers' expectations are similar. Comfort means ease of use and speed, together with the ease of registering and checkout (A.T. Kearney, 2013, p. 9).

However, it should be stressed that studies on demanded features of payment instruments show that consumers also really value other features of payment instruments such as safety or the cost of use. This is confirmed by results of over 100 research projects that have been conducted all over the world since the middle of 1990s, the aim of which was to identify factors influencing the adoption (that is the decision to acquire or use a specific payment instrument for the first time) and the continued use of various payment instruments. Although the identified variables seem to differ depending on the circumstances of payment and the socio-demographic characteristics of the respondents (the most important of them is the age), those cited as the key factors are costs, security and perceived ease of use (European Central Bank, 2012, p. 78).

Finally, it ought to be emphasised that if electronic payments are to replace traditional payments based on paper documents and cash, it should be assessed by consumers better in terms of convenience but also safety and cost, or with respect to a majority of these features. It is not going to be easy because in many countries, especially those less wealthy, with strong preference for using cash in which societies show strong attachment to cash, like for example in Poland, cash is considered the most comfortable and safest form of payment that at the same time allows for better control of expenses in comparison with non-cash payments. In these countries, the use of cash in daily payments largely results from a habit, but also from the absence of financial knowledge and lack of trust in financial institutions. The change in these habits needs time as well as development of incentives aiming at this change with accompanying educational measures.

2.2.4 Innovative payment instruments as a substitute for cash

Displacing cash in face-to-face transactions may become in the coming years easier, thanks to the development of payment innovations. This is because they largely fill the gap that banks were not interested in as they were focused on traditional, classical payment instruments offered for many years. The gap is formed by low-value payments, particularly micropayments that are still made with the use of cash.

The significance of payment innovations is still rather small; however, forecasts show that by 2020 their share in the number of non-cash transactions in Europe may even reach 20% – see Figure 2.12. At the same time, the share of credit transfers and direct debit is expected to fall by more than one-fifth and the share of debit and credit cards will remain quite stable.

The majority of payment innovations occurring recently favour development of non-cash transactions, yet only a few may become direct competitors for cash. Identification of this type of innovations among all that have been occurring in the market recently is not easy due to

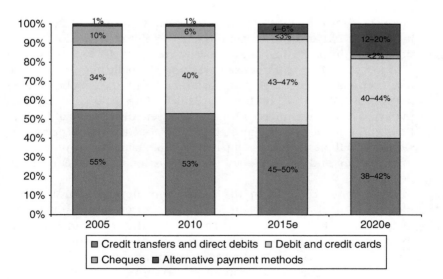

Figure 2.12 Change in payment mix in Europe, 2005–2020e
Source: Based on A.T. Kearney (2013, p. 6).

their large number and diversity. In recent years two large-scale surveys aiming at identification of innovations in retail payments have been conducted.

As a result of the survey conducted by the World Bank in 2010 among 101 central banks, 173 payment innovations were identified. P2B payments and P2P payments were the most common types of payment offered by the providers of innovative payment instruments and methods. Less than 10% of the instruments and methods support government payments. New instruments and methods of payment, mainly implemented by non-banking PSPs, are usually initiated via electronic channels and have well-developed price models. However, their fundamental drawbacks include very limited interoperability, absence of direct connection to the clearing and settlement infrastructure and relatively low level of safety (World Bank, 2011, pp. 44–45).

In a similar survey conducted a year later by CPSS, 122 innovations in retail payments were reported by thirty central banks. They could be divided into process-oriented and product-oriented innovations. Process-oriented innovations are mostly focused on back-office processes, the area of the payment process where innovation is generally only observed by payment service providers. These innovations are aimed at increase in effectiveness of the payment process. On the other hand, product-oriented innovations apply the intuitive features of a payment instrument that are obvious from the user's point of view. The innovations that can be further categorised by, for example, types of device used to initiate payment (for example cards or mobile phones) or channels that enable its completion (for example Internet, mobile phone network or POS). In a report from the Bank for International Settlements five types of product-oriented innovations were distinguished: innovations in the use of card payments, Internet payments, mobile payments, electronic bill presentment and payment (EBPP), and improvements in infrastructure and security (Bank for International Settlements, 2012, pp. 12–15).

Innovations occurring in the retail payment market usually are product-oriented (new payment instruments) or process-oriented (new methods/ways to made payments perceived as the process including its initiation, processing, settlement and clearing, and receiving payment). The majority of new solutions recently occurring on the retail payment market are incremental innovations (for example contactless cards or EMV cards). On the other hand, radical innovations appear much more rarely – this category includes mobile payments, online payments, e-money and virtual currencies (Harasim and Klimontowicz, 2013, pp. 88–89).

Considering the pace of development and the rate of adoption of the basic types of payment innovations, it should be stated that contactless payments constitute the most promising alternative for cash. They include contactless cards (based on RFID technology) and mobile proximity payments, and especially NFC (Near Field Communication) payments – see Table 2.5. E-money and virtual currencies are going to have much smaller potential in this field in the nearest future. On the other hand, innovative payment instruments used in online transactions are first of all a competition to traditional non-cash payment instruments such as payment cards (mainly credit cards), credit transfer and direct debit.

Table 2.5 Payment innovations as a substitute for cash

Payment instruments	Innovation range		Transaction type		Substitute for cash
	incremental	radical	face-to-face	online	
Contactless cards	X		X		+++
Proximity mobile payments (NFC)		X	X		+++
Remote mobile payments		X		X	+
Online payments		X		X	+
e-purse/e-wallet (e-money)		X	X	X	++
Virtual currencies		X		X	++
e-credit transfer	X			X	+
e-direct debit	X			X	+
EMV cards	X		X	X	+

Source: Own work.

2.2.5 Determinants of diffusion of contactless payments

However, many factors determine whether contactless payments will become a real competition for cash. They can be divided into three major groups (see Figure 2.13):

- factors resulting from specific features of payment market,
- conditions on the part of payment services providers,
- conditions on the part of payment services users – consumers and merchants.

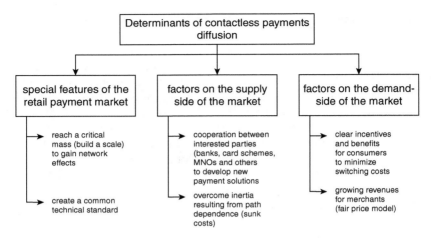

Figure 2.13 Determinants of contactless payments' diffusion
Source: Own work.

Reaching a large customer and merchant base quickly is crucial to succeed in payment innovations. As regards contactless payments, conditions associated with specific features of the payment market are in a short period more advantageous for contactless cards than for mobile proximity payments. In the case of cards, reaching the critical mass is much easier because the contactless function is usually added (frequently free of charge) to newly issued cards, which brings fast growth in the number of cards. Dissemination of contactless cards is also favoured by a relatively low number of applied technological standards; two of them have fundamental importance here: PayPass technology implemented by MasterCard and PayWave implemented by Visa. Poland can serve as an example of a fast achievement of critical mass with reference to contactless cards, where at the end of 2009 there were 320 thousand contactless cards in circulation. This represented around one % of issued payment cards, whereas five years later, the number of cards with contactless function reached 25.7 million and their share in the market increased to 71.3% (National Bank of Poland, 2015, p. 10). However, the British market is the largest market of contactless cards in Europe. In 2014 there were fifty-eight million contactless cards in circulation there. According to the UK Cards Association (The UK Cards Association, 2015), UK consumers used their contactless cards 319.2 million times in 2014 and spending on contactless cards more than trebled over 2014, reaching a record £2.3 billion (it was more than double that of all the previous six years combined).

The situation is slightly worse in the case of mobile proximity payments. Even though the number of smartphones and tablets is dynamically growing, it is not equivalent with fast adoption of mobile payments. The multitude of technological solutions is one of the major reasons for this situation. However, so far none of them has become a standard that might be adopted by a majority of market participants. The greatest hopes are recently associated with NFC technology, but for the time being, a universal standard has not been developed yet. Experiences of the countries of South-Eastern Asia, including Japan, where mobile payments are developing rapidly, show that overcoming these obstacles (and thereby the possibility of critical mass achievement) demands not a competition, but cooperation of all interested parties (telecoms, banks and technical solutions providers). However, as previous experiences show, it is not easy because their interests are often contrary. The situation is different if we consider contactless cards, and different in the case of mobile proximity payments.

Banks (in cooperation with cards schemes) are leaders in the implementation of contactless cards while occupying the predominant position in the market of retail payments. Contactless cards are an incremental innovation and are not a competitor for other payment instruments offered by banks; on the contrary, they complement each other and make their offer richer. This is because the majority of payments with the use of traditional payment cards are between USD 15 and 150, whereas contactless card is used in low-value payments in which cash has been mostly used so far. The contactless function is generally added to newly issued debit or credit cards, which allows market players (merchants, merchant processors, merchant acquirers, card networks, card processors, issuers and many other suppliers) further mitigation of sunk investments in equipment, software and people.

On the other hand, new competitors from outside the sector (for example mobile devices producers or telecoms) are initiators of mobile proximity payments. The ability to identify customers' needs that have not been properly satisfied by traditional payment instruments ought to be considered the largest competitive advantage of new PSPs (Sullivan and Wang, 2007). New competitors also have significantly developed customer databases that are much larger in numbers than of single banks. For example, Apple has over 500 million customers, the largest mobile network operator, Vodafone, has around 400 million customers, while Citigroup and Santander have 'only' about 100 million customers each. New PSPs know perfectly the purchasing habits of consumers and can identify their needs in an excellent way. Their interest in the retail payment market results from the willingness to offer the customers an integrated package composed of products offered by them and simple payment instruments enabling making payments. Therefore, payment ought to be ideally integrated with the selling process and made in the way that is most 'friendly' for a customer. Experience gained in the retail sector results in the larger flexibility, innovativeness and simplicity of instruments proposed by them. In comparison with traditional payment instruments offered by banks, they satisfy to a larger extent the needs of customers in terms of speed, cost and simplicity of payment while ensuring at the same time a relatively high level of protection from abuse and faster and easier procedures concerning refunds or complaints. Moreover, new competitors make decisions, implement new solutions and react to market changes faster than banks (Harasim, 2013, pp. 97–98).

The latter group of factors determining success of contactless payments is associated with expectations of their users. There are two groups of end users in two-sided markets: consumers and merchants. For consumers the most important are convenience and usefulness of payment (including its speed and ease of use), as well as security and cost, whereas for merchants relationship between profits obtained from acceptance of a particular payment instrument (for example in the form of increased income) and incurred costs (for example in the form of payments for POS terminals or other services associated with supporting payments) are particularly important.

From the consumer's point of view the largest advantages of contactless payments are their ease of use and speed. This is confirmed by both national and foreign research. The results of studies conducted in 2010 by Edgar, Dunn & Company show that speed of making payments and reduction of queue waiting time were considered by respondents to be the most important advantages resulting from implementation of contactless payments. It ought to be stated here that these benefits must occur simultaneously – because if the queue waiting time is not reduced, the fact that payment will last a few seconds shorter will not be important any longer (Edgar, Dunn & Company, 2011). Research conducted in Poland showed that all forms of contactless payments (that is contactless card, off-line contactless card, RFID sticker on telephone and NFC phone with PIN) are faster than payments made via traditional cards. However, only off-line contactless cards proved to be competitive in relation to cash in terms of speed (Polasik *et al.*, 2013, p. 13). The convenience of contactless payments is also associated with the absence of the necessity to sign confirmation of transaction or to enter a PIN. On the other hand, the absence of the need to carry cash that so far has been necessary to make low-value payments represents larger safety even though contactless payments are not considered as a very safe form of payment.

Large-scale adoption of contactless payments can also bring a lot of benefits to the merchants. Major profits gained by them are associated with the possibility of income increase. This is because reduction of service time allows for serving a larger number of customers which is particularly important in the case of mass services of restaurants, transport and so on.[5] Moreover, consumers making contactless payments in general spend more (by 20–30%) than those who pay in cash and are more satisfied which results in further purchases. Acceptance of contactless payments also allows for reduction of costs related to cash, including its insurance or losses from theft. But many merchants perceive these costs as fixed costs and envisage only limited savings resulting from their reduction. Weighting these savings against the fees they pay for card acceptance, some merchants assess critically the economic viability of contactless cards. Despite of this, the majority of merchants understand that suitably deployed contactless technology has substantial benefits for end users, particularly in specific merchant sectors (Edgar, Dunn & Company, 2011, p. 18). Apart from financial benefits, merchants may gain more information about consumers' preferences and their purchasing habits, which could be helpful while creating loyalty programs or in other marketing activities.

It could be noted that some expectations of consumers and merchants are similar and can be the source of mutual benefits (for example those associated with the speed of payment), but others remain contradictory, like for example those concerning the cost of payment. Therefore, development of business models considering the interests of all market players, including a price strategy that assumes proper division of costs between interested parties, is going to be of key importance in payment innovations adoption. However, generally in practice, in the early stages at least, one way to reach a critical mass may be a pricing strategy that lets the less price-sensitive side of the market subsidise the more price-sensitive one (Bank for International Settlements, 2012, p. 19).

2.2.6 The role of regulatory framework in reducing the cash usage and fostering the growth of non-cash transactions

Regulations may affect the payment market and its participants in a different ways. In this chapter the notion of regulation is approached broadly. It comprises not only the government regulations, but also bottom-up initiatives that have the nature of self-regulations[6] undertaken by market participants (most often PSPs, for example SEPA) and all initiatives and programs, which could be helpful for reducing the cash usage (for example Digital Agenda for Europe). A large number of regulations concerning the payment market, their diversified nature (top-down or bottom-up) and scope (global, regional or national) make it difficult to assess their influence on the cash usage and the development of non-cash transactions. This is because regulations implemented recently are aimed at various issues mostly related to increase in market efficiency. Furthermore, a lot of them refer at the same time to many aspects associated with provision of payment services for example access to market, its transparency, standardisation, innovation, consumer protection and so on. According to Capgemini, RBS and EFMA the regulations reflect some trends in the payment market clearly observed in recent years. They include systemic risk reduction and control, transparency of services, innovations, standardisation and convergence (Capgemini *et al.*, 2012, p. 27). Table 2.6 shows the most important European and worldwide regulations directly or indirectly referring to the payment market and the way they influence its shape and functioning, while considering the most important trends observed in payment markets in recent years.

Table 2.6 Influence of regulatory framework on the payment market

Sphere of regulation	Examples of impact of regulation on payment market	Selected regulations
Systemic risk reduction and control	Searching by banks for the most stable, long-term sources of financing (including resources on retail customers' accounts and prepaid cards) (+) Reduction of efficiency of payment systems due to increase in the costs of payment processing and slowdown of the process of direct processing on the way from the ordering entity to the beneficiary (STP – Straight Through Processing) (–) Growth in safety and reliability of payment systems, and trust in payment instruments (+)	AML/ATF (2005) Basel III (2010)
Transparency of services	Increase in transparency of the structure of payment costs and prices of payment services (+) Reduction of the possibility to collect hidden fees (e.g., interchange fees, debit-card swipe fees) (+) Reduction of bank revenues (–)	PSD (2007) PAD directive (2014) MIF Regulation (2015)

Continued

Table 2.6 Continued

Sphere of regulation	Examples of impact of regulation on payment market	Selected regulations
Innovations	Increase in competitiveness in the market and change in its subjective structure (through admission of non-banking suppliers of payment services or establishment of cooperation between banks and other entities from outside the financial sector in the case of innovative forms of payment, among others) (+) Occurrence of new payment instruments / forms of payments (e.g., mobile payments and online payments) (+) Change in preferences of the users of payment services and their payment habits Increase in the scale of using financial services (financial inclusion) through development of non-cash transactions and related infrastructure (+) Popularisation of non-cash transactions and services accompanying them (e-invoicing) in settlements with public institutions (+)	PSD (2007) EMD directive (2009) The Digital Agenda (2010) PAD directive (2014)
Standardisation	Facilitation of achievement of critical mass in the case of new solutions (+) Stimulating competition through development of a common market standard (+) Automation of the payment service, reduction of its costs and creation of new sources of income (+) Reduction of diversity of payment solutions applied in domestic and foreign settlements (+) Reduction of motivation to implement innovation after popularisation of a common standard (–) Difficulties in making changes in existing standard or replacing it with another one (–)	SEPA SEPA – SCT, SDD and SCF standards
Convergence	Increase in competitiveness in market through blurring the differences between various types of settlement and clearing systems	TARGET2 evolution ACH Frequent Settlement

Note: (+) – Positive impact, (–) – Negative impact.

Source: Own case study on the basis of Capgemini and RBS 2013).

While making an attempt to assess regulations impact on the cash usage at the beginning, it ought to be emphasised that only a small part of regulations shown in Table 2.6 directly refers to cash transactions. The limitation on cash payments in Europe has been installed in the anti-money laundering legislation (AML/ATF). This limit amounts to EUR 15,000; however, it concerns payments made between professional entities (entrepreneurs). However, in EU legislation there are no uniform regulations reducing the use of cash in payments made by consumers. Still, regulations introducing amount limits for making cash payments, also binding for natural persons, exist in some EU Member States – see Table 2.7. Payments higher than the limit determined by law must be made in non-cash form, and in Denmark it is additionally required that they should be made electronically.

Table 2.7 Cash payment restrictions in European countries: an overview

Country	Date of introduction	Cash limits	Reporting entities
Belgium	1 January 2014	3,000 EUR	
Bulgaria	16/22 February 2011	15,000 BGN	Natural persons and entrepreneurs
Czech Republic	1 January 2013	350,000 CZK	Natural persons and entrepreneurs (with exceptions)
Denmark	1 July 2012	10,000 DKK	Natural persons and entrepreneurs
France	1 January 2002	3,000 EUR 15,000 EUR	Residents and non-resident traders Non-resident consumers
Greece	1 January 2011	1,500 EUR 3,000 EUR	Payment between entrepreneur and consumer B2B payments
Hungary	1 January 2013	1,500,000 HUF	Legal persons
Italy	6 December 2012	1,000 EUR	
Portugal	14 May 2012	1,000 EUR	
Slovakia	1 January 2013	5,000 EUR 15,000 EUR	Natural persons (being not entrepreneurs)
Spain	19 November 2012	2,500 EUR 15,000 EUR	Residents (at least one side is entrepreneur)

Source: Own work based on European Consumer Centre France (2014) and National Bank of Poland (2013).

It should be stressed that in the majority of the countries these limits have occurred quite recently, or they have been tightened in recent years. Furthermore, generally the countries that limit the use of cash suffered more than other countries as a result of crisis; it can also be supposed that the limits were the response to decline in trust in non-cash transactions for the benefit of trust in cash, which is a phenomenon quite typical of the periods of economic uncertainty. However, counteracting terrorism and money laundering as well as the phenomenon of tax avoidance, but also, even though in a smaller degree, the phenomenon of tax evasion on income coming from business activity were fundamental reasons for implementation of limits on cash usage. These limits also provide the possibility to trace the flow of financial resources while ensuring their larger transparency. The efficiency of these limits is questioned by some people (for example Beretta, 2014), and it seems that they do not have significant impact on reduction of the cash usage in the field of its previous predominance, that is, in low-value face-to-face transactions.

Reduction of cash usage is more favoured by regulations which stimulate the development of electronic payments and payment innovations including those that could be an alternative for cash. Over several recent years, dynamic development of regulatory framework has been observed all over the world, although Europe, unlike many emerging markets such as India, China and Brazil, presents conservative attitudes as regards regulations aiming at stimulation of innovations. For many years both EU and national regulations have been strengthening the traditional structure of the market, with a predominant role for banks in the whole payment execution process, while creating barriers for non-banking PSPs in access to each of its stages. Despite growing pressure concerning transparency of costs of payment services and their prices, there were no definite actions taken by regulators aiming at ensuring fair redistribution of incomes and costs between particular groups of market participants. Therefore regulations were a serious barrier for increase in efficiency of the payment market, particularly in the area of retail payments.

The situation was not significantly changed by the most important regulations concerning payments implemented in recent years in the European Union, that is, the PSD or SEPA. They concern mainly traditional payment instruments (direct debit, credit transfer and payment cards). Although payments made electronically (they do not include cash payments or those based on paper documents) are the object of the directive, it does not create conditions for development of innovations. During consultations conducted in 2010 concerning the E-Commerce

Directive, payments have been identified as one of the main barriers to the future growth of e-commerce. On the other hand, in 'Green Paper. Towards an Integrated European Market for Card, Internet and Mobile Payments', the lack of a concrete European framework addressing the main concerns, such as technical standards, security, interoperability and the cooperation between market participants and risks perpetuating a fragmented e-payments and m-payments market in Europe were considered the major barrier for development of e-payments and m-payments. Furthermore, for both e- and m-payments, (potential) market participants seem reluctant to invest as long as the legal situation regarding scope for applying collective fee arrangements, such as for payment cards, has not been settled (European Commission, 2012a, pp. 5–6).

Regulations aiming at stimulating competition in the payment market and increasing its efficiency, such as the MIF Regulation or PSD2, started to occur in Europe only recently with significant delay in comparison with other regions. Regulations included in the MIF Regulation foster competition and in the Revised Directive on Payment Services (PSD2) that is to be adopted in 2015, ought to provide support for development of innovations. As the European Commission declares: *The new measures will ensure that all payment providers active in the EU are subject to supervision and appropriate rules. This should create the right incentives for the emergence of new players and the development of innovative mobile and Internet payments in Europe. This means more choice and better conditions for consumers and businesses* (European Commission, 2015). A definite majority of regulations occurring recently, while opening access to new markets for new PSPs, leads to defragmentation of the payment process. As a result, the payment value chain will be disaggregated and a payment process will be handled by specialised PSPs. Establishment of legal frameworks for payment innovations stimulates their development, establishes trust in them and encourages using them in payments. This, in turn, may lead to change in payment habits, particularly in reducing cash transactions.

2.3   Conclusions

The moment we may stop using cash seems to be really close. This statement is supported by many factors including dynamic development of ICT technologies, expansion of e-commerce and also social and cultural changes. The changes comprise growing virtualisation and digitalisation resulting in changes of lifestyles and behaviours of contemporary consumers. In the opinions of many entities, cash is becoming a relic of the past, a payment form that does not match contemporary lifestyles and the speed of life. It is also not adjusted to the type of concluded transactions and the way they are conducted. However, are we really ready to abandon cash? And if we are, what should it be replaced by?

The analysis conducted in this chapter does not give an explicit answer to this question. It is certain that financial institutions, including banks or card schemes, and recently also other PSPs engaged in development of payment innovations, are major supporters of elimination of cash from circulation. In many countries also state authorities aim at reducing cash usage. Their major goal is to limit the shadow economy and reduce the costs of cash circulation. However, it seems that theses aims are not shared by a quite big group of consumers. In many countries people show strong commitment to cash and still perceive it as the most convenient, the fastest, the cheapest and safest payment form, particularly in P2P or C2B transactions. Cash also has an additional value that must not be ignored – anonymity. It ensures privacy to consumers, which is currently becoming a rare and increasingly appreciated good in the world where mass surveillance is becoming a general practice.

As a result, in Europe we can find countries such as Sweden or Denmark where the use of cash is low and is still decreasing, and also such as Greece, Bulgaria or Romania where more than nine per ten retail transactions are conducted with its use.

Due to these reasons, replacement of cash by other payment instruments is not going to be as easy and fast as it may seem. Considering the pace of development and the rate of adoption of the basic types of payment innovations, it should be stated that contactless payments constitute the most promising alternative for cash in face-to-face transactions. They include contactless cards (based on RFID technology) and mobile proximity payments, and especially NFC payments. Their popularisation mostly depends on consumers' willingness to change existing payment habits and fast establishment of a large merchant base. Achievement of the first goal demands holding intense educational actions leading to increase in the scale of financial inclusion and activities aiming at reducing barriers in access to basic financial services (for example payment account with basic features). Reaching a large merchant base quickly demands in turn development of business models considering interests of all market players, including a price strategy that assumes proper division of costs between interested parties. However, before this happens, it is necessary to develop the technical standards that might be approved by a majority of market players. In the case of contactless cards this barrier has actually been overcome; however, in the case of mobile proximity payments it is still an obstacle to reaching critical mass in the market.

Notes

1. In the summer of 2011, the Federal Reserve Board of Governors issued a final rule governing debit card interchange fees. This regulation, named Regulation II (Debit Card Interchange Fees and Routing), was required by the Durbin Amendment to the Dodd-Frank Act. The regulation, which went into effect on 1 October 2011, limits the maximum permissible interchange fee that a covered issuer can collect from merchants for a debit card transaction. The Board's Regulation II provides that an issuer subject to the interchange fee standard (a covered issuer) may not receive an interchange fee that exceeds 21 cents plus 0.05% multiplied by the value of the transaction, plus a 1-cent fraud-prevention adjustment, if eligible.
2. There is, as yet, no single, precise definition of micropayments. In the payments industry they are defined as transactions under 5 USD, but in the case of PayPal in the UK it is the amount below 5 GBP.
3. They were: Denmark, Estonia, Finland, Greece, Hungary, Ireland, Italy, Latvia, Netherlands, Portugal, Romania, Spain and Sweden.
4. Financial inclusion is the process of ensuring access to appropriate financial products and services needed by vulnerable groups such as weaker sections and low-income groups at an affordable cost in a fair and transparent manner by mainstream institutional players (Reserve Bank of India, 2011). Financial inclusion includes access to and usage of a broad range of affordable, quality financial services and products, in a manner convenient to the financially excluded, unbanked and under-banked, in an appropriate, but simple and dignified manner with the requisite consideration to client protection. Accessibility should be accompanied by usage which should be supported through the financial education of clients (The Banking Association of South Africa, 2015).
5. A board member of an American fast food restaurant chain estimated that reducing the time of payment with the use of POS by one second allows for increasing the annual company turnover by USD one million.
6. *Self-regulation* may be forced by the very state (like for example SEPA), but it can also be initiated by market participants for the purpose of protection of their interests (for example agreement concerning *interchange fee*). At the same time, the results of self-regulation can be varied for particular groups of participants in the payment market (generally different for suppliers and users of payment services).

References

Aghion, P., and Bolton, P. (1997) 'A theory of trickle-down growth and development', *Review of Economics Studies*, Vol. 64, No. 2, pp. 151–172.
Allen, F., Demirguc-Kunt, A., Klapper, L., and Martinez Peria, M.S. (2012) *The foundations of financial inclusion understanding ownership and use of formal accounts*,

Policy Research Working Paper 6290 (The World Bank, Development Research Group, Finance and Private Sector Development Team).

A.T. Kearney (2013) *European payment strategy report. Winning the growth challenge in payments*, https://www.atkearney.de/documents/856314/1545047/BIP_Winning_the_Growth_Challenge_in_Payments.pdf/49ecf6a4-66d4-4a48-a7ac-dd5ad999da56, date accessed 17 May 2015.

Banerjee, A., and Newman, A. (1993) Occupational Choice and the Process of Development, *Journal of Political Economy*, Vol.101, No. 2, pp. 274–298.

Bank for International Settlements (2002) *Policy issues for central banks in retail payments*, Report of the Working Group on Retail Payment Systems (Basel: Committee on Payment and Settlement Systems, Bank for International Settlements).

Bank for International Settlements (2012) *Innovations in retail payments*, Report of the Working Group on Innovation in Retail Payments (Basel: Committee on Payment and Settlement Systems), May.

Bank for International Settlements (2013) *Statistics on payment, clearing and settlement systems in the CPSS countries – figures for 2012* (Basel: Committee on Payment and Settlement Systems, Bank for International Settlements).

Bank for International Settlements (2014) *Statistics on payment, clearing and settlement systems in the CPSS countries – figures for 2013* (Basel: Committee on Payment and Settlement Systems, Bank for International Settlements).

Beck, T., Demirgüç-Kunt, A., and Martinez Peria, M.S. (2007) 'Reaching out: Access to and use of banking services across countries', *Journal of Financial Economics*, 85, pp. 234–266.

Beretta, E. (2014) 'The irreplaceability of cash and recent limitations on its use: Why Europe is off the track', http://www.bundesbank.de/Redaktion/EN/Downloads/Tasks/Cash_management/Conferences/2014_09_16_cashs_irreplaceability_and_recent_limitations_on_its_usage.pdf?__blob=publicationFile, date accessed 12 May 2015.

Capgemini, and RBS (2013) *World payments report*, https://www.capgemini.com/thought-leadership/world-payments-report-2013, date accessed 11 May 2015.

Capgemini, and RBS (2014) *World payments report*, https://www.capgemini.com/thought-leadership/world-payments-report-2014-from-capgemini-and-rbs, date accessed 14 May 2015.

Capgemini, RBS, and EFMA (2011) *World payments report*, https://www.capgemini.com/resources/world-payments-report-2011, date accessed 10 May 2015.

Capgemini, RBS, and EFMA (2012) *World payments report*, https://www.capgemini.com/resource-file-access/resource/pdf/The_8th_Annual_World_Payments_Report_2012.pdf, date accessed 10 May 2015.

Deloitte Center for Banking Solutions (2008) *Catalyst for change. The implications of gen Y consumers for banks*, December, http://www.deloitte.com/assets/Dcom-Shared%20Assets/Documents/us_fsi_GenY_Consumers_april08.pdf, date accessed 18 May 2015.

Demirguc-Kunt, A., and Klapper, L. (2012) 'Measuring financial inclusion. The Global Findex Database', Policy Research Working Paper 6025 (The World Bank, Development Research Group, Finance and Private Sector Development Team), April.

Demirguc-Kunt, A., Klapper, L., and Randall, D. (2013) 'The Global Findex Database measuring financial inclusion in Europe and Central Asia', *Findex Note*, 06 (The World Bank), April.

Demirguc-Kunt, A., Klapper, L., Singer ,D., and Van Oudheusden, P. (2015). 'The Global Findex Database 2014 measuring financial inclusion in the World', Policy Research Working Paper No. 7255 (The World Bank, Development Research Group Finance and Private Sector Development Team), April.Denecker, O., Sarvady, G., and Yip, A. (2009) *Global perspective on payments. The McKinsey global payments map*, April,

Deutsche Bundesbank (2012) *Payment behaviour in germany in 2011, an empirical study of the utilisation of cash and cashless payment instruments*, https://www.bundesbank.de/Redaktion/EN/Downloads/Publications/Bulletins_and_surveys/payment_behaviour_in_germany_in_2011.pdf?__blob=publicationFile., date accessed 25 April 2015.

E-commerce Foundation (2014a) *European B2C e-commerce report 2014*, https://www.ecommercebenchmark.org/pl/report-info/13/European-B2C-E-commerce-LIGHT-Report-2014, date accessed 30 April 2015.

E-commerce Foundation (2014b) *Global B2C e-commerce report 2014* https://www.ecommercebenchmark.org/pl/report-info/16/Global-B2C-E-commerce-LIGHT-Report-2014. date accessed 30 April 2015.

Edgar, Dunn & Company (2011) *Advanced payments report*, http://www.edgar-dunn.com/press/issues-and-opportunities/90-2011-advanced-payments-report. date accessed 4 May 2015.

EFMA and McKinsey & Company (2012) *Digital transformation in 10 building blocks to boost customer experience and ROE* (Copenhagen and New York), October.

ECB (2012) 'Towards an integrated European card payments market', *ECB Monthly Bulletin*, January.

ECB (2015) *Payment statistics,* http://sdw.ecb.europa.eu/reports.do?node=1000001964, date accessed 25 April 2015.

European Commission (2008) *Financial services provision and prevention of financial exclusion* (Brussels), May.

European Commission (2012a) 'Green Paper. Towards an integrated European market for card, internet and mobile payments' (Brussels, 11 January 2012, COM(2011) 941 final).

European Commission (2012b) *Special Eurobarometer on retail financial services* (Brussels), February.

European Commission (2015) 'Press release commissioner hill welcomes agreement on the revised payment services directive' (Brussels), 5 May http://europa.eu/rapid/press-release_IP-15-4916_en.htm?locale=en, date accessed 22 May 2015.

European Consumer Centre France (2014) Cash payment limitations, http://www.europe-consommateurs.eu/en/consumer-topics/buying-of-goods-and-services/cash-payment-limitations/, date accessed 8 May 2015.

Górka J. (2009) *Konkurencyjność form pieniądza i instrumentów płatniczych* (Warszawa: CeDeWu).

Gumuła W. (2013) 'Pieniądz gotówkowy i bezgotówkowy w Polsce' in H. Żukowska and M. Żukowski (eds) *Obrót bezgotówkowy w Polsce* (Lublin: Wydawnictwo KUL).

Harasim J. (2013) *Współczesny rynek płatności detalicznych – specyfika, regulacje, innowacje* (Katowice: Wydawnictwo Uniwersytetu Ekonomicznego w Katowicach).

Harasim, J., and Klimontowicz, M. (2013) 'Payment habits as a determinant of retail payment innovations diffusion: The Case of Poland', *Journal of Innovation Management*, No. 2.

ING (2015) *ING International survey, the rise of mobile banking and the changing face of payments in the digital age* (Paris: Ipsos for ING Group), April.

King, B. (2013) *Bank 3.0. Why banking is no longer somewhere you go but something you do* (Singapore: Brett King and Marshall Cavendish (International) Asia Pte Ltd.).

Koźliński, T. (2013) *Zwyczaje płatnicze Polaków* (Warszawa: NBP, Departament Systemu Płatniczego), May.

National Bank of Poland (2013) Diagnoza stanu rozwoju obrotu bezgotówkowego w Polsce (Warszawa: NBP, Departament Systemu Płatniczego), December.

National Bank of Poland (2015) *Informacja o kartach płatniczych IV kwartał 2014* (Warszawa: Departament Systemu Płatniczego), Marzec.

Polasik, M., Górka, J., Wilczewski, G., Kunkowski, J., Przenajkowska, K., and Tetkowska, N. (2013) 'Time efficiency of point-of-sale payment methods: The empirical results for cash, cards and mobile payments', http://papers.ssrn.com/sol3/papers.cfm?abstract_id=1769922, date accessed 25 March 2015.

Reserve Bank of India (2011) Financial Inclusion | A road India needs to travel, https://rbi.org.in/scripts/BS_SpeechesView.aspx?Id=607, date accessed 10 May 2015, date accessed 15 May 2015.

Schmiedel, H., Kostova, G., and Ruttenberg, W. (2012) 'The social and private costs of retail payment instruments. A European perspective', *European Central Bank Occasional Paper Series*, No. 137, October.

Sullivan, B.J., and Wang, Z. (2007) 'Nonbanks in the payments system: Innovation, competition and risk – a conference summary', *Federal Reserve Board of Kansas City Economic Review*, No. 3.

Sveriges Riksbank (2015) 'The payment behaviour of the Swedish population', http://www.riksbank.se/en/Statistics/The-payment-behaviour/, date accessed 12 May 2015.

The Banking Association of South Africa (2015), Working definition of financial inclusion, http://www.banking.org.za/what-we-do/overview/working-definition-of-financial-inclusion, date accessed 10 May 2015, date accessed 15 May 2015.

The UK Cards Association (2015) 'Consumers turn to contactless as usage surges', http://www.theukcardsassociation.org.uk/news/Contactless_surgeJan2015.asp, date accessed 17 May 2015.

The World Bank (2011) *Payment systems worldwide – a snapshot. Outcomes of the Global Payment Systems Survey 2010*, http://www-wds.worldbank.org/external/default/WDSContentServer/WDSP/IB/2012/06/25/000425970_201206251043 00/Rendered/PDF/701580ESW0P1230bal0Survey0Book02010.pdf.

3
Could "Nudges" Steer Us towards a Less-Cash Society?

Leo Van Hove

3.1 Introduction: more than the latest fad?

Every now and then academics write a popularising book on economics that effectively becomes wildly popular. *Information Rules* by Carl Shapiro and Hal Varian comes to mind, and in 2008 there was *Nudge – Improving Decisions about Health, Wealth, and Happiness* by Richard Thaler and Cass Sunstein, a book described by one website as "the Harry Potter of the policy world this summer".[1] In the book, behavioural economist Thaler and law professor Sunstein, then both at the University of Chicago, argue that seemingly small changes in the choice context – "nudges" – can have massive effects on people's behaviour. Other books, such as Daniel Kahneman's (2011) *Thinking, Fast and Slow* and *I'll Have What She's Having* by Bentley, Earls and O'Brien (2011) have since ridden the wave of interest in behavioural economics.

This chapter puts Thaler and Sunstein's "libertarian paternalism" – which has been embraced by Barack Obama, David Cameron and other key policy makers – to the test. Specifically, I was eager to find out whether it could offer fresh answers to an old problem in payment economics: how to reduce people's cash usage? On the face of it, *Nudge* should be able to provide clues. After all, payment behaviour *is* behaviour. Also, Thaler and Sunstein themselves argue that "the range of potential applications [of libertarian paternalism] is much broader than the topics [they] have managed to include" in the book (2008, p. 252). They add that "one of [their] main hopes is that an understanding of choice architecture, and the power of nudges, will lead others to think of creative ways to improve human lives in other domains" (ibidem). At the same time, *Nudge* triggered quite some criticism, both in the financial press and in academia. A *Financial Times* editorial contended that "the policy options [libertarian paternalism] opens up are rather limited".[2] Neuroscientist Dean Buonomano in his book *Brain Bugs* argued that nudging is "ultimately limited in reach [...] the effects are often relatively small, helping some people, but far from all, improve their decision" (2011, p. 233).[3]

Is the backlash justified, or can the Thaler/Sunstein framework really yield promising policy suggestions, at least where the War On Cash (WOC) is concerned? In this chapter, I present my findings in the following way. In Section 3.2, I first explain what nudging is all about. Section 3.3 then deals with the preliminary question as to whether the WOC qualifies as a policy problem susceptible to nudging in the first place. It also explains an even more basic premise: why would policy makers want to reduce cash usage? Section 3.4 then confronts the nudging theory with the WOC problem. I point out a number of nudges that have already been tried out in the payments sector (even though they were probably not recognised as such at the time), and I suggest a number of others that might work. Section 3.5 then takes a look at the limited academic research so far Section 3.6 concludes.

3.2   The theory

As pointed out in the introduction, between 2008 and now several other relevant books besides *Nudge* have been published. Also, both *Nudge* and these other books are based on extensive academic research – in psychology, economics and other fields. However, for the sake of brevity I will in this section limit myself to the Thaler and Sunstein book, containing as it does all the concepts that are needed in later sections.

Nudge applies behavioural economics to business practices and, in particular, government policy. Thaler and Sunstein's starting point is straightforward: you, me, everybody, we are all not as smart as we think we are. Humans, Thaler and Sunstein point out, are less rational than policy makers and economists make them out to be. People make bad choices quite often; choices they should not make, and do not really want to make, either. In other words, we all have a bit of the impulsive and weak-willed Homer Simpson in us. (The book uses several Homer quotes to good illustrative effect.) Hence, people could use some help in making better choices.

Enter libertarian paternalism, or "nudging". Nudging is all about steering people in the "right" direction by making subtle changes to the choice context. An example given in the book consists in changing the way food is displayed and arranged in school cafeterias in order to increase consumption of healthy foods. Placing carrot sticks at eye-level and desserts last, for example. The nudging is done by "choice architects": business leaders and policy makers in particular, but, as the food example shows, basically anyone who "has the responsibility for organising the context in which people make decisions" (Thaler and Sunstein, 2008, p. 3).

The paternalistic aspect of Thaler and Sunstein's policy recipe lies in the assumption that there is someone – either a person or an institution – who knows what is best for everybody else, and "in the claim that it is legitimate for choice architects to try to influence people's behavior in order to make their lives longer, healthier, and better" (o.c., p. 5). The libertarian aspect lies in the insistence that people should be free to choose. In other words, libertarian paternalism is a "soft, and nonintrusive type of paternalism [where] choices are not blocked, fenced off, or significantly burdened" (ibidem). If people want to eat a lot of chips instead of carrot sticks, they should be allowed to do so. Thaler and Sunstein repeatedly stress that for it to count as a mere nudge, the intervention should not significantly change people's economic incentives (o.c., p. 6). Hence, increasing material costs does *not* qualify; even additional cognitive costs should be low (o.c., p. 8). For the case analysed in this chapter, the implication is that, say, introducing or increasing fees for ATM withdrawals – as part of a move towards cost-based pricing of payment instruments (Van Hove, 2002, 2004, 2008) – cannot be considered to be a nudge.

In their book, Thaler and Sunstein also explain at length why humans are prone to making bad choices and how choice architects can harness the systematic biases in the way we think. Thaler and Sunstein portray the human brain as containing two semi-autonomous selves, a Reflective System and an Automatic System. The Reflective System is our conscious thought, the Mr Spock (of *Star Trek* fame) lurking within us. The Automatic System is our gut reaction, or everyone's inner Homer Simpson. The Automatic System is rapid and intuitive, and "it does not involve what we usually associate with *thinking*" (2008, p. 19; emphasis in original). In a complex world where most of us are busy, the Automatic System comes in handy as we cannot afford to reflect heavily on every choice we have to make. However, it sometimes turns us into mindless, passive decision makers, with a tendency to go along with the status quo or default option.

In addition, when we have to make judgments, we use heuristics, or simple rules of thumb, to help us. Thaler and Sunstein discuss three such heuristics and the biases that are associated with each. For our purposes, the anchoring heuristic will prove particularly instrumental. When we are asked to make a guess, we start with some number – a number we know or that is suggested to us – and then adjust it in the direction we think is appropriate. The problem with this process is that the adjustments are typically insufficient, and, worse, that our guess is influenced by the anchor, even if the anchor is plainly irrelevant. Hence, as Thaler and Sunstein point out, anchors can serve as nudges: "We can influence the figure you will choose by ever-so-subtly suggesting a starting point for your thought process" (o.c., p. 24).

Another interesting observation is that people are loss averse, and that, roughly speaking, losing something makes one twice as miserable as gaining the same thing makes one happy (o.c., p. 33). Thaler and Sunstein stress that, just like mindless choosing, loss aversion produces inertia; that is, a strong desire to stick with our current holdings, even when changes are very much in our interest.

Finally, Thaler and Sunstein point out that one of the most effective ways to nudge is via social influence (o.c., p. 54), for the simple reason that we like to conform. Thaler and Sunstein distinguish two categories of social influences: information and peer pressure. In some cases, simply informing people about what other people are doing can do the trick: "sometimes the practices of others are surprising, and hence people are much affected by learning what they are" (o.c., p. 65). In a particularly salient illustration given in the book, some three hundred households in San Marcos, California were informed about how much energy they had used in a certain period. They were also provided with figures on average household consumption in their neighbourhood. In the following weeks, the above-average energy users significantly decreased their consumption (o.c., p. 68).[4] Peer pressure, for its part, works because people care about what other people think about them.

3.3 The problem

As explained in the Introduction, my objective in this chapter is to find out whether libertarian paternalism – as set out in *Nudge* and related literature – might suggest new ways to discourage the use of cash. However, before I can tackle this question, I obviously first need to explain *why* one would want to discourage cash usage. A related question is whether the WOC actually fits in the Thaler-Sunstein framework.

3.3.1 The social cost of cash

The main problem with cash is its relative inefficiency, as reflected by its high social cost. The social cost of a payment service refers to the resources that society as a whole consumes in providing and using it. It is computed by adding up the private costs of all stakeholders (consumers, merchants, commercial banks, the central bank, etc.) and eliminating any transfer payments, in order to avoid double counting.[5]

It is intuitively clear that the circulation of notes and coins is labour intensive and thus costly. However, until a couple of years ago, estimates of the social cost of cash were scarce and not very reliable. Luckily, at least where Europe is concerned, this lack of hard evidence has progressively been remedied by studies conducted by central banks. Especially a study by the Dutch central bank (De Nederlandsche Bank, 2004) has proven ground-breaking. In the second half of the 2000s it was followed by studies for Belgium (Steering Committee, 2005; National Bank of Belgium, 2006), Austria,[6] Sweden (Bergman *et al.*, 2007), Finland (Takala and Virén, 2008) and Norway (Gresvik and Haare, 2008b, 2009).[7] Comparing the results of these studies should be done with caution because they not only differ in timing but also in scope (that is, the payment instruments and stakeholders covered), as well as in costing methodology. In this respect, a recent study by the European Central Bank, in cooperation with multiple national central banks, constitutes an important milestone (Schmiedel *et al.*, 2012). Not only does it examine the social and private costs of the most important payment instruments in thirteen different EU countries, it does so, at least in principle, based on a common methodology. Several participating national central banks, though not all, have since published more details in national reports.[8]

When one overviews this body of research, three major observations stand out: first, in many countries the social cost of cash is substantial; second, the level depends on the state of development of the retail payment system; and third, there are substantial cost savings to be reaped by discouraging the use of cash. Let us first talk levels. The ECB study examines cash, cheques, debit and credit cards, as well as direct debits and credit transfer payments up to EUR 50,000. The ECB finds that the total social cost of these payment instruments for the year 2009 amounts to EUR 45 billion, which corresponds to 0.96% of GDP for the sample of participating countries. This figure does not include the costs for households and consumers. Schmiedel *et al.* (2012, p. 42) point out that recent data for Denmark and Hungary suggest that this would increase the estimate with about 0.2% of GDP.[9] For the purposes of the present paper, an important finding is that the social cost of cash accounts, overall, for nearly half of the total, i.e., 0.49% of GDP (o.c., Table 7, p. 27).[10] As Schmiedel *et al.* (o.c., p. 6) correctly stress, this is in fact only natural given that cash is still the most frequently used retail payment instrument: in 2009, 69% of the transactions in the sample countries were made in cash (o.c., p. 22).

However, this average hides dramatic inter-country differences: the market share of cash ranges from a low of 27% in Sweden to a high of no less than 95% in Greece and Romania (o.c., Table 4, p. 23). As a result, the relative importance of the social cost of cash also differs dramatically: it lies between 0.25% and as much as 0.76% of GDP (o.c., Table 7, p. 27). The ECB study does not identify the respective countries,[11] but the underlying national reports do provide some clues. Together with the earlier studies they indicate that, overall, the social cost of cash is higher in the more cash-centric countries. To start with the ECB study, in Figure 3.1 I have plotted, for the seven countries that I was able to identify, the social cost of cash as a % of GDP (excl. consumers) against the market share of cash. As can be seen, there is, overall, effectively a positive relationship between the two indicators: the correlation amounts to 0.76 and without the two outliers (Portugal and Hungary) it is even near perfect (0.99).

Looking back to the early studies yields the same conclusion. Of the countries studied, Austria, the Netherlands and Belgium are the more cash-centric.[12] This is also reflected in the estimates: the cost of cash for society (excl. consumers) would, respectively, have amounted to 0.47%,

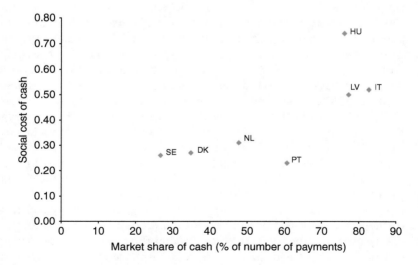

Figure 3.1 Social cost of cash, as a percentage of GDP

Sources: Schmiedel *et al.* (2012), Ardizzi and Giucca (2012), and Latvijas Banka (2013).

0.48% and 0.58% of GDP (with data for 2005, 2002 and 2003). Given that all the other countries are from Scandinavia, where card usage is higher, it comes as no surprise that the estimates are lower. Bergman *et al.*'s (2007) estimate for Sweden is 0.28–0.33% of GDP in 2002, depending on whether consumers' withdrawal time costs are included or not. Takala and Virén (2008) put the cost of cash in Finland – the country with at the time the highest number of card payments per capita in the EU – at only 0.12% of GDP in 2005, excluding costs for consumers. The figure for Norway, where card usage is even higher than in Finland, is, at 0.15% of GDP (in 2007), somewhat higher. But then this figure includes costs for households.

The fact that there has been more than one study for the Netherlands also allows us to examine the evolution of the cost estimates over time.[13] Interestingly, the combined social cost of cash and debit card payments in the Netherlands has declined from 0.57% of GDP in 2002 to 0.42% in 2009 and an estimated 0.40% in 2012 (Jonker, 2013). This is a first indication that there are substantial cost savings to be reaped by discouraging the use of cash, because between 2002 and 2012 the Dutch more than doubled their usage of debit cards (o.c., p. 13), to the detriment of cash.

A second indication can be obtained by comparing the marginal social cost of cash with that of its electronic competitors. To be clear: the marginal social cost is the cost, for society, of making one additional payment with a given payment instrument. When thinking about ways to improve the overall efficiency of the payment system, this is the yardstick that one should use – rather than average social costs. This is because the latter are, by definition, affected by the volume of payments that are made with the respective instruments. Because of the important economies of scale in payment services, the implication is that, no matter how cost efficient it is, a fledgling payment instrument will always have a higher average social cost than the incumbent instruments. In other words, as Schmiedel *et al.* (2012, p. 27) stress, the fact that cash payments have, in most countries, still the lowest unit social cost "does not necessarily mean that cash is the most cost-efficient payment instrument, because low unit costs may be due to the high volume of cash payments". By contrast, if the *marginal* social cost of payment instrument Y is lower than that of payment instrument X, this implies that the total social cost will go down if payments with instrument X are displaced by payments with instrument Y – provided that no substantial additional investments are needed.[14]

The ECB study makes no attempt to compute marginal social costs and therefore "does not allow for direct efficiency comparisons among payment instruments" (Schmiedel *et al.*, 2012, p. 25, footnote 17). But the central bank studies for Belgium, the Netherlands, Sweden and Denmark do provide indications. The general picture that emerges is one where cash is still more economical than debit cards for small payments, but not for larger transactions – the reason being that, unlike for cards, the marginal cost of cash increases with the transaction amount. The policy implication is that for transactions above the cash-cards "switching point", the overall social cost of the payment system would drop if cash payments were displaced by debit card payments.

Interestingly, whereas the early studies for Belgium and the Netherlands put the social switching point between cash and cards at, respectively, EUR 10.24 (in 2003) and EUR 11.63 (in 2002), recent studies find a much lower threshold.[15] For the Netherlands, Bolt *et al.* (2008, pp. 8–9) use newly available cost information for 2005–2006 and find that the threshold has more than halved in five years' time, to roughly EUR 5. More recently, still concerning the Netherlands, Jonker (2013) shows that cash usage declined considerably between 2002 and 2009, whereas debit card usage more than doubled. In addition, she highlights rapid developments in IT as well as cost-cutting measures taken by the central bank, retailers, and commercial banks. Jonker then studies the impact of these developments and finds that in 2009 the variable social cost of an additional cash payment exceeded the variable social cost of an additional debit card payment for transaction sizes above EUR 3.06 (o.c., p. 32). Jonker argues that it is likely that this break-even point has continued to decline since 2009, "as IT developments have made debit card payment processing even more efficient" (ibidem). Jonker's findings correspond well with recent findings for Denmark and Sweden. Jacobsen and Pedersen (2012), in their study for Denmark, put the social cash-cards switching point at DKK 29 (EUR 3.90). In Sweden, the break-even point has come down as dramatically as in the Netherlands – that is, by some 75%; namely from SEK 72 (EUR 7.80) in 2002 (Bergman *et al.*, 2007) to a mere SEK 20 (EUR 1.88) in 2009 (Segendorf and Jansson, 2012). The message is clear: society benefits from substituting debit card payments for cash.

This said, an important qualification is that costs are only one side of the coin. The benefits of payment instruments should also be taken into account. As Schmiedel *et al.* (2012, p. 8) put it, the goal should be "to minimise the total social cost of making payments without sacrificing the availability or quality of the services". For example, the anonymity of cash may, in certain circumstances, be a major benefit, and this for perfectly lawful reasons of privacy. Proponents of libertarian paternalism could see this as an additional justification for their position that people should remain free to choose, and that outright bans are too intrusive. As far as I know, only Garcia-Swartz *et al.* (2004) – for the US – and Simes *et al.* (2006) – for the case of Australia – try to calculate *net* social costs; that is, social costs corrected for social benefits.[16]

To sum up, this brief review of the literature has shown, first of all, that in many countries the total social cost of cash is substantial. To make it more tangible, in the Netherlands the social cost of cash would, in 2009, have amounted to some 245 euro per family per year (down from 305 euro in 2002),[17] which is actually an excellent way of looking at it because ultimately consumers end up footing the bill (cf. infra, in subsection 3.3.2). A second conclusion is that for many payments there are more cost-effective alternatives than cash. The consensus that is emerging concerning the relative efficiency of cash and cards can be summarised as follows. First, different payment instruments are socially efficient at different transaction sizes. Second, not all payment cards are by definition cost-efficient: compared to debit cards, credit cards are socially suboptimal – unless perhaps when benefits are included, and then only for larger payments. Third, leaving aside electronic purses[18] (which have largely disappeared because of a lack of success), cash still appears to be efficient for (very) small payments, but as the transaction size increases a break-even point is reached where debit cards overtake cash as the socially optimal payment instrument. Hence, for payments above this threshold society would benefit from using less cash.

3.3.2   The invisible cost of cash

Part of the problem in convincing economic agents of the point just made is that the social cost of cash – and that of many other payment instruments, for that matter – is a hidden cost. In a recent study for Australia, Stewart *et al.* (2014, p. 1) note that the costs of payment instruments "are typically not transparent to policymakers or end users of payment systems". In particular, in many countries – Belgium being a case in point – consumers face no or hardly any direct, transaction-based fees when withdrawing cash.[19] As a result, cash is perceived to be free. And we all know what happens with services that are free of charge: they are overused. In other words, with the current pricing structure, consumers have no incentive to optimise their payment behaviour, and as a result, the efficiency of our payment system is suboptimal. There is also an issue of fairness. When banks cannot recoup the costs caused by the distribution of cash directly from account holders, they will resort to cross-subsidisation. Banks might, for example, offer lower interest rates on deposits. As a result, the costs of payment services are not necessarily borne by those who enjoy the benefits. Seen from the opposite angle, even the most avid users of electronic payment instruments continue to pay their share of the social cost of cash because they are charged the same prices in shops as cash users, and are offered the same interest rates by banks. In other words, users of electronic payment instruments subsidise cash users.

Encouragingly, central bank economists are increasingly becoming aware of the absence of incentives for consumers to optimise their payment behaviour. Concerning Italy, Ardizzi and Giucca (2012, p. 6) note:

> The picture that emerges is of a price policy that does not give users the indications they need in order to make a rational selection of which instruments to use.

For the Netherlands, Jonker (2013, p. 17) stresses:

> Consumers do not pay any transaction fees for card payments, cash withdrawals or cash depositions at the ATM, nor do they receive any tangible rewards. Thus banks in the Netherlands tend not to make consumers directly aware of the costs associated with their payment behaviour or to provide any incentives towards more cost efficient payment behaviour.

Stronger still, in their study for Sweden, Segendorf and Jansson (2012, pp. 30–32) demonstrate that that when it comes to the choice between cash and card payments, consumers' private costs are not aligned at all with social costs: the private cash-debit card threshold lies at no less than SEK 173, compared to a social threshold of SEK 20 (cf. supra). Segendorf and Jansson (o.c., p. 36) conclude that "the consumers' choice of payment method is not consistent with what is socially optimal. Consumers pay too high values in cash and therefore use cash too often and cards too seldom."

When combining the cost analyses discussed in Section 3.3.1 with the observations just made, the logical conclusions are, in my view, (1) that the use of cash should be actively discouraged[20] and the use of debit cards and e-purses, if any, actively encouraged and (2) that, in order to do so, consumers should be made aware of the social cost of payment instruments. For society as a whole, the resulting increased efficiency of the payment system would have the same effect as any reduction in the cost of inputs.[21] In an international perspective, it would improve a country's competitive position. And, importantly, everyone would benefit, including consumers. Assuming that there is sufficient competition, merchants, for example, would pass on their cost savings to consumers in the form of lower prices.

The most straightforward way to discourage cash usage would obviously be to introduce or increase ATM fees. Gradually, more and more policy makers are becoming convinced of the merits of cost-based pricing.[22] Even an increasing number of central bankers have been speaking out in favour of such a pricing method. For example, in a January 2008 interview with the *Financial Times*, Gertrude Tumpel-Gugerell, who was at the time the member of the Executive Board of the ECB responsible for Payment Systems and Market Infrastructure, said: "I would prefer it if banks could spend the money they spend on handling cash on investing in their systems and the development of new products".[23] She added that operators should be encouraged to offer discounts for card payments, following the example of London's Oyster card for public transport services.[24] The National Bank of Belgium, for its part, suggested in its 2014 annual report that in order to ensure their lasting profitability Belgian financial institutions should explore "more systematic charges for the services offered, more in line with the true cost of the business" (2015, p. 30). It added that "[i]n the more specific case of financial market infrastructures, it would be better for the activities to be remunerated directly via fee payments, rather than indirectly in the form of interest income obtained by investing the deposits of users of these infrastructures" (ibidem). Finally, in a recent speech, Erkki Liikanen, governor of the Bank of Finland, was particularly outspoken. He explained that the Bank of Finland has defined five criteria that should serve as guiding principles when assessing present payment systems and future developments, and that "efficient and cost-based pricing" was one of these criteria (Liikanen, 2015). Liikanen elaborated that this criterion "requires that the pricing of payment methods is transparent and reflects the costs of producing such services. Prices relative to production costs give the right signals that should guide users to adopt the most cost-efficient payment method in any given situation."[25]

There is some evidence that cost-based pricing of payment instruments would incite (some) consumers to switch to less costly payment methods; see Lam and Ossolinski (2015) and the references therein.[26] However, in practice, policy makers have been loath to take action. Part of the reason is probably that making cash more expensive will not be popular with consumers. Commercial banks, for their part, find themselves in a (related) prisoners' dilemma of sorts: collectively banks would gain from a shift to cost-based pricing, but no individual bank wants to be the first to make the move – for fear of losing market share.[27] And a coordinated move is basically not an option, as it would be seen as collusive by antitrust authorities. All this makes it all the more interesting to investigate the potential of softer, less intrusive measures – in other words, to look into the "gentle power of nudges" (Thaler and Sunstein, 2008, p. 8).

3.3.3 Does libertarian paternalism apply?

However, upon reading the first two chapters of the Thaler/Sunstein book – entitled "Biases and Blunders" and "Resisting Temptation", respectively – I had my doubts on whether the WOC really fitted into their framework. As pointed out in Section 3.2, *Nudge* is all about "how people systematically go wrong" (o.c., p. 19). However, as is clear from the evidence presented in Section 3.3.2 above, from an individual perspective paying with cash is, in the current circumstances, not irrational – quite the contrary, even. Nor is it – at first sight – a case where "private...decisions may be improved if judgements can be nudged back in the direction of true probabilities" (o.c., p. 26) or where people are dynamically inconsistent (o.c., p. 41). As a matter of fact, with the current pricing structure, people who try to use more efficient electronic payment instruments may end up being charged *more* by their bank. Let me illustrate this with an example from my own personal experience. When I first started using Proton, the Belgian (now defunct) electronic purse, I had to pay an annual fee of roughly EUR 5 on top of what I was already paying for my current account. (Back then I did not yet have a "package deal" that includes current account services and selected payment cards for a fixed fee.) At the same time, my reduced use of cash and, consequently, my reduced use of my bank's ATM services did not save me any money because my bank did not charge me any explicit fees for ATM access. For me personally, the convenience of the e-purse was worth the additional 5 euro per year. But given such perverse pricing incentives, it would be far-fetched to call those who said no to the e-purse, and continued to use cash, irrational.

Another reason for my doubts was Thaler and Sunstein's insistence that libertarian paternalism should make people's lives "go better (*as judged by their own preferences*, not those of some bureaucrat)" (o.c., p. 10; my emphasis).[28] Thaler and Sunstein point out, for example, that "the overwhelming majority of smokers say that they would like to quit" (o.c., p. 44). Stronger still, "many smokers, drinkers, and overeaters are willing to pay third parties to help them make better decisions" (o.c., p. 7). I do not think that cash users see their payment behaviour as problematic. Also, in chapter 4 of their book, Thaler and Sunstein answer the question in the title of the chapter – "When do we need a nudge?" – as follows: "people will need nudges for decisions that are difficult and rare, for which they do not get prompt feedback, and when they have trouble translating aspects of the situation into terms that they can easily understand" (o.c., p. 72). None of these conditions seem to hold in the case of POS payments: it is something we do every day, feedback is immediate (or so it seems) and – as I will highlight below – making a payment can be done on automatic pilot.

On the other hand, I felt encouraged to continue reading when I spotted references, albeit brief, to the so-called no-surcharge rule[29] imposed by credit card networks (o.c., p. 36) and the complex pricing schemes of credit cards (o.c., p. 93). Eventually I was reassured of the applicability of *Nudge* when I read that "choice architects need to know how to encourage … *socially beneficial* behavior" (o.c., p. 54; my emphasis). Clearly, this ties in directly with the "social cost of cash" issue set out in the first part of this section. In fact, there are interesting parallels with the problem of pollution that Thaler and Sunstein analyse in chapter 12 of their book. For one, Thaler and Sunstein note that polluters impose externalities on others (o.c., p. 184). This is also true for cash users (cf. supra).[30] Second, in both cases incentives are not properly aligned and there is a "tragedy of the commons". Just as polluters "do not pay the full costs that [they] impose on the environment" (ibidem), cash users can in part free ride on others. The result, in both cases, is the overuse of socially costly resources. Third, Thaler and Sunstein point out that a "problem that contributes to excessive pollution is that people do not get feedback on the environmental consequences of their actions" (o.c., p. 185). Likewise, people are not fully aware of the social costs that come from their payment behaviour. (This qualifies my earlier statement that feedback at the POS is immediate. While it is immediately apparent whether a payment was successful or not, payers are not told whether they have done well from a social point of view.)

Furthermore, given that the nature of the problem is similar, it is not surprising that the solutions advocated by Thaler and Sunstein on the one hand and by myself and other payments scholars on the other are also analogous. Thaler and Sunstein argue that governments should make the environmental costs more visible and realign people's incentives by imposing taxes or penalties on those who pollute (o.c., pp. 185–186).[31] Similarly, the purpose of cost-based pricing of payment instruments is to make their social cost visible by means of explicit, transaction-based fees. A final similarity is that both policy proposals face comparable difficulties, as is evidenced by the juxtaposition of the following quotes:

> Although we think that the most important step in dealing with environmental problems is getting the prices (that is, incentives) right, we realize that such an approach is politically difficult. When voters are complaining about the high price of gasoline, it can be hard for politicians to unite on a solution that raises this price. A key reason is that the costs of pollution are hidden, while the price at the pump is quite salient. So we suggest that along with getting the prices right (or while we are waiting for the political courage to set the prices right), we should take other nudge-like steps that can help to reduce the problem in politically more palatable ways. (Thaler and Sunstein, 2008, pp. 188–189)

> The problem is obviously that making cash more expensive is not going to win elections; nor will it earn central bankers or Eurocrats plaudits. Indeed, explaining cost-based pricing to consumers is not easy: the costs are very visible – on purpose – and the claimed benefits – lower prices at the POS, higher interest rates – much less so. The key question therefore is: who will have the political courage to sell cost-based pricing of retail payments – cash included – to the general public? In the meantime less brave policymakers could start by educating consumers and merchants about the real cost of cash. (Van Hove, 2007, p. 43)

A final reason why nudges can, after all, be applied in the WOC is related to the nature of the demand for payment instruments. In their book, Thaler and Sunstein elaborate at length on the so-called status quo bias, or the tendency for people to stick with their current situation (o.c., p. 34). One of the causes of this bias is simply a lack of attention (o.c., p. 35). These observations seem particularly relevant for the payments industry. Leinonen (2008, p. 2) argues that "over time, [consumers] develop payment habits that govern their instrument choices in repetitive situations". These payment habits are notoriously slow to change, and one of the explanations for the inertia may well be that people do not give much thought to payments. Indeed, the demand for payment instruments is only a derived demand: what consumers really want is the goods or services that they can pay for with the payment instruments. Spencer (2003, p. 305), for example, talks about "convenience goods", "wanted not for [their] own sake but as a way to access other goods and services". One of the implications is that (the proper functioning of) a payment service is hardly noticed by consumers and that it is not something that they derive a lot of utility from. As the Netherlands Bankers' Association (NVB) once put it: "payments (services) are a hygiene factor; a dissatisfier (as opposed to being a motivation factor or satisfier). This means that the nature of the services is such that a faulty provision of services leads to dissatisfaction and complaints. On the other hand, a proper delivery of services does not lead to additional satisfaction.".[32] In the terminology used by Thaler and Sunstein, one could argue that, when making payments, people rely to a large extent on their Automatic System (see Section 3.2). If this is the case, then the two generic ways to change people's payment behaviour seem to be either to harness people's mindless choosing by making electronic the default option *or* to move making payments from the Automatic to the Reflective System by prompting people to think about them (and, in this way, eventually change their payment habits). The next section tries to come up with concrete nudges that fit into either category.

3.4   The confrontation

Now that I have explained what nudging is all about (Section 3.2) and why the WOC qualifies as a "nudge-able" policy problem (Section 3.3), this section confronts the nudging theory with the WOC problem and presents a number of possible nudges, some of which already exist. Rather than listing these nudges according to the type of cognitive bias that they try to exploit, I present them per choice architect.

This said, most proposed nudges are of two main types. A first type of nudges could be described as increasing the "hassle factor", and consist, for example, in making cash withdrawals somewhat less convenient. A second type relies on altering the default option. This should not come as a surprise. Indeed, a central observation in Thaler and Sunstein's book is precisely that the power of inertia should not be underestimated, and, crucially, that it can be harnessed. Thaler and Sunstein point out that "the combination of loss aversion with mindless choosing implies that if an option is designated as the 'default', it will attract a large market share" (o.c., p. 35). Hence, they argue, "if private companies or public officials think that one policy produces better outcomes, they can greatly influence the outcome by choosing it as the default" (o.c., p. 8).

In the same line, Goldstein *et al.* (2008, p. 100) argue that "defaults are the building blocks of [choice] architecture", and propose a taxonomy of defaults. At the highest level, they place defaults into two categories: "mass" and "personalised". Mass defaults apply to all customers of a product or service, without taking individual characteristics or preferences into account. Given that the present chapter deals with the promotion of changes in our collective behaviour in order to lower the *social* cost of our payment system, the default options discussed below are without exception mass defaults.

A final preliminary remark is that all stakeholders can obviously engage in consumer education, and can disseminate information in order to increase the general awareness of the social cost of payment instruments. By publishing the cost studies discussed in Section 3.3, central banks are in fact already doing this.

3.4.1 The government as a nudger

Thinking, first of all, of governments as nudgers, it is interesting to observe that governments have in fact selected a default when it comes to payments: they have made cash legal tender. As explained in more detail in Van Hove (2005), typically the legal tender status of cash has the legal effect that it is incumbent on the creditor to accept legal tender notes and coins as valid discharge of pecuniary debts unless – at least in most countries – the parties have contracted to use an alternative means of payment. One could contend that perhaps the time is ripe to "modernise" the default. In an intervention at the 2008 Eurofi conference,[33] Jean-Michel Godeffroy, then director-general for Payment Systems and Market Infrastructure at the ECB, stressed that there is a major cultural problem in that many people still feel about money the same way their grandparents did, meaning that they consider cash to be the "normal" money. However, Godeffroy said, the reality is different: "Today, normal money is scriptural money moved around electronically".[34]

Interestingly, in 2000, the Board of Commissioners of Currency, Singapore (BCCS) – the government agency that at the time had the sole right to issue banknotes and coins in Singapore[35] – was apparently convinced that a change in mind-set was indeed overdue, and aired its vision "to establish an *electronic* legal tender system by 2008" (my emphasis).[36] This did, however, not materialise. More recently, a Philippine lawmaker proposed the "E-Peso Act of 2014" (House Bill 4914). The e-peso would be the electronic equivalent of the paper peso and would be legal tender for debt, taxes, and goods and services transacted through the Internet.[37]

This said, in most countries the direct impact on POS payment behaviour of making an electronic payment instrument legal tender instead of cash would be limited.[38] Indeed, contrary to popular understanding of legal tender, such a change would – in most countries – *not* imply that merchants would be *obliged* to accept the payment instrument; they would remain free to set payment conditions. The distinction between repaying a debt and making a payment in an everyday POS transaction is crucial here, as indicated in the following quote about the US: "The question of legal tender is irrelevant to retail transactions...because consumers are negotiating an exchange, not repaying an existing debt. Retailers are therefore within their rights to specify the types of payment they will accept to consummate a transaction" (CBO, 1996).

However, even in the absence of a statutory obligation to accept, there might still be a positive impact on the uptake of electronic payment instruments: a change in the legal tender law might enhance consumer confidence (CBO, 1996).[39] This is in line with the following remark by Thaler and Sunstein: "In many contexts defaults have some extra nudging power because consumers may feel, rightly or wrongly, that default options come with an implicit endorsement from the default setter, be it the...government, or [another choice architect]" (o.c., p. 35).

3.4.2   The central bank as a nudger

Turning to central banks, an important way in which they could change the choice context for POS payments is by altering the number and/ or face value of the coins and banknotes that they issue. The literature on this topic argues that in determining the denominational structure, a central bank should primarily bear in mind the so-called principle of least effort, which holds that the settlement of cash transactions should, on average, involve as few tokens – coins and/or banknotes – as possible (Van Hove, 2001; Bouhdaoui *et al.*, 2011). This will, so the argument goes, improve convenience for transactors, speed up transactions, and curb the bulk and weight carried about by the cash-using public. If, however, the maxim is that the use of cash should be discouraged, then central banks might try to make cash payments *less* convenient.

The case of the ECB is particularly interesting in this respect because it issues as many as 15 different denominations, and because its biggest banknote has a face value of no less than EUR 500. Focusing first on the latter aspect, let me point out that the social cost figures presented in Section 3.3.1 clearly show that cash payments for which the EUR 500 banknote would prove useful should not be encouraged – quite the contrary. If the ECB were to withdraw the EUR 500 banknote from circulation, and why not the EUR 200 and EUR 100 banknotes as well, then cash users would be forced to use ten 50 euro notes for every 500 euro note.[40] Let me emphasise that restricting the nominal value of the largest euro banknote to EUR 50 would not inconvenience the vast majority of consumers as they provision themselves with banknotes at ATMs that typically only churn out banknotes no larger than EUR 50.[41] This nudge would therefore conform to Thaler and Sunstein's "golden rule of libertarian paternalism": "offer nudges that are most likely to help and least likely to inflict harm" (o.c., p. 72). It could also be framed in the "asymmetric paternalism" advocated by Camerer *et al.* (2003), which is about helping the least sophisticated people while imposing minimal harm on everyone else.[42] Note that EUR 50 need not be the endpoint; the upper limit could progressively be restricted further.

Jumping from the upper to the lower limit of the denominational structure, the same lower-convenience logic can also be applied to the case of the 1 and 2 euro cent coins. A majority of Eurozone citizens have for years been in favour of getting rid of the 1-cent and 2-cent coins.[43] However, from a social efficiency point of view, if consumers find these coins inconvenient, then it is best to leave them in circulation in order not to lower the relative attractiveness of e-purses and debit cards. A final remark along the same lines concerns the possible replacement of the EUR 1 and EUR 2 coins by banknotes. This idea was considered by the ECB in 2002–2004. Several member states supported the plan, arguing that it might help curb price rises.[44] In the logic advocated here, if anything, the ECB should make the EUR 1 and EUR 2 denominations less pocket friendly, not more. (Note that in November 2004, the Governing Council of the ECB eventually decided not to issue low-denomination banknotes.)[45]

Going one step further, particularly proactive central banks could, in parallel to lowering the upper limit of their banknote series, move into e-territory themselves. The debate about the societal benefits of a central-bank-sponsored digital currency is certainly heating up. In a recent article, *Financial Times* journalist Izabella Kaminska argues that "now, more than ever, is the time for central banks to launch their own official e-money".[46] Even the Bank of England – the "Old Lady" among central banks – is pondering the implications of issuing its own digital currency. In its "One Bank Research Agenda", the BoE (2015, p. 31) notes, under the heading "Response to fundamental change", that "while existing private digital currencies have economic flaws which make them volatile, the distributed ledger technology that their payment systems rely on may have considerable promise. This raises the question of whether central banks should themselves make use of such technology to issue digital currencies." Almost simultaneously, David Andolfatto, Senior Vice President and Director of Research at the Federal Reserve Bank of St. Louis, on his personal blog, floated the idea of an open-source Bitcoin-like "Fedcoin" issued by the Federal Reserve.[47]

3.4.3   Commercial banks as nudgers

Commercial banks and/or payment service providers could also try to capitalise on the fact that many people will take the path of least resistance. This said, for the vast majority of POS payments, it is not technically possible to make electronic payment the default option since cash and cards make use of different user interfaces and/or acceptance infrastructures (cash registers vs. POS terminals). It is, however, possible to nudge – or coerce – people in their choice between different cards. In France, for example, if a consumer has a Moneo electronic purse incorporated in her debit card (as opposed to a stand-alone Moneo e-purse), then for amounts below EUR 10, the payment will automatically be an e-purse (read: prepaid) payment. For amounts between EUR 10 and EUR 30, the consumer can choose between Moneo and debit (Bounie *et al.*, 2008, p. 75, note 22). While this specific configuration does not qualify as a nudge – because cardholders have no choice for payments below EUR 10 – it is possible to conceive of a set-up where consumers are presented with a default option that they can overrule; that is, they are allowed to pick a different card if they want. Norway provides a good example here. Gresvik and Haare (2008a, p. 56) point out that

> most physical plastic cards issued in Norway are combined [credit/debit] cards, and the combination Visa/Bank-Axept is by far the most common. The Visa logo is on the front of the card, while the Bank-Axept logo is on the back. When the card is used in a card terminal which accepts Bank-Axept, the Bank-Axept card function is used by default.

However, the cardholder can override the debit default, and turn the payment into a credit (Visa) payment by orally informing the cashier of her preference.[48]

Compared to POS payments, so-called Unattended POS (U-POS) payments offer additional room for nudging. If a vending or ticketing machine, for example, also accepts cash, it is perfectly possible to make card payment the default, and to force consumers to push an additional button and/or go to a next screen if they insist on paying cash. The instructions alerting users to the possibility of a cash payment could also be kept low-key on purpose (bottom of screen, smaller font, etc.). In Goldstein *et al.*'s taxonomy, this would be an example of a "hidden" option, where "the default is presented as a customer's only choice, although hard-to-find alternatives exist" (Goldstein *et al.*, 2008, p. 103). An example given by Goldstein *et al.* relates to Dell. Dell sells computers with either Windows or Linux operating systems, but the Linux option does not appear in the main product configurator, where customers can select the features they want; it can only be accessed through an obscure link on the site (ibidem). An intriguing real-life illustration of the possible impact of nudges in a U-POS context relates to Germany and Austria. Since 1 January 2007, cigarette vending machines in both countries are required by law to check, prior to purchase, a legal-age digital certificate on the local debit card that also carries an e-purse. Once the age-check is done, smokers are still able to pay with cash, but an increased number opted to simply make use of the GeldKarte, c.q. Quick e-purse that they had to insert anyhow. Tellingly, in Germany, the number of GeldKarte transactions jumped by 58% year-on-year in January 2007.[49] Also, a survey showed that the number of GeldKarte users who also use their e-purse at cigarette vending machines doubled from 12% to 24%.[50] In Austria, the number of Quick transactions increased by 21.8% in the first quarter of 2007, whereas in 2006 the growth rate over the same period was only 8.5%.[51] This appears to be in line with Thaler and Sunstein's observation that "many people will take whatever option requires the least effort" (2008, p. 83). By the same token, supermarkets wanting to promote card payments could try to harness people's natural inertia by incorporating their loyalty application on a popular payment card, requiring customers to insert/wave this card into/at a terminal as a *conditio sine qua non* to accumulate loyalty points, and then asking customers whether they also want to pay with the same card. Also, in view of the higher "nudgeability" of U-POS payments, an interesting development, at least in Belgium, is that some supermarkets have turned POS payments into U-POS payments by deploying so-called self-pay terminals. This opens up nudging possibilities in the traditional retail environment that are similar to the U-POS context.

In their efforts to reduce cash usage, banks could also try to exploit the anchoring heuristic. As explained in Section 3.2, the number people will choose in a particular situation can be influenced by suggesting a starting point – a nudge – for their thought process. Thaler and Sunstein give the example of donations for charities and point out that people will give more if the options are $100, $250, $1,000, $5,000 and "other", than if the options are $50, $75, $100, $150 and "other". More generally, "in many domains, the evidence shows that, within reason, the more you ask for, the more you tend to get" (o.c., p. 24).

Transposed to our case, this suggests that banks, at their ATMs, could experiment with an approach in the spirit "the less we offer, the less people will tend to take". When I withdraw cash at an ATM of my bank in Belgium, the screen with standard amounts reads (in euro): 20, 50, 80, 100, 140, 240, 500, "other amount". When I was in Nice for a conference some years ago, the menu on an ATM that I used was simply (again in euro): 10, 20, 30, 40, 50, 60, 70, "other amount". Clearly, if banks want to reduce cash usage, the second option makes vastly more sense. Obviously, one should not confuse cause and effect: the amounts are lower in France because, compared to Belgium, French consumers rely less on cash and more on cards and cheques. Nevertheless, it would be interesting to test whether lower default amounts would change Belgian consumers' perception of what's a lot, and what's not.[52]

Still concerning ATMs, banks can obviously also simply reduce the number of ATMs, and in this way increase the "hassle cost" involved. After all, it is no coincidence that spatial demand-for-money models use the distance to the nearest ATM as a measure of the transaction cost of obtaining cash. Empirical research for the Netherlands and Finland, for example, shows that there is indeed a link between the number of ATMs and the share of cash in the value of aggregate retail payments, c.q. cash holdings (DNB, 2006; Snellman and Virén, 2009). Finland is an especially interesting case because it is the only country in the EU15 where the number of ATMs has indeed been reduced since the mid-1990s – in part because of the banking crisis (Takala and Virén, 2007, Figure 5, p. 53). Although, to repeat, the correlation probably goes both ways, it is tempting to link this observation with the fact that the use of cash in Finland is "among the lowest in the world" (Takala and Virén, 2008, p. 33).[53] Moreover, in a survey of 5,000 households conducted by the Bank of Finland in February 2007, 25% of the respondents felt that the ATM network is not as dense as it should be, while none regarded it as being too dense (o.c., p. 23). This is an indication that in Finland the hassle cost has indeed increased.[54]

To conclude this subsection, let me point out that Belgian banks, when they wanted to discourage cheque usage in the early 1990s, not only introduced fees,[55] but also took a number of seemingly trivial accompanying measures that made life just a little bit harder for cheque users. In other words, they tried to nudge their clients – in the direction of debit cards. Kredietbank (now KBC), for example, reduced the number of cheques per chequebook from 20 to 10. At the same time, the maximum number of chequebooks per client was trimmed down to two. Moreover, as long as a client still had ten or more unused cheques – the number of which was tallied by means of a central counter – she could not request a new chequebook. First she had to report the outstanding numbers as lost or damaged so that they could be cancelled centrally.[56] The drop in cheque usage in Belgium in the 1990s is probably primarily due to the introduction of (and gradual increase in) transaction fees, and the final blow was clearly given by the abolition of the Eurocheque guarantee at end-2001.[57] Still, the nudges described here may have helped.

3.4.4 Merchants as nudgers

In some countries, some merchants surcharge for low-value card payments. Although, as Jonker (2013) describes, the situation has changed markedly; according to a survey commissioned by the Dutch central bank, in the autumn of 2006 over one-fifth of retailers who accepted debit cards charged their customers for paying small amounts by debit card (Bolt et al., 2008 p. 21). The typical charge was 10–15 euro cents for purchases below EUR 10.[58] However, as already explained, such charges cannot be called nudges. Where real nudges are concerned, Canadian evidence indicates that merchants do little, if anything, to influence the payment behaviour of their customers. Evidence for Europe paints a slightly more nuanced picture.

In Canada, the Bank of Canada had a stratified survey carried out amongst 500 merchant representatives in March–May 2006. Prior to this national survey, there was also a pilot survey. Interestingly, none of the thirty-five merchants interviewed in the pilot survey "reported any type of practice to dissuade customers from paying with any of the payment instruments surveyed" (Arango and Taylor, 2008, p. 17, note 24). In their paper, Arango and Taylor analyse the full survey results and find additional evidence for the hypothesis that, aside from the initial decision to accept a payment instrument, merchants exert little influence over the payment decisions made by their customers. For one, of those merchants who do not accept credit cards, the highest number (29%) said that lack of demand was the main barrier to acceptance (o.c., p. 9). Also, merchant acceptance levels do not necessarily reflect merchants' relative preferences. For example, when merchants who accept *all three* payment instruments surveyed (cash, debit and credit) were asked which one they prefer consumers to use the most often, 53% favoured debit cards, 39% favoured cash, and only 5% favoured credit cards – whereas they do accept them. Together, this indicates that, within certain limits, a merchant will accommodate consumer demand, particularly in a competitive environment. A second piece of evidence is that Arango and Taylor find that, as consumers use a payment instrument more intensively, merchants increasingly value their choice. For example, the more cash-oriented a merchant's business, the lower he will rank debit and credit cards (o.c., p. 16). Finally, Arango and Taylor estimate payment instrument shares as a function of, on the one hand, merchant perceptions regarding cost, risk and reliability, and, on the other hand, variables that are meant to proxy consumer payment behaviour.[59] The probit analysis reveals that merchant perceptions – which obviously drive merchant preferences – do *not* help in explaining payment shares (after controlling for acceptance). Proxies for consumer payment behaviour, such as average transaction value and transaction frequency, on the other hand, do have explanatory power.

In Europe, McKinsey in 2007 interviewed small-ticket merchants in two cash-centric countries (Italy and Germany) and two more card-oriented countries (France and the UK).[60] All merchants surveyed – 476 in total – received a majority of their payments in amounts less than EUR 15 and were active in one of three sectors: butchers, delicatessens and fishmongers; fruit and vegetable markets/greengrocers; and bookshops, stationers and newsstands. Overall, in contrast with the Canadian evidence, about one-third of the merchants declared that they steered consumer behaviour at least occasionally and that they succeeded two-thirds of the time (De Ploey *et al.*, 2008, p. 39).[61] Unfortunately, many merchants steered customers ... towards cash. Almost all merchants in the four countries surveyed preferred cash for transactions below EUR 15. More than two-thirds of the German and Italian merchants still preferred cash for transactions above EUR 100. In France, the price threshold at which the appeal of cash dwindled was noticeably lower. This said, there were notable differences in the way in which merchants reacted when a customer tried to pay a low amount by card that the merchant believed should be paid in cash. In Germany, 43% of the surveyed merchants refused the card payment, while 29% accepted the card only if the customer had no other way to pay. However, in Italy, the other cash-centric country, a mere 3% of the merchants refused the payment, 38% accepted the card only if the customer was unable to pay with another payment instrument, and 56% accepted it without making a fuss.

Still in Europe, Bounie *et al.* (2010) conducted a national survey amongst 4,601 French retailers in March–May 2008 and found – by means of univariate analyses (pp. 13–14) – that merchant acceptance of in particular the local "Cartes Bancaires" (CB) debit card is influenced by customer characteristics such as sex, age, financial situation and "origin" (local-regional-international). This could be seen as indications that merchants adapt to consumer demand. It is, for example, striking that 73% of French merchants with a "well-off clientele" accepted the CB card vs. only 53.6% of merchants with "patrons of very modest financial means" (my translations). Unsurprisingly, merchants with an international clientele also accept the card more often. Another interesting result is that the degree of competition seems to matter: the more a retailer (thinks he) has market power, the lower the acceptance of the CB card (o.c., p. 15). The logic seems to be that (quasi-)monopolists see less need to accommodate customers by accepting (costly) cards. Finally, not unlike Arango and Taylor (2008), Bounie *et al.* go further than just looking at acceptance and also try to link usage of payment instruments to a number of variables that would seem to be relevant for retailers. However, none of the results reported by Bounie *et al.* seem to provide evidence of possible nudging. For example, usage of payment instruments is not significantly correlated with reported fraud rates per payment instrument (o.c., p. 20). Also, transaction fees paid by retailers for card payments do have some impact on usage, but the correlation is positive (o.c., p. 19), whereas if merchants steered customers away from costly payment instruments, one would need to find the opposite.

In a recent paper, Górka (2014) reports on a 2012 national merchant survey among 1,006 Polish merchants. Interestingly, when asked, about half (49%) of the respondents *who accept cards* in fact prefer their customers to pay in cash. Only 4% had a clear preference for cards. Again this shows that many merchants accept cards not because their expected net private benefits are higher than for cash, but in order to please their customers.

Finally, a recent survey commissioned by the Dutch central bank among 1,340 retailers in six sectors (DNB, 2015) finds that while retailers generally prefer debit card payments over cash – for reasons of safety and costs – they hardly ever pro-actively steer their customers' payment behaviour so as to reduce their cash volumes.[62] In fact, 81% of those retailers who do not prefer cash payments indicate that they *never* ask their customers to pay by card. And those who do only do so in specific circumstances – for example, in case of a shortage of small change.

To sum up, overall, merchants will often accommodate consumer preferences and will not be inclined to nudge. There is, however, a host of things that they could do if they wanted to steer customers towards cards. In some cases, the visibility of the POS terminal on the counter could be improved. Shops with multiple check-out lanes could experiment with card-only lanes.[63] Shop assistants could also simply be instructed to talk to customers and inform them that card payment is possible or, stronger, indicate what the preferred payment method is for a given amount.[64]

Finally, social influence could be a powerful tool too, as indicated by the energy use example mentioned in Section 3.2. Thaler and Sunstein also refer to the finding that people are more likely to recycle if they learn that lots of people do it (2008, p. 66). Hence, merchants could, in principle, consider informing their customers about the payment behaviour of other customers. However, the problem is that, in many retail situations, cash is still more popular than cards. In the words of Thaler and Sunstein, this is a scenario where "the incidence of undesirable behaviour is high" (o.c., p. 66). Hence, it is not something for all merchants. But, say, supermarkets where the majority of customers already pay electronically could try to nudge even more customers to do so by displaying signs at the check-out that state: "The majority of our customers ($x\%$) pay by card" – or another message along these lines.[65]

Again, in reality, merchants do not often make use of such nudges. However, in 2007–2008 Dutch supermarkets became an exception to the rule. In May 2007, Currence, the product owner of the Dutch PIN debit card and the Chipknip e-purse, launched a promotional campaign to stimulate consumers to use their debit card for small purchases as well.[66] The main slogan was "Klein bedrag? PINnen mag!" Translated literally: "Small amount? Debit allowed!" (it sounds much better – and rhymes – in Dutch). Gradually a number of large supermarkets and store chains joined in,[67] and September 2008 saw the kick-off of a large-scale joint campaign – with the same message – by Currence, Centraal Bureau Levensmiddelenhandel (the Dutch professional federation for food retail) and the Stichting Bevorderen Efficiënt Betalen (Foundation for the Promotion of Efficiency in Payments, FPEP).[68] All Dutch supermarkets were involved and the campaign was centred on a TV commercial and simultaneous in-store promotion. Buttons, stickers, posters, etc., all carried the slogan already mentioned or variants such as "Liever PIN dan contant" ("We prefer PIN over cash"). Special attention was also devoted to reminders that customers would see just prior to and at the moment of making a payment: the slogans appeared on so-called "beurtbalkjes" (supermarket checkout item separators) and even on small cards mounted on the POS terminal itself. There was also an educational campaign to inform supermarket personnel about the goal and background of the campaign, and several chains offered prizes for the branch that achieved the biggest increase in debit card payments. Interestingly, the educational video and leaflets encourage cashiers to actively – but in a friendly manner – stimulate consumers to use their debit card. The suggested comment was: "U mag ook PINnen, hoor" – in English: "Feel free to pay by debit card".[69]

The campaign was continued, albeit with differing intensity and with interventions targeting different sectors, until the first half of 2012; see Jonker *et al.* (2015) for details. In 2012, the FPEP decided to change the message to "U pint toch ook?", which is hard to translate but essentially tries to convey a message along the following lines: "Surely you pay by debit card too?" (like most other people).[70] In May 2013 the FPEP launched a third slogan: "Pinnen? Ja, graag!" ("Debit card? Yes, please!"). Note that rather than focusing on low-value payments, the new slogans promoted debit card payments in general. Also, as Jonker *et al.* stress, whereas the initial campaign used a "behaviour expansion strategy" (o.c., p. 8), encouraging consumers who were already using their debit card for medium- and high-value payments to also use it for low-value payments, the new slogans tried

> to encourage consumers to use their debit cards more often in situations where its use was rather uncommon, such as in the catering industry and on street markets. As a result, consumers may have experienced a stronger discrepancy between the existing payment behaviour and the proposed behaviour than during the first years of the campaign. This may have hampered the transfer of these later interventions to real payment situations. (o.c., pp. 10–11)

The paper by Jonker *et al.* (2015) evaluates in detail the long-term impact of the campaign and is discussed in Section 3.5. But early results suggested that the campaign had the intended impact. In September 2008, the month in which the campaign was the most intense, the number of PIN transactions in supermarkets increased by 14.7% year-on-year vs. only 9.1% elsewhere.[71] The effect was particularly marked for transactions below EUR 10, which – again compared to September 2007 – jumped by 28.5% in supermarkets. This said, the number of low-value PIN transactions also increased by 22.2% in the other segments, which indicates that the campaign may have had spill-over effects. As a matter of fact, in October the year-on-year growth in the number of PIN transactions of less than EUR 10 was more pronounced in the other segments (+25.1%) than in supermarkets (+21.8%).

3.5   Empirical research

As mentioned in the introduction, empirical research on the effectiveness of nudges in the payments sector is still limited. I am aware of only four studies, all of which look into the impact of pro-card slogans. Three of the papers exploit Dutch data, the fourth is on Belgium. I discuss them in chronological order.

Leenheer *et al.* (2012) use a large panel that is representative for Dutch society to conduct both a survey as well as experiments. In addition, they also conduct controlled lab experiments with students. Overall, Leenheer *et al.* conclude that payment behaviour is influenced by three factors: perception and attitudes, wallet content and habits. In their research set-up, several hard and soft interventions prove effective, but the impact varies depending on the user segment. For instance, prompts (small messages at the checkout with variants of the slogan "pleases use cards") are effective for users who chose their payment instrument based on the sector and the value of the transaction, but not for persistent cash users. Unfortunately, Leenheer *et al.* do not present figures as to the magnitude of these effects.

Van der Horst and Matthijsen (2013), in their paper, conjecture that payment choice is fundamentally based on habits and cannot therefore easily be manipulated. Besides a small-scale neuro-scientific study, van der Horst and Matthijsen conduct a virtual-reality study with a representative Dutch panel. In particular, participants had to play a game in which they were asked to shop in a virtual supermarket and visit a virtual restaurant for a meal. Respondents were told that the study was about their choice between healthy and less healthy options. In reality, the aim of the game was to test for the effect of surcharges and pro-card signs. Van der Horst and Matthijsen find that actively promoting card usage by means of signs decreases the likelihood that respondents pay in cash in restaurants (by 33%), but not in supermarkets. Conversely, surcharges on card payments increase the probability to pay in cash in both restaurants and supermarkets (by 45% and 43%, respectively). Crucially, however, none of these effects is significant.

In a study on Belgium, Aydogan and Van Hove (2014) set up a field experiment in a university canteen frequented by both students and university personnel. In an attempt to steer consumers towards card payments, they mounted, during a period of eight weeks, posters with a pro-card slogan on the cash registers. The slogan read *"Less cash = safer for the VUB. Payment by card preferred"* – VUB being the name of the university. The slogan was meant to appeal to patrons' sense of loyalty and connection with their alma mater. Interestingly, the impact of the posters proved to differ between students and employees. For students, Aydogan and Van Hove could not detect any effect in their time series analysis. For employees, the posters would appear to have increased card usage (by 3%), but only towards the end of the experiment. Also, while employees' card usage was still higher in the first week after the removal of the posters, the effect disappeared in the second week. Aydogan and Van Hove suggest that the differential effect could be due to the fact – underpinned by a post-experiment survey – that employees feel more connected to the university than students.

Finally, Jonker *et al.* (2015) evaluate the impact of the Dutch public campaign discussed in Subsection 3.4.4. They do so by analysing weekly debit card transaction data for 2005–2013. The authors conclude that "[t]he overall results show positive effects of a national campaign to promote debit card usage, both in the short and in the long run" and also that "[t]he effects are the most significant at the early stages of the campaign, while appearing to wear off after a few years of interventions" (o.c., p. 1).

Concerning the short-run, "impulse" effects, my own reading of the Jonker *et al.* results is less rosy. For one, only one type of intervention generated a significant short-term impact, namely interventions aimed at large-scale retailers (o.c., p. 18). Moreover, there is only a significant positive impact in one of the four years – namely in 2007 – and then only at the 10% significance level. In 2008 and 2009 the effect is not significant and in 2010 there is a highly significant *negative* effect (that is bigger in size than the positive effect of 2007). Jonker *et al.* explain this as follows: "The negative result for the year 2010 suggests that while the interventions had a positive effect on the number of debit card transactions at the early stages of the campaign, near the end of its lifecycle this type of intervention had lost its impact on consumer behaviour" (ibidem). This explanation could justify the absence of an effect for the 2010 interventions, but does not, in my view, explain why they would lower the number of debit card transactions by 5.6%. To be clear: we are looking at impulse effects here; that is, effects that are present during the intervention period but disappear afterwards.

Turning to the fixed long-term, "step" effects, Jonker *et al.* include in their model thirteen different "cluster variables" that each identify not individual interventions, but a cycle of nationwide interventions that "were clustered in periods of several months" (o.c., p. 12). Of these thirteen variables, (only) two have significant positive coefficients, namely cluster 3 (in 2009) and cluster 7 (in 2011). The long-run increase in the number of debit card payments would amount to 2.5% and 5.2%, respectively. Interestingly, both clusters again include interventions in large retail chains (o.c., p. 19). However, there are also two clusters with significant *negative* coefficients, namely cluster 6 (−2.9%) and 10 (−2.4%). This is again, as Jonker *et al.* acknowledge, "less straightforward to explain than the positive effects" (o.c., p. 19). Jonker *et al.* think that the effects "actually reveal the dampening of the positive long-term effects of cluster 3 and the partial dampening of the long-term effect of cluster 7" (o.c., p. 20). They then compute that the net long-term effect over the period 2007–2013 would amount to 352 million extra debit card transactions (or +2.0%), that the return on investment of the campaign is – at roughly 500% – clearly positive, but that the annual cost savings (of EUR 8 million) are "rather modest" (o.c., p. 23) compared to the total social cost of cash and debit card payments in 2009, which amounted to EUR 2.4 billion. On a final note, Jonker *et al.* find no evidence that the introduction of new slogans, in 2012 and 2013, contributed to increased debit card usage.

To conclude, the existing empirical research would seem to indicate that the impact of nudges on consumers' payment behaviour is limited, especially when it comes to lasting effects. Part of the explanation might lie with the persistency of habits. In an intriguing recent paper, van der Cruijsen *et al.* (2015) show, for the case of the Netherlands, that there are major discrepancies between people's payment preferences or stated behaviour from surveys and their actual behaviour (as gleaned from payment diaries). Concretely, while seven out of ten Dutch consumers report that "under normal circumstances" they prefer paying by debit card, only seven out of twenty actually pay by debit card most of the time (even after correcting for situations where people could not use their preferred payment instrument). In other words, a substantial share of consumers – 34% to be exact, or about half of those who report a preference for debit cards – overestimate their debit card usage. Conversely, only 4% of consumers (or 13% of those who report a preference for cash) overstate their cash usage. In addition, van der Cruijsen *et al.* find that the likelihood that reported preferences and actual behaviour are not in sync increases with income, education and age. Van der Cruijsen *et al.* argue that in particular the age effect – consumers aged 55 and older are seven percentage points more likely to overestimate their debit card usage than the 35–45 reference group – indicates that the habit of paying cash is an important explanation of the observed overestimation of debit card usage. This is in line with results from the survey conducted by van der Cruijsen *et al.*: 69% of cash-likers mention "habit" as one of the reasons behind their preference (making it the second most important reason), and it is also the second most important reason given by the 34% of debit card-likers who prefer to pay cash for amounts below EUR 5. Overall, van der Cruijsen *et al.* (o.c., p. 24) conclude that "changing payment patterns is a challenging task; even when consumers have fallen in love with the debit card they find it hard to divorce from cash". This is in line with the results of Leenheer *et al.* and Van der Horst and Matthijsen.

3.6 Conclusion: nudging might help

As mentioned in the introduction, when I started reading *Nudge*, I was eager to find out whether libertarian paternalism could offer new insights into this old problem of mine. What have I learned? First, as echoed by a number of commentators,[72] nudging is nothing new, not even in the payments industry. The legal tender status of cash is a nudge. Central banks nudge when they determine the denominational structure of their coin and banknote series. Reducing the number of cheques per chequebook is a nudge. Second, nudging has its limits. Richard Thaler has been quoted as saying: "I don't think we're going to nudge Osama Bin Laden. But maybe we can make progress on litter".[73] Similarly, where payment behaviour is concerned, it is an illusion to think that those active in the underground economy can be nudged into reducing their cash usage.[74] Third, I agree with *Undercover Economist* Tim Harford when he points out that "there is no idea so good that it cannot be spoilt by politicians" and that nudging can become "an excuse for doing little when something serious must be done – for instance, on climate change".[75] On the social cost of cash, I remain convinced that the shove of cost-based pricing would prove more effective.

However, and this is conclusion number four, every bit can help, especially since the political courage required to promote cost-based pricing seems to be lacking. This said, as documented in Section 3.5, the (limited) empirical research so far is not so encouraging. However, all four studies by and large look into the effectiveness of the same type of nudge, namely pro-card slogans. Crucially, such a nudge requires a meditated action from consumers – that is, from their Reflective System; cf. Section 3.2 – to either start following the behaviour of others or to adapt to the preferences of retailers. Perhaps other types of nudges – in particular nudges that harness people's tendency to go along with the default option – hold more promise. Because then our Automatic System could bring about the desired behavioural change.

Notes

I am indebted to Olaf Gresvik and Harald Haare (Norges Bank) for background information on the Norwegian Visa/Bank-Axept card; to Bart Guns, former Senior General Manager Group Payments at KBC, for providing me with information on KBC's cheque policy; to Simon Lelieveldt, formerly of the Netherlands Bankers' Association, for background information on the Dutch case; to Piet Mallekoote, CEO of Currence, for data and information on the "Klein bedrag? PINnen mag!" campaign in the Netherlands; to Jakub Górka for providing me with additional details on the Polish merchant survey that I discuss; and to Valérie-Anne Bleyen (Vrije Universiteit Brussel), Olivier Denecker (McKinsey), Malte Krueger (University of Applied Sciences Aschaffenburg) and Harry Leinonen (Ministry of Finance, Finland) for comments on earlier versions of this paper.

1. See PIRC, "A Nudge and a Think", news story, no date, <http://www.pirc.co.uk/news/story242.html> (no longer available; last visited on October 1, 2009).
2. "There Is More to Life than Nudging", *Financial Times*, 5 August 2008. See also: "Wink, Wink", *The Economist*, 24 July 2008.
3. See also Schlag (2010).
4. On the other hand, in what is called a boomerang effect, some of the below-average energy users significantly increased their energy use. But such effects can be contained.
5. See Schmiedel *et al.* (2012, pp. 15–16) for more details.
6. Discussed briefly in Schautzer (2007, p. 148).
7. The central bank of Portugal has also looked into the costs of retail payment instruments (Banco de Portugal, 2007), but has focussed on the costs for the banking sector. Outside Europe, I am aware of studies by Simes *et al.* (2006), the Reserve Bank of Australia (2007) and Stewart *et al.* (2014) for Australia, and one on the US by Garcia-Swartz *et al.* (2004, 2006a, 2006b).
8. See the references in Schmiedel *et al.* (2012) and Jonker (2013). Separately, Krueger and Seitz (2014) present recent estimates for Germany in a study commissioned by the Deutsche Bundesbank.
9. In line with this, Stewart *et al.* (2014, p. 14) estimate that the resource costs of consumers would add about 0.17% of GDP to their estimate for Australia.
10. Expressed as a percentage of the total social cost of point-of-sale (POS) payments, the social cost of cash is obviously even higher; see the early cost studies for figures.
11. Probably for reasons of confidentiality, when reporting the total social costs on the country level – in Table 11 on p. 35 – Schmiedel *et al.* (2012) use numbers between 1 and 13. The discussion of the national reports, in Table 12 on p. 36, does reveal the identity of four of these countries.
12. To illustrate this, in 2003 cash would still have been used in no less than 81% of POS transactions in Belgium (Steering Committee, 2005) vs. a mere 24% in Norway in 2007 (Gresvik and Haare, 2008b, 2009).
13. The results of the cost studies for Sweden cannot really be compared because of a change in methodology; see Segendorf and Jansson (2012, p. 7).
14. Indeed, marginal-cost analysis only looks at variable costs; fixed costs are not included. In other words, the implicit assumption is that the infrastructure is already available.

15. The value of EUR 15 for Finland reported by Takala and Virén (2008, p. 41) is a back-of-the-envelope calculation, which, moreover, relates to average instead of marginal costs.
16. In both studies, adding benefits improves the efficiency ranking of credit cards compared to debit cards. Since the relative position of cash is not affected – that is, above a certain threshold, there is always at least one electronic alternative that is more efficient – this point is not elaborated further here.
17. Source: own calculations based on Jonker (2013, Table 4, p. 26).
18. An electronic purse is a card, usually a chip card, that can store multipurpose prepaid value and that is used for small retail or other payments; see CPSS (2003a, p. 22). The early cost studies for Belgium and the Netherlands showed that for low-value payments, electronic purses are even more cost-effective than cash. In the Netherlands, one additional e-purse payment would, in 2003, have cost society a mere 3 euro cents, compared to 11 euro cents for a cash payment.
19. The same was/is true for Portugal (Banco de Portugal, 2007, p. 13), Sweden (Bergman *et al.*, 2008, p. 49), Finland (Takala and Virén, 2008, p. 30; Leinonen, 2008, p. 25) and the Netherlands (Jonker, 2013, p. 17; van der Cruijsen *et al.* 2015, p. 4).
20. For a dissenting voice, see Krueger (2008, p. 34): "On the whole, there may be good reasons to believe that cash use will continue its decline for some time. But there is little reason for regulators to speed up this process." Shampine (2007), for his part, demonstrates that the calculations of Garcia-Swartz *et al.* for the US are highly sensitive to variations in the assumptions and argues that "at this stage, such estimates should be used in policy debates only with great caution" (o.c., p. 508). Garcia-Swartz *et al.* (2007) do not fully agree with Shampine's critique, but they do agree with his conclusion; cf. "more (and more comprehensive) cost-benefit studies should be conducted before introducing policy measures that affect the distribution of payment instruments in the population of transactions" (o.c., pp. 521–522). Finally, Takala and Virén (2008) are also not keen on policy action. They seize upon their low estimates for Finland (cf. supra) to argue that the Finnish example "clearly indicates that it is possible to arrive at very low values of economy-wide payment costs indicating that earlier estimates of the 'burden of payment systems' do not seem to be representative for Finland, at least" (o.c., p. 42). They concede that there are considerable cross-country differences so that "in some countries benefits are considerable" (o.c., p. 40), but even then, they argue, one has to keep in mind that "great efficiency gains could already be obtained by changing the way different payment systems operate in different countries. If the most efficient way of producing payment services is reached (in other words, the system is at the efficient frontier) *changes in the market shares of different payment media may not produce great large* [sic] *social efficiency gains*" (o.c., pp. 40–41; my emphasis).
21. See Bergman *et al.* (2008, p. 6).
22. In this respect, it is revealing to compare my earlier account of the state of the debate on cost-based pricing, in Van Hove (2004), with a later overview of the positions of policy makers in Van Hove (2007, pp. 31–34).
23. "Europeans Still Addicted to Cash", *Financial Times*, January 28, 2008.

24. At around the same time Deputy Governor Lars Nyberg of the Sveriges Riksbank also commented approvingly on discounts for card payments: "At a coffee shop chain in Stockholm one can buy a plastic [smart] card for SEK 20 and then charge it with cash in any of the chain's shops. If one uses the card one receives a discount when buying coffee and sandwiches. ... It is evidently rational management at the sales outlets and, moreover, is appreciated by the consumers" (Source: Nyberg, L., "Cash and Payments – What Lies Ahead?", speech, Stockholm, 5 February 2008 <http://www.riksbank.com/templates/Page.aspx?id=26857>).

25. It should not come as a surprise that the most explicit central bank statements in favour of cost-based pricing come from members of Scandinavian central banks – for the case of Finland, see also Hakkarainen (2009, p. 34) – and in particular from the Norwegian central bank as Norway is the poster child for cost-based pricing of payment instruments; see Van Hove (2002) and Enge and Øwre (2006). At the presentation of Norges Bank's 2007 *Annual Report on Payment Systems*, Governor Svein Gjedrem pointed out that there were signs that banks were reducing prices for many payment services or offering them free of charge. He commented that "this is not in bank customers' best interests. ... A reduction in earnings may reduce banks' capacity and willingness to invest in improved infrastructure. Furthermore, without cost coverage, payment services will have to be financed by earnings from other services. This sends the wrong signal to customers and may result in the inefficient use of resources" (Source: Norges Bank, "Payment Services Free of Charge are not in Bank Customers' Best Interests", press release, 8 May 2008 <http://www.norges-bank.no/templates/article___69212.aspx>).

26. See also Section 3.4.4.

27. The travails of the Raiffeisenlandesbank NÖ-Wien in Austria in 2002 (Van Hove, 2004, pp. 95–96) and Fortis in Belgium in 2003 (Van Hove, 2007, p. 29, note 19) – two banks that tried to introduce charges for ATM withdrawals but were forced to withdraw them because of public outcry – are salient illustrations.

28. See also: " ... make choosers better off, *as judged by themselves*" (Thaler and Sunstein, 2008, p. 5; emphasis in original).

29. In short: a rule that forbids participating retailers to charge credit customers more than cash customers.

30. See also Segendorf and Jansson (2012, p. 4) who note that users of payment instruments "may not internalize the effect of their choice on other parties".

31. Thaler and Sunstein stress that such economic incentives have a strong libertarian element: "Liberty is much greater when people are told, 'You can continue your behavior, so long as you pay for the social harm that it does' than when they are told, 'You must act exactly as the government says'." (2008, p. 186).

32. Source: Nederlandse Vereniging van Banken, Reply of Dutch banks to the Second Interim Report on Current Accounts and Related Services, letter to the European Commission, October 12, 2006, p. 9.

33. Panel on "Electronic payments, an underused opportunity" at the 2008 Eurofi conference on "EU priorities and proposals from the financial services industry for the Ecofin council", Nice, September 11–12, 2008.

34. Source: author's notes. Godeffroy also added that consumers who want to leave this electronic circuit should pay a price because of the cost attached to cash payments.
35. In the meantime it has been merged with the Monetary Authority of Singapore.
36. Source: <http://www.bccs-sin.com/bccsinfo.html>, visited on 17 January 2001 (no longer available). The statement also appears on p. 3 of the 2000 Annual Report of the BCCS.
37. Source: Romero, P. S, "Solon Pushes E-Peso Act", *The Philippine Star*, October 5, 2014 <http://www.philstar.com/business/2014/10/05/1376516/solon-pushes-e-peso-act>, visited on March 31, 2015.
38. This would obviously be different in countries that adhere to a strict interpretation of legal tender, where currency must be accepted as payment for *all* types of transactions. South Korea seems to be a (rare) example of such a country: "Banknotes and coins are issued solely by the Bank of Korea and cannot be refused, as legal tender, *in any transactions*" (EMEAP, 2002, p. 237; my emphasis). However, in this setting, making an electronic payment instrument legal tender would not qualify as a nudge.
39. As the CPSS (2003b, p. 96) puts it: "Although legal tender status is of limited direct relevance in the majority of transactions, it nevertheless helps to build the reputation of banknotes as being safe and unique assets".
40. The suggestion that the ECB should place the upper limit of its banknote series at EUR 50 instead of EUR 500 was first put forward in Van Hove and Vuchelen (1996). However, their main concern was not so much to lower the social cost but rather to squeeze the underground economy. Takala and Virén (2008, p. 28) refer to Bank of Finland studies that show that in Finland the larger denominations are used for "car purchases, large durable purchases, real estate deals and for several miscellaneous other uses". A recent argument in favour of a more proactive strategy for phasing out the use of paper currency, especially large-denomination notes, can be found in Rogoff (2014). However, as in Van Hove and Vuchelen (1996), Rogoff's concern is not so much the social cost of cash, but rather its use in the underground and illegal economy, and, in addition, the fact that the existence of currency makes it difficult for central banks to take interest rates much below zero.
41. Takala and Virén (2007, Table 1, p. 58) report that of the EMU12 countries only ATMs in Austria, Germany and Luxembourg contained EUR 100 banknotes.
42. Camerer, C. F., Issacharoff, S., Loewenstein, G. F., O'Donoghue, T., and M. Rabin, 2003. "Regulation for Conservatives: Behavioral Economics and the Case for 'Asymmetric Paternalism'", *University of Pennsylvania Law Review*, 151, 1211–1254, as mentioned in Thaler and Sunstein (2008, p. 72).
43. In October 2005, 58% and 52% of Euro-citizens were in favour of removing the 1-cent and 2-cent coins, respectively (Source: TNS Soffres/EOS Gallup Europe, "The Euro, 4 Years after the Introduction of the Banknotes and Coins", *Flash Eurobarometer*, European Commission, no. 175, November 2005 <http://ec.europa.eu/public_opinion/flash/fl175_en.pdf>).
44. Source: "ECB May Issue One Euro Note to Curb Price Rises", *Financial Times*, 12 December 2002.
45. Cf. European Central Bank, *Annual Report 2004*, p. 98.

46. Source: Kaminska, I., "The Time for Official e-Money is NOW!", *FTAlphaville*, 12 January 2015 <http://ftalphaville.ft.com/2014/01/22/1748152/the-time-for-official-e-money-is-now/>.
47. Source: Andolfatto, D., "Fedcoin: On the Desirability of a Government Cryptocurrency", *MacroMania* blog, 3 February 2015 <http://andolfatto.blog-spot.be/2015/02/fedcoin-on-desirability-of-government.html>.
48. Source: Haare, H., personal e-mails, June 12, 2009 and Gresvik, O., personal e-mail, July 27, 2009.
49. Source: EURO Kartensysteme, "GeldKarte: Fulminanter Start ins Neue Jahr mit 90% Mehr Ladevolumen – Jugendschutzmerkmal als Antrieb für den Goldenen Chip; Positive Ausstrahlungseffekte auch auf Andere Akzeptanzbereiche", press release, 22 February 2007 <http://www.geldkarte.de/> (no longer available).
50. Source: Initiative GeldKarte, "Allensbach-Studie: GeldKarte auf Erfolgstour durch Jugendschutzmerkmal – Breite Zustimmung für Einsatz des Chips am Zigarettenautomaten", press release, 13 August 2007 <http://www.geldkarte.de/> (no longer available).
51. Source: Europay Austria, "Quick Hebt ab – 2007 Schon 50.000 Neue Nutzer", press release, 3 May 2007 <http://www.paylife.at/>.
52. Takala and Virén (2007, p. 57) suggest a completely different nudge, which also goes against the withdrawal of high-denomination euro banknotes proposed in Section 3.4.2: "If the ATMs provide only large denomination notes, so that the minimum withdrawal is large, that represents a kind of implicit transaction cost for the consumers, which may reduce the use of cash".
53. According to Takala and Virén (2008), the currency circulation in Finland was presumably close to 2% of GDP in 2007.
54. Note that consumers can limit the nuisance by making increased use of cash-back at the POS or by making larger withdrawals. The introduction of *ad valorem* ATM fees would curb the latter behaviour.
55. Dexia, for example, introduced a fee of BEF 5 (EUR 0.12) per cheque in 1992.
56. Source: Guns, B., personal e-mail, October 16, 2008. Bart Guns was at the time Senior General Manager Group Payments at KBC.
57. Under the Eurocheque guarantee, merchants were guaranteed payment for cheques up to BEF 7,000 (roughly EUR 175). Once that guarantee had disappeared, many merchants simply stopped accepting cheques.
58. The DNB research shows that consumers are sensitive to such fees and adapt their payment behaviour accordingly. Three-quarters of the respondents replied that they were unwilling to pay the surcharge, and around two-thirds indicated they would rather pay cash; 4% use their e-purse and 5% shop elsewhere (Bolt et al., 2008, p. 14).
59. The proxies are derived from earlier research on consumers' payment choices, and comprise, for example, the average transaction value and the number of transactions per terminal. For the first, the assumption is that the cash payment share will decrease with the average transaction value because cash tends to be inconvenient for high-value payments. The second variable proxies for waiting times in line. According to Arango and Taylor, consumers in busy stores with long lines may get impatient and may prefer to use cash. [Note that Arango and Taylor rely on tender time estimates obtained in the

study led by the Dutch central bank (DNB, 2004). According to these estimates, cash payments are the speediest.] Clearly, these variables are rough proxies for consumer payment behaviour. Still, the results do complement the other evidence mentioned in the main text.

60. See De Ploey *et al.* (2008).
61. Note that "steering" was not explicitly defined in the interviews. As a result, it is not clear whether surcharging is included or not. McKinsey itself thinks it unlikely, given the nature of the question. Source: De Ploey, W., personal e-mail, 8 December 2008.
62. In line with this, van der Cruijsen *et al.* (2015, p. 5) find that Dutch consumers hardly experience any constraints when making POS payments: in 2013 only 1% of the payments could not be made with consumers' preferred means of payment.
63. van der Cruijsen *et al.* (2015, p. 25) also make this suggestion. As a matter of fact, a number of supermarkets in the Netherlands, such as Albert Heijn, have been doing this (MOB, 2007, p. 23).
64. This comes with a major caveat. The implicit assumption here is that what is best for a merchant is also best for society; in other words, the assumption is that private and social costs are aligned. In the current situation, this will often not be the case. As explained in Section 3.3, in the Netherlands, in 2002 the social switching point between cash and debit cards was EUR 11.63. However, as demonstrated in Van Hove (2004, p. 86, Figure 1), for Dutch merchants, the cut-off point was at the time no less than EUR 67; that is, it was only for amounts above this threshold that debit cards became more cost-effective from merchants' *private* perspective. This shows why private and social costs should be aligned by means of cost-based pricing.
65. Note that I have followed Thaler and Sunstein's advice that a positive message is more effective than a negative message (2008, p. 67).
66. Source: Currence, "Estelle Gullit Geeft Goede Voorbeeld met PINnen Klein Bedrag", press release, 22 May 2007 <http://www.currence.nl/Currence. nl/22052007.html> (no longer available). Note that the Chipknip e-purse – which from a social perspective is even more cost-effective (cf. Section 3.3) – has not proved much of a success in the retail environment. As a result, Currence repositioned Chipknip as a niche product for U-POS payments in the parking and vending segment (Source: "Chipknip Verdwijnt uit Praktisch Iedere Winkel", *Het Financieele Dagblad*, 20 September 2007).
67. Source: Currence, "Supermarkten Stimuleren PINnen", press release, 5 July 2007 <http://www.currence.nl/Currence.nl/05072007.html> (no longer available).
68. Source: Stichting Bevorderen Efficiënt Betalen, "Supermarkten Zetten Pinnen in Tegen Stijgende Overvallen", press release, 12 June 2008. The Stichting was created as a result of the "Payment Services Covenant 2005" (Convenant Betalingsverkeer 2005), an agreement between banks and retailers to promote the efficiency of the Dutch payment system. The banks have put EUR 10 million in the fund managed by the Stichting; see: <http://www. efficientbetalen.nl/>.
69. Source: Currence, educational material. Coincidence or not, the leaflet directed at cashiers stresses that they can give customers "een duwtje in de goede richting" – in English: "a ... nudge in the right direction".

70. Jonker *et al.* (2015, p. 8) translate it as "Why not use your debit card?", but this would seem to miss the social-norm aspect of the slogan. Cf. "The later slogans no longer focused ... on following behaviour of others" (o.c., p. 24).
71. Source: Currence. Note, firstly, that the use of debit cards in Dutch supermarkets increased in preceding months too, and, secondly (and relatedly), that the campaign started in May 2007 and was *intensified* in September 2008. This makes it difficult to isolate the impact of the September 2008 initiative. However, over the period January-August 2008 (and excluding February because of the leap-day), the total number of PIN transactions in supermarkets grew on average by 12.3% year-on-year vs. 14.7% in September 2008. For PIN transactions below EUR 10, the corresponding figures are 18.8% and 28.5%.
72. See Jacobs, E., "Book Review: Nothing New When Push Comes to Shove", *Financial Times*, 21 August 2008 and Harford, T., "It Is Markets That Nudge, Not States", *Financial Times*, 22 August 2008.
73. Jacobs, E., "Book Review: Nothing New When Push Comes to Shove", *Financial Times*, 21 August 2008.
74. As Leinonen (2008, p. 12) explains, even explicit transaction-based pricing of cash would not drive out underground cash payments since "the value of anonymity is perceived as much higher than the additional costs".
75. Harford, T., "It is Markets That Nudge, Not States", *Financial Times*, 22 August 2008.

References

Arango, C., and V. Taylor. 2008. "Merchant Acceptance, Costs, and Perceptions of Retail Payments: A Canadian Survey", Discussion Paper 2008–12, Bank of Canada <http://www.bankofcanada.ca/2008/08/discussion-paper-2008-12/>. Accessed on November 3, 2015.

Ardizzi, G., and P. Giucca. 2012. "The Social Costs of Payment Instruments in Italy. Surveys of Firms, Banks, and Payment Service Providers", <https://www.bancaditalia.it/pubblicazioni/tematiche-istituzionali/2012-costo-sociale/social_costs_payment_instruments_Italy.pdf>. Accessed on November 3, 2015.

Aydogan, S. and L. Van Hove. 2014. "Nudging Consumers towards Card Payments: A Field Experiment", in *The Usage, Costs and Benefits of Cash – Revisited*. Conference book of the 2014 International Cash Conference, Deutsche Bundesbank, 589–630.

Banco de Portugal. 2007. *Retail Payment Instruments in Portugal: Costs and Benefits* <https://www.bportugal.pt/SiteCollectionDocuments/DPG-SP-PUB-Instrumentos-Pagamento-Retalho-Est-en.pdf>. Accessed on November 3, 2015.

Bank of England (BoE). 2015. "One Bank Research Agenda", Discussion Paper <http://www.bankofengland.co.uk/research/documents/onebank/discussion.pdf>. Accessed on November 3, 2015.

Bentley, A., Earls M. and M. J. O'Brien. 2011. *I'll Have What She's Having – Mapping Social Behavior*, Cambridge: MA: MIT Press.

Bergman, M., G. Guibourg, and B. Segendorf. 2007. "The Costs of Paying – Private and Social Costs of Cash and Card Payments", Working Paper No. 212, Sveriges Riksbank.

Bergman, M., G. Guibourg, and B. Segendorf. 2008. "Card and Cash Payments from a Social Perspective", *Economic Review,* Sveriges Riksbank, 2, 42–59.

Bolt, W., N. Jonker, and C. van Renselaar. 2008. "Incentives at the Counter: An Empirical Analysis of Surcharging Card Payment and Payment Behaviour in the Netherlands", Working Paper No. 196, De Nederlandsche Bank.

Bouhdaoui Y., Bounie D., and L. Van Hove. 2011. "Central Banks and Their Banknote Series: The Efficiency-Cost Trade-off", *Economic Modelling,* 28, 1482–1488.

Bounie, D., M. Bourreau, A. François, and M. Verdier, "La Détention et l'Usage des Instruments de Paiement en France", *Revue d'Economie Financière,* 91, 2008, 53–76.

Bounie, D., J.-P. Buthion, and F. Abel. 2010. "Une analyse des facteurs de l'acceptation et de l'usage des instruments de paiement par les commerces en France", *Revue d'Economie Financière,* 96, 187–213.

Buonomano, D. 2011. *Brain Bugs: How the Brain's Flaws Shape Our Lives,* New York: Norton.

Congressional Budget Office (CBO). 1996. "Emerging Electronic Methods for Making Retail Payments" <http://www.cbo.gov/doc.cfm?index=14>. Accessed on November 3, 2015.

Committee on Payment and Settlement Systems (CPSS). 2003a. "A Glossary of Terms Used in Payments and Settlement Systems" <http://www.bis.org/publ/cpss00b.htm>. Accessed on November 3, 2015.

Committee on Payment and Settlement Systems (CPSS). 2003b. "The Role of Central Bank Money in Payment Systems", CPSS Publications 55 <http://www.bis.org/publ/cpss55.pdf>. Accessed on November 3, 2015.

De Nederlandsche Bank (DNB). 2004. "The Cost of Payments", *Quarterly Bulletin,* March, 57–64.

De Nederlandsche Bank (DNB). 2006. "Towards a Cashless Society?", *Quarterly Bulletin,* March, 63–70.

De Nederlandsche Bank (DNB). 2015. "Card or Cash? Customer Preferences Dictate Retailers' Approach", *DNBulletin,* 30 April <http://www.dnb.nl/en/news/news-and-archive/dnbulletin-2015/dnb321621.jsp>. Accessed on November 3, 2015.

De Ploey, W., T. Natale, and A. Proko. 2008. "Mission Impossible? The Cashless Payments Proposition for 'Small-Ticket' Merchants", *McKinsey on Payments,* February, 38–43.

EMEAP Working Group on Payment and Settlement Systems. 2002. "Payment Systems in EMEAP Economies", Executives' Meeting of East Asia–Pacific Central Banks and Monetary Authorities <http://www.emeap.org/wp-content/uploads/2015/04/redbook.pdf>. Accessed on November 3, 2015.

Enge, A., and G. Øwre. 2006. "A Retrospective on the Introduction of Prices in the Norwegian Payment System", *Economic Bulletin,* Norges Bank, 77, 162–172.

Garcia-Swartz, D.D., R.W. Hahn, and A. Layne-Farrar. 2004. "The Economics of a Cashless Society: An Analysis of the Costs and Benefits of Payment Instruments", Related Publication 04-24, AEI-Brookings Joint Center for Regulatory Studies.

Garcia-Swartz, D.D., R.W. Hahn, and A. Layne-Farrar. 2006a. "The Move toward a Cashless Society: A Closer Look at Payment Instrument Economics", *Review of Network Economics,* 5, 175–198.

Garcia-Swartz, D.D., R.W. Hahn, and A. Layne-Farrar. 2006b. "The Move toward a Cashless Society: A Closer Look at Payment Instrument Economics of a Cashless Society: Calculating the Costs and Benefits", *Review of Network Economics*, 5, 199–228.

Garcia-Swartz, D.D., R.W. Hahn, and A. Layne-Farrar. 2007. "Further Thoughts on the Cashless Society: A Reply to Dr. Shampine", *Review of Network Economics*, 6, 509–524.

Goldstein, D.G., E.J. Johnson, A. Herrmann, and M. Heitmann. 2008. "Nudge Your Customer toward Better Choices", *Harvard Business Review*, December, 99–105.

Górka, J. 2014. "Merchant Indifference Test Application – A Case For Revising Interchange Fee Level in Poland", in *The Usage, Costs and Benefits of Cash – Revisited*. Conference book of the 2014 International Cash Conference, Deutsche Bundesbank, 75–151.

Gresvik, O., and H. Haare. 2008a. "Payment Habits at Point of Sale. Different Methods of Calculating Use of Cards and Cash in Norway", Staff Memo 6/2008, Norges Bank <http://www.norges-bank.no/upload/publikasjoner/staff%20 memo/2008/staff_memo_2008_06.pdf>. Accessed on November 3, 2015.

Gresvik, O., and H. Haare. 2008b. "Costs in the Norwegian Payment System 2007 – A Brief Overview of the Surveys and Results", Staff Memo9/2008, Norges Bank <http://www.norges-bank.no/upload/publikasjoner/staff%20memo/2008/ staff_memo_0908.pdf>. Accessed on November 3, 2015.

Gresvik, O., and H. Haare. 2009. "Costs in the Norwegian Payment System", Staff Memo No. 4/2009, Norges Bank, <http://www.norges-bank.no/upload/publikasjoner/staff%20memo/2009/staff_memo_0409.pdf>. Accessed on November 3, 2015.

Hakkarainen, P. 2009. "The Future of Retail Banking: More Competition Needed, *Settlements, Payments, E-money & E-trading Development (SPEED)*, 4, 34–39.

Jonker, N. 2013. "Social Costs of POS Payments in the Netherlands 2002–2012: Efficiency Gains from Increased Debit Card Usage", Occasional Studies, 11(2), De Nederlandsche Bank.

Jonker, N., M. Plooij, and J. Verburg. 2015. "Does a Public Campaign Influence Debit Card Usage? Evidence from the Netherlands", Working Paper No. 470, De Nederlandsche Bank.

Jacobsen, J.G.K., and A.M. Pedersen. 2012. "Costs of Cash and Card Payments in Denmark", *Monetary Review*, Danmarks Nationalbank, 2nd Quarter, 109–121.

Kahneman, D. 2011. *Thinking, Fast and Slow*, New York: Farrar, Straus & Giroux.

Krueger, M. 2008. "Cash – The Familiar Stranger", *European Card Review*, 15(5), September/October, 30–34.

Krueger, M., and F. Seitz. 2014. *Costs and Benefits of Cash and Cashless Payment Instruments – Module 1: Overview and Initial Estimates*, Frankfurt am Main, Germany: Deutsche Bundesbank.

Lam, T., and C. Ossolinski. 2015. "The Value of Payment Instruments: Estimating Willingness to Pay and Consumer Surplus", Research Discussion Paper 2015–03, Reserve Bank of Australia.

Latvijas Banka. 2013. *The Bank of Latvia Review of Social Costs of Retail Payment Instruments in Latvia*.

Leenheer, J., M. Elsen, and R. Pieters. 2012. "Consumentenprikkels voor Efficiënt Betalen – Management Summary", CentERdata, Tilburg.

Leinonen, H. 2008. "Could Transparent Pricing Increase Payment Efficiency and Competition at Point of Sale?", mimeo, Bank of Finland, 3 November.

Liikanen, E. 2015. "Enhancing Reliability and Efficiency of Future Payments: Five Criteria", speech at the joint European Central Bank and Bank of Finland Retail Payment Conference, Helsinki, 4 June.

Maatschappelijk Overleg Betalingsverkeer (MOB). 2007. "Rapportage Maatschappelijk Overleg Betalingsverkeer 2006", report to the Minister of Finance <http://www.dnb.nl/binaries/Rapportage%20MOB%202006%20-%20 april%202007_tcm46-153444.pdf>. Accessed on November 3, 2015.

National Bank of Belgium. 2006. "Costs, Advantages and Drawbacks of the Various Means of Payment", *Economic Review*, National Bank of Belgium, 41–47.

National Bank of Belgium. 2015. Annual report.

Reserve Bank of Australia. 2007. "Payment Costs in Australia" <http://www.rba. gov.au/payments-system/resources/publications/payments-au/paymts-sys-rev-conf/2007/7-payment-costs.pdf>. Accessed on November 3, 2015.

Rogoff, K. S. 2014. "Costs and Benefits to Phasing out Paper Currency", Working Paper 2016, National Bureau of Economic Research.

Schautzer, A. 2007. "Cash Logistics in Austria and the Euro Area", *Monetary Policy & the Economy*, Oesterreichische Nationalbank, No. 1, 138–149.

Schlag, P. 2010. "Nudge, Choice Architecture, and Libertarian Paternalism", *Michigan Law Review*, 108, 913–924.

Schmiedel, H., G. Kostova, and W. Ruttenberg. 2012. "The Social and Private Costs of Retail Payment Instruments: A European Perspective", Occasional Paper Series No. 137, European Central Bank.

Segendorf, B. and T. Jansson. 2012. The Cost of Consumer Payments in Sweden. Working Paper 262, Sveriges Riksbank.

Shampine, A. 2007. "Another Look at Payment Instrument Economics", *Review of Network Economics*, 6, 495–508.

Simes, R., A. Lancy, and I. Harper. 2006. "Costs and Benefits of Alternative Payments Instruments in Australia", Working Paper 2006–08, Melbourne Business School.

Snellman, H., and M. Virén. 2009. "ATM Networks and Cash Usage", *Applied Financial Economics*, 19, 841–851.

Steering Committee over de toekomst van de betaalmiddelen. 2005. "Kosten, Voor-en Nadelen van de Verschillende Betaalmiddelen", National Bank of Belgium.

Stewart, C., I. Chan, C. Ossolinski, D. Halperin, and P. Ryan. 2014. "The Evolution of Payment Costs in Australia", Research Discussion Paper 2014–14, Reserve Bank of Australia.

Spencer, P. D. 2003. "Market Structure, Innovation and the Development of Digital Money", in Balling, M., F. Lierman, and A. Mullineux (eds), *Technology and Finance: Challenges for Financial Markets, Business Strategies and Policy Makers*, Routledge, London, 302–313.

Takala, K., and M. Virén. 2007. "Impact of ATMs on the Use of Cash", *Communications & Strategies – International Journal of Digital Economics*, 66, 47–62.

Takala, K., and M. Virén. 2008. "Efficiency and Costs of Payments", Discussion Paper No. 11/2008, Bank of Finland.

Thaler, R., and C. Sunstein. 2008. *Nudge – Improving Decisions about Health, Wealth, and Happiness*, New Haven & London: Yale University Press.

van der Cruijsen, C., L. Hernandez, and N. Jonker. 2015. "In Love with the Debit Card but Still Married to Cash", Working Paper No. 461, De Nederlandsche Bank.

Van der Horst, F., and E. Matthijsen. 2013. "The Irrationality of Payment Behaviour", *Occasional Studies*, 11(4), De Nederlandsche Bank.

Van Hove, L. 2001. "Optimal Denominations for Coins and Bank Notes: In Defense of the Principle of Least Effort", *Journal of Money, Credit, and Banking*, 33, 1015–1021.

Van Hove, L. 2002. "Electronic Money and Cost-based Pricing", *Wirtschaftspolitische Blätter*, 49, 128–136.

Van Hove, L. 2004. "Cost-Based Pricing of Payment Instruments: The State of the Debate", *De Economist*, 152, 1, 79–100.

Van Hove, L. 2005. "Making Electronic Money Legal Tender: Pros & Cons", Working paper, Free University of Brussels, October.

Van Hove, L. 2007. "Central Banks and Payment Instruments: A Serious Case of Schizophrenia", *Communications & Strategies – International Journal of Digital Economics*, 66, 19–46.

Van Hove, L. 2008. "On the War On Cash and Its Spoils". *International Journal of Electronic Banking*, 1, 36–45.

Van Hove, L., and J. Vuchelen. 1996. "Who Needs High-Denomination Euro Banknotes? A Note on the Proposed Denominational Structure of the Euro", *Rivista Internazionale di Scienze Economiche e Commerciali*, 43, 4, 791–803.

4
Cash Holdings in Germany and the Demand for "German" Banknotes: What Role Is There for Cashless Payments?

Nikolaus Bartzsch and Franz Seitz

4.1 Introduction*

Generally speaking, all euro-area national central banks issue euro banknotes. Following the introduction of euro cash at the start of 2002, the cumulated net issuance of euro notes by the Deutsche Bundesbank ("German" euro notes) increased from an initial €73 billion to €508 billion at the end of 2014. Figure 4.1 shows that the volume of these German euro banknotes outstanding has grown very much faster than could have been expected on the basis of earlier growth rates of D-Mark currency. For the first two years after the launch of euro cash, this strong growth could be explained by the need to replenish stocks of hoarded banknotes both inside and outside the euro area after the currency changeover. However, this should have ceased to have an effect at the end of 2003 when the volume of German banknotes outstanding returned to the hypothetical level that would have been reached had euro cash not been introduced. Nevertheless, the pace of growth in the volume of banknotes outstanding continued to be much more dynamic than in the D-Mark era in the 1990s. As shown in Bartzsch *et al.* (2011a), this huge surge is due to foreign demand for euro banknotes. They find that, at the end of 2009, around 70% of the cumulated net issuance was held outside Germany. Of

* The authors thank E. Gladisch and R. Setzer for their helpful comments. We are particularly grateful to S. Arz for his valuable contribution. The opinions expressed in this paper do not necessarily reflect those of the Deutsche Bundesbank.

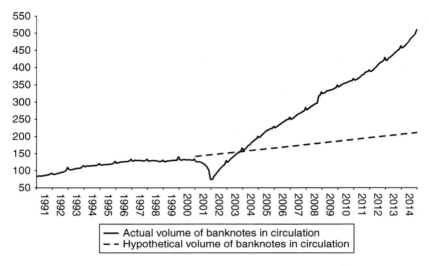

Figure 4.1   German banknotes in circulation (€ billion)

Note: The actual volume of banknotes in circulation in the period from January 1991 to December 2001 corresponds to the volume of D-Mark banknotes outstanding (converted to euros with the irrevocably fixed exchange rates of 1 January 1999) and following the introduction of euro cash in January 2002, the volume of Bundesbank-issued euro banknotes outstanding. For the sake of simplicity, the volume of D-Mark banknotes outstanding in the period from January 1991 to December 2000, extrapolated using its linear trend, is taken as the hypothetical volume of banknotes in circulation as of January 2001.

Sources: Deutsche Bundesbank and the authors' own calculations.

this, the lion's share (roughly 50%) was in non-euro-area countries, with the remainder in other euro-area countries. This also means that only a relatively small share – approximately 30% – was used for transaction purposes and hoarding in Germany.[1] In their opinion, 20% is a realistic figure for banknotes hoarded in Germany. Consequently, only around 10% were used for transaction purposes in Germany. This was equivalent to around €430 *per capita* at the end of 2009.

While Bartzsch *et al.* (2011a, 2011b) have split up the cumulated net issuance of euro notes by the Deutsche Bundesbank into its components (transaction balance, hoarding and foreign demand), we want to further analyse the role of these underlying motives of banknote demand. These should differ for the individual denominations. Therefore, we estimate models of banknote demand for small, medium and large German euro banknotes. In these structural models, the demand for banknotes is explained by proxy variables for the motives of holding banknotes. Amongst others, we estimate the interest (semi-)elasticities of banknote demand. This allows us to answer the question whether portfolio shifts from short-term bank deposits into cash are to be expected owing to the very low level of interest rates. Moreover and specifically, we ask what role cashless payment media play in the evolution of the demand for banknotes. Our paper is closely related to the work of Seitz and Setzer (2009), who also estimate structural models of the demand for German banknotes. With data available only up until the end of 2007 they use a mixed D-Mark/euro series from 1991 to 2007. By contrast, our models are estimated for the euro era only with data ranging from 2002 to 2011.

The paper is structured as follows. Section 4.2 contains a literature survey on banknote demand models with special emphasis on Germany and the role of card payments. In Section 4.3, some stylised facts are presented concerning the development and composition of banknotes in circulation in Germany and the rest of the euro area as well as some figures on cashless payments. The data we use to estimate banknote demand models are described in Section 4.4. In Section 4.5, we estimate structural models of banknote demand for the three denomination categories. The results are summarised together with other conclusions in Section 4.6.

4.2 Literature review

The following literature survey focuses on more recent work since the beginning of the 2000s. For an overview of older papers on currency demand, see Boeschoten (1992, subsection 1.4.2).

Doyle (2000) estimates foreign demand for US, German and Swiss currency. He obtains higher foreign shares than in previous studies. His results are based on currency demand equations within a cointegration framework. Doyle obtains different results when he splits up currency into large and small-value denominations. The signs and significance of the coefficients are unchanged with just large-denomination notes. By contrast, when only small-denomination notes are used, those same coefficients tend to be insignificant or have the wrong signs. These smaller notes are the ones that Doyle expects will more likely be used in the legitimate US economy. Therefore, he concludes that this result might indicate an invalidation of traditional explanations of currency demand or simply movements away from small to large notes (in real terms), or from cash to other payment instruments.

Khamis and Leone (2001) find strong evidence that real currency demand in Mexico remained stable throughout and after the financial crisis in Mexico which started at the end of 1994. They find a strong cointegration relationship between currency balances, private consumption expenditures and the interest rate. The sample period from 1983 to 1997 includes the inflationary debt crisis period, the stabilisation period under the 1987 stabilisation plan, the ensuing financial crisis in December 1994 and the recovery period thereafter. The paper concludes that the significant reduction in currency demand in the course of the financial crisis can be appropriately explained by a change in the variables that historically explain cash demand in Mexico quite well.

Akinci (2003) models currency in circulation in Turkey using data between 1987 and 2003. Cointegration analysis reveals that there is a long-run relationship between currency issued, private consumption, interest rates and a bilateral exchange rate. The results reveal that economic agents are more sensitive to interest rate movements than to exchange rate movements in the long run. The exchange rate elasticity is more effective in the short run. This indicates that the exchange rate might be a powerful indicator in terms of capturing the dynamics of the demand for cash. Moreover, this implies the existence of currency substitution in Turkey. In the long run, however, real income and the interest rate variables appear to be the main determinants of the demand for cash balances.

Amromin and Chakravorti (2009) analyse cash demand for thirteen advanced economies from 1988 to 2003 with panel regressions by separating cash into three denomination categories to disentangle its store of value and payment functions. They isolate the transactional role of cash by focusing on the small-denomination class, which they define as banknotes (including coins) that are lower in value than those which are commonly dispensed by ATMs. Amromin and Chakravorti econometrically test a money demand equation where the currency-to-GDP ratio is a function of the alternative payment infrastructure, the cash infrastructure, the proportion of small merchants and the opportunity cost of cash. They also report results for the aggregate currency-to-GDP ratio. The substitution effects with respect to electronic payments are largely confined to the demand for small denominations. Moreover, they find that the demand for small-denomination currency is not affected by changes in the interest rate. By contrast, the demand for high-denomination notes decreases as interest rates rise but is unaffected by changes in debit card usage. The interest rate sensitivity of demand for high-denomination notes is especially high in countries that do not have significant proportions of their currency stock circulating outside their borders. This suggests a persistent role for cash as a store of wealth.

Nachane *et al.* (2013) identify various factors influencing currency demand in India from 1989 to 2011 in a vector error correction framework for aggregate currency demand as well as for various currency sub-groups. They argue that the homogeneity postulate with respect to prices might be too restrictive. Hence, they model currency in nominal terms, using wholesale prices as price measure. The trends in currency in circulation at the individual denomination level show considerable fluctuations, in particular, which renders econometric modelling a complex task. However, there exists a cointegrating relationship between (total) currency circulation, real GDP, prices and deposit rates. The income elasticity of currency is found to be somewhat higher than is observed in similar studies for advanced countries.

Cusbert and Rohling (2013) analyse the strong increase in the demand for currency in Australia which began in mid-October 2008, around one month after the collapse of Lehman Brothers and concurrently with policy responses of the Reserve Bank of Australia and the Federal Government. They attempt to capture the effects of the global financial crisis on currency demand in three ways. First, they add dummy variables for the last quarter of 2008 until the second quarter of 2009 to their baseline model. Second, they introduce confidence, financial market and wealth variables to their model. They expect increases in the stock of currency to be associated with declines in confidence and wealth and rises in financial volatility. Finally, they examine whether these variables retain any explanatory power in the presence of dummy variables. In their baseline model, currency in circulation is modelled in a single equation error correction framework to exploit the possible cointegration between currency holdings, nominal GDP and interest rates. They also include ATMs, EFTPOS (electronic funds transfer at point of sale) terminals, bank branches per capita and the ratio of self-employed to total employment in the long-run relationship. They estimate the model using data from 1993 to 2011 and find that only around 20% of the rise in Australian currency demand during the financial crisis can be attributed to the normal response of currency holdings to the lowering of interest rates and to the increase in income from the government stimulus. The remaining 80% may be due to an increase in precautionary holdings in response to financial market uncertainty, which is consistent with the larger increase in demand for high-denomination banknotes. In addition, Cusbert and Rohling estimate separate models of currency demand of the bank and non-bank sectors for different denominations. The interest coefficients are broadly consistent with the idea that demand for larger denominations should be more interest sensitive. The insignificance of the financial crisis dummy variables in the low-denomination regression confirms that only larger denominations were behaving unusually in this period.

Besides these time series models, there is one paper which estimates currency demand using micro data. Briglevics and Schuh (2014) investigate US consumer demand for cash using panel micro data for 2008–2010 with a special emphasis on the role of low interest rates and different kinds of credit cards. They find that cash demand by consumers using credit cards for convenience is much more interest elastic than those using credit cards to borrow. These findings may have implications for the welfare cost of inflation because consumers who revolve credit card debt are less likely to switch from cash to credit.

There are only three papers which concentrate on the euro area. Fischer *et al.* (2004) analyse currency in circulation in the euro area since the beginning of the 1980s. They develop a theoretical model which extends traditional money demand models to also incorporate arguments for the informal economy and foreign demand for specific currencies. In the empirical part, they estimate the total demand for euro legacy currencies and for small and large denominations within a vector error correction framework. They find significant differences between the determinants of holdings of small and large denominations as well as overall currency demand. While the long-run demand for small-value banknotes is mainly driven by domestic transactions, the demand for large-value banknotes in the cointegrating relation depends on a short-term interest rate, the exchange rate of the euro as a proxy for foreign demand and inflation variability. Therefore, large-value banknotes seem to be used to a large extent as a store of value both domestically and abroad.

An approach similar to that of Fischer *et al.* (2004) is taken by Seitz and Setzer (2009). They estimate the demand for small, medium and large denominations of German banknotes in a vector error correction framework for the period from the first quarter of 1991 to the fourth quarter of 2007. These comprise D-Mark banknotes and euro banknotes which were put into circulation by the Deutsche Bundesbank. They include the DM period, as the time series for the euro era alone was too short at that time. In the case of small and medium denominations, what stands out in the results is the obvious impact of the transaction volume. The large denominations, by contrast, appear to be unaffected by this. In their case, however, non-resident motives are important: first, via a long-term impact of the house prices in the euro area, whose dynamics are determined mainly by the real estate market outside Germany, and second, via private consumption in the euro area excluding Germany. Additionally, demand from non-euro-area countries is important for all denominations. Moreover, an influence of the shadow economy on banknote demand cannot be ruled out for any of the three banknote categories. Finally, opportunity costs in the form of interest rates seem to be of relevance only for the small denominations. Alternative means of payment (especially card payments) evidently influence only the small denominations, too. The error correction term indicates the fastest adjustment for the small denominations and the longest for the large denominations.

Bartzsch *et al.* (2015) take Seitz and Setzer (2009) as starting point, but concentrate on genuine euro area data. Their models reveal a strong foreign influence on the demand for "German" banknotes, but no significant repercussions from card payments as alternatives to cash. This might be attributed to the poor quality of their proxy variable, the number (value) of card payments published by the Deutsche Bundesbank in its payments statistics. Due to redefinitions, this series exhibits a counterintuitive and unexplained downward shift in 2007 (see Section 4.4 for details). In contrast, in Seitz and Setzer (2009), who use a similar framework with data before the redefinition, this variable exerted a significant influence on small-denomination notes.

Our paper analyses cash demand using genuine euro data since 2002. As regards card payments, we take another data series into account which does not suffer from the statistical break.

4.3 Stylised facts

In this section we present a number of stylised facts about the cumulated net issuance of euro banknotes by the Deutsche Bundesbank ("German" euro banknotes in circulation) and the Eurosystem as well as the role of cashless payments in Germany. The development of euro banknotes in circulation is shown in Figure 4.2. After the euro cash changeover at the beginning of 2002, the cumulated net issuance of German euro banknotes increased from an initial €73 billion to €508 billion (10.7 billion notes) at the end of 2014. This corresponds to an average annual growth rate of more than 16%. In the euro area, banknotes in circulation increased during the same period from an initial €221 billion to €1,017 billion (17.5 billion notes). Thus, the German share in the value of the cumulated net issuance of euro banknotes has increased from 33% to 50% since the euro cash changeover. This share is clearly above Germany's share in the European Central Bank (ECB) capital of 25.7%, which is determined on the basis of the size of its population and its GDP.

The vast growth in German euro banknotes in circulation up until the end of 2003 can be attributed to the replenishment of stocks of hoarded banknotes both inside and outside the euro area (see Figure 4.1). From 2004, the growth rates of banknotes in circulation began to decline steadily. In 2006, they stabilised at a level of about 10%. In the wake of the financial crisis, German households made considerable shifts in

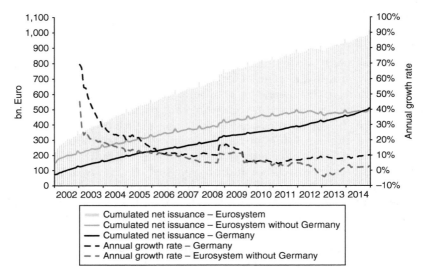

Figure 4.2   Euro banknotes in circulation

Note: Left scale: Cumulated net issuance; right scale: annual growth rate.

Sources: Deutsche Bundesbank and ECB.

their financial investment in the fourth quarter of 2008 (see Deutsche Bundesbank, 2009, p. 52f). This led to sharp inflows into liquid and (relatively) secure short-term types of investment, which also boosted the demand for cash. As a result, the German net issuance of banknotes rose by €16 billion in October 2008. In that month alone, the annual growth rate of the cumulated net issuance of German euro banknotes increased by six percentage points.

As can be seen in Figure 4.2, the hoards of German euro banknotes resulting from the crisis were partially reduced in the course of 2009 in the sense that the growth rates in Germany developed more in line with those in the rest of the euro area.

Since the beginning of 2012, the volume of German euro banknotes in circulation, which has seen annual growth rates of between 7% and 10%, has again been showing much stronger growth than the circulation of banknotes issued by other Eurosystem member states (see Figure 4.2). Some euro-area countries have even recorded negative rates of increase. These differences in the development of euro banknotes in circulation can be explained by the large share of the Bundesbank's cumulated net issuance of euro banknotes in circulation outside

Germany. A number of different approaches can be used to measure the foreign demand for German euro banknotes (see Bartzsch *et al.*, 2011a, 2011b). In this connection, the regional distribution of the cumulated net issuance is determined using the "net shipments and foreign travel" approach (Bartzsch *et al.*, 2011b, section 3.1). The volume of German euro banknotes in circulation abroad is estimated using data collected as part of a household survey by the Bundesbank on foreign travel as well as available data on net shipments of euro banknotes by banks (international foreign currency traders) to countries outside the euro area. These net shipments correspond to the difference between the outpayments by the Bundesbank to international foreign currency traders and the inpayments by the international foreign currency traders at the Bundesbank. The estimated regional distribution of euro banknotes issued in Germany estimated using this approach can be seen in Figures 4.3 and 4.4.

At the end of 2013, the largest share of the Bundesbank's cumulated net issuance in the amount of just over €460 billion was accounted for by banknotes in circulation abroad (€330 billion, or just over 70% of the cumulated net issuance), with the lion's share in circulation outside the euro

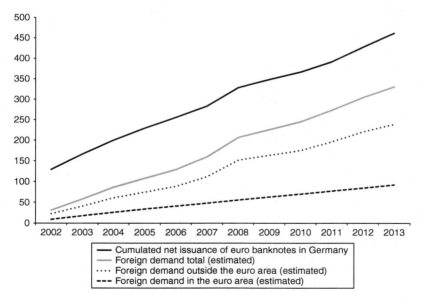

Figure 4.3 Regional distribution of euro banknotes issued in Germany (in € billion)
Sources: Deutsche Bundesbank and authors' own calculations.

area (just under €240 billion, or over 50% of the cumulated net issuance). Germany was, however, also a major net exporter of euro banknotes – especially via foreign travel – to the rest of the euro area (just over €90 billion, or 20% of the cumulated net issuance). The banknotes in circulation outside the euro area can be attributed to foreign travel and to the net shipments, with the latter (cumulated) accounting for the greatest share (just over €140 billion, or just over 30%) at the end of 2013. In summary, the growth in the cumulated net issuance of banknotes in Germany can be primarily explained by the volume of German-issued euro banknotes held abroad (foreign demand), whereas the domestic demand for banknotes (for transaction and hoarding purposes) remains largely constant and therefore does not make a notable contribution to the growth in the cumulated net issuance. The percentage share of the Bundesbank's cumulated net issuance of euro banknotes in circulation abroad has therefore increased significantly since the introduction of euro cash (see Figure 4.4).

To complete the picture, Figure 4.5 shows the cumulated net shipments from Germany and from the Eurosystem as a whole. Both time series lie close together over the entire time horizon and have been virtually congruent since the end of 2010. In other words, virtually all of

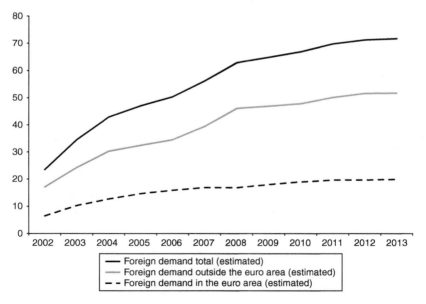

Figure 4.4 Regional distribution of euro banknotes issued in Germany

Note: Percentage shares in the cumulated net issuance.

Sources: Deutsche Bundesbank and authors' own calculations.

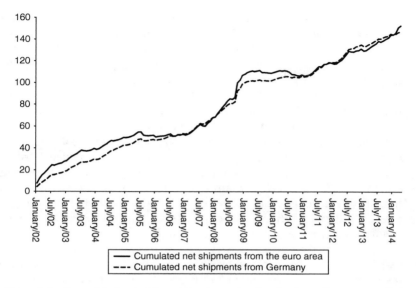

Figure 4.5 Cumulated net shipments of euro banknotes from Germany and the euro area (€ billion)

Sources: Deutsche Bundesbank and ECB.

the Eurosystem's total cumulated net issuance originates from Germany on balance. This can be explained, in part, by Germany's long-standing strong involvement since the D-Mark era in the international wholesale banknote market, its central geographical location and also by the role of Frankfurt airport. In addition to the cumulated net shipments, the (total) volume of euro banknotes in circulation outside the euro area is fed by other channels, such as foreign travel or cash sent home by foreign workers. The cumulated net shipments therefore only represent a lower limit. According to estimates by the ECB, around 25% of all euro banknotes issued by the Eurosystem are outside the euro area (ECB, 2014, p. 23). At the end of 2013, this was equivalent to just under €240 billion. This corresponds exactly to the estimated value of the cumulated net issuance of "German" euro banknotes in circulation outside the euro area (see Figure 4.3).

In summary, the dynamic development of the cumulated net issuance of euro banknotes by the Bundesbank – unlike those issued by other Eurosystem member states – can be explained as follows. Practically the entire volume of euro banknotes in circulation abroad issued by the Eurosystem seems to originate from Germany. Furthermore, Germany is a major (net) exporter of euro banknotes to other euro-area countries.

Moreover, the growth in the cumulated net issuance in Germany is almost exclusively driven by foreign demand. In the meantime, foreign demand is presumably also the greatest driving force behind the development of the foreign demand for euro banknotes for the Eurosystem as a whole.[2] In Germany's euro-area partner countries, the volumes of banknotes held for transaction purposes are likely to have grown less strongly owing to the subdued economic growth and the generally lesser significance of cash as a means of payment.

The lion's share of euro banknotes in circulation outside the euro area is presumably not used for transaction purposes, but is hoarded. Bartzsch *et al.* (2011b, section 3.4) estimate that stocks of hoarded banknotes account for 70% of the total volume of German euro banknotes in circulation outside the euro area. This hypothesis is also supported by the breakdown (by denomination) of the shipments from Germany (by value). Figure 4.6 illustrates this by way of example for 2013, which is when inpayments at central banks, i.e., the purchases by wholesale currency banks, started being recorded by denomination. With regard to outpayments and inpayments, the bulk of these banknotes is accounted for by the €500, €100 and €50 denominations. The €500 and €100 banknotes are denominations that are typically used for hoarding, whereas the €50 note is probably used for both hoarding and transaction purposes.

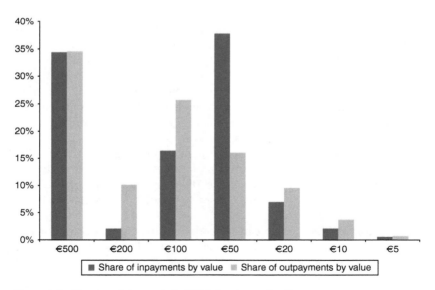

Figure 4.6   German shipments in 2013, by denomination
Source: Deutsche Bundesbank.

The breakdown by denomination of the number of banknotes put into circulation is shown in Figure 4.7 for the Bundesbank and in Figure 4.8 for the Eurosystem without Germany. It is striking that the share of €5 notes and €10 notes for Germany (together 40%) is quite large, whereas it is negative for the rest of the euro area.[3] This means that the demand for these denominations is completely met by the Deutsche Bundesbank. Moreover, the share of €50 notes is much higher in the Eurosystem without Germany (61% compared with 28%).[4]

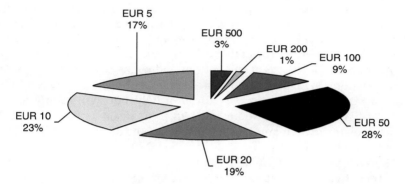

Figure 4.7   Denominational structure of the number of euro banknotes put into circulation by the Deutsche Bundesbank

Note: Percentage shares in the cumulated net issuance as at 15 June 2014.

Source: Deutsche Bundesbank.

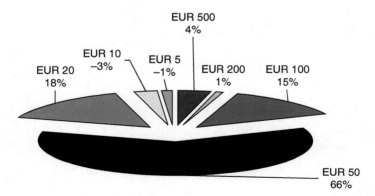

Figure 4.8   Denominational structure of the number of euro banknotes put into circulation by the Eurosystem without Germany

Note: Percentage shares in the cumulated net issuance as at 15 June 2014.

Source: ECB.

As regards cashless payments, Figure 4.9 reveals that according to the annual surveys conducted by the Institute for Payment Systems in Retail Trade the share of payments accounted for by cash on a value basis fell from 79% in 1994 to 54% in 2013, while card payments rose from 6% to just under 43% in the same period. As illustrated, the two shares are increasingly converging. The rate of convergence is slowing down, however, which could mean that, in the long run, the two will have an equal share of sales.

Figure 4.10 compares the number of card payments in selected EU countries between 2002 and 2013. The values have increased in every country. The highest levels of growth, starting from a low base level, are evidently in the Baltic States and in Poland. In 2013, the Scandinavian EU countries were clearly at the top with more than 200 transactions per inhabitant. Greece was at the bottom end of the scale with only seven transactions. With a score of forty-five transactions, Germany is on a par with Malta and Lithuania, just ahead of Italy, but significantly behind France, Austria and the Netherlands. In comparison with the rest of the EU, growth in Germany has been slower. Outside the EU, the number of transactions per capita was 248 in the US (2012), 70 in Japan (2012), 89 in Switzerland (2013) and 10 in China (2013). Therefore, according to these figures and bearing in mind the level of development, the value for Germany is relatively low.

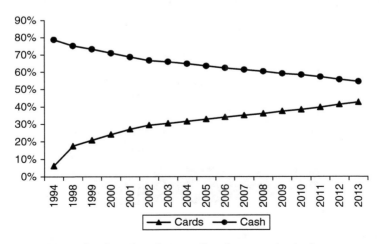

Figure 4.9   Share of cash and cards in retail trade on a value basis
Source: EHI.

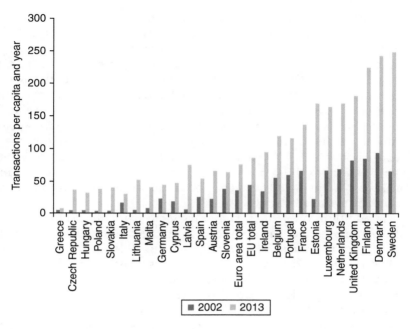

Figure 4.10 Card payments in the EU
Source: ECB.

4.4 Data and determinants of banknote holdings

The main objective of this section is to present the data used in the econometric analysis and to explain the determinants of the demand for "German" euro notes in circulation. The procedure is eclectic to the extent that we use a large set of variables which reflect the various motives for holding banknotes and which we test for statistical significance. This approach is followed by a look at limited data availability – a factor which is mainly related to the characteristic feature of banknotes, their anonymity.

In total, **we identify five different purposes of holding cash (or banknote) balances.** These are (1) transaction motives, (2) store-of-wealth (and, in this connection, opportunity cost) considerations, (3) the availability of alternative means of payment, (4) the size of the shadow economy and (5) demand by non-residents. In the following paragraphs, we describe the coding of these variables in the empirical analysis.[5]

In terms of the **transaction variable**, it would be optimal to include a variable capturing all cash transactions (Snellman and Vesala, 1999; Snellman *et al.*, 2000). Since no data are available on the number of cash transactions in Germany, one solution is to resort to total private consumption, retail sales or GDP as is the case in conventional money demand studies. This is, however, only a rough proxy given the large number of cashless transactions in an economy. Therefore, we additionally construct a variable based on those components of domestic private consumption which are primarily carried out in cash (real "cash consumption", *ccr*). These include (1) accommodation and hospitality services; (2) clothing and footwear; (3) leisure, entertainment and culture; (4) food and beverages; and (5) other purposes, such as body care and personal articles.

In addition to its function as a payment medium, cash also serves as a **store of value**. This is the case in particular for high-value and, to a certain extent, also for medium-value banknotes. Since cash bears no interest, interest rate levels can be used as an opportunity cost measure for holding cash.[6] Appropriate choices include the three-month money market rate or the ten-year government bond yield. Following Friedman (1977), we also include a measure of the whole term structure of interest rates as estimated, for instance, by the Nelson-Siegel-Svensson method; see Deutsche Bundesbank (1997) for details. The term structure of interest rates provides a precise measure of expectations in the money and bond markets. Its pattern can thus provide information about expected changes in interest rates or inflation – both variables which are directly related to the opportunity costs of cash holdings. Moreover, this procedure circumvents multicollinearity problems when taking more than one interest rate into account in empirical applications. Friedman argues that a demand-for-currency equation should include the key characteristics of the whole structure of yields: the "general" level, the "tilt" of the term structure to maturity and the difference between real and nominal yields. A steepening of the tilt of the term spread with an unchanged mean, for example, which implies higher long-term rates and lower short-term rates, will tend to reduce cash balances, and vice versa (Friedman, 1977, p. 408).[7] The formula used for estimating the term structure specifies the interest rate as the sum of a constant and various exponential terms and reads as (Deutsche Bundesbank, 1997, p. 63f)

$$i(T, \beta) = \beta_0 + \beta_1 \left(\frac{1 - \exp(-T/\tau_1)}{(T/\tau_1)} \right)$$

$$+ \beta_2 \left(\frac{1 - \exp(-T/\tau_1)}{(T/\tau_1)} - \exp(-T/\tau_1) \right)$$

$$+ \beta_3 \left(\frac{1 - \exp(-T/\tau_2)}{(T/\tau_2)} - \exp(-T/\tau_2) \right)$$

Here, $i(T, \beta)$ denotes the interest rate for maturity T as a function of the parameter vector β. β_0, β_1, β_2, β_3, τ_1 and τ_2 are the parameters to be estimated. We include β_0 as a measure of the complete interest range into the analysis (*int*). It may be interpreted as a shift parameter to represent the generally prevailing interest rate level. An increase in this parameter means that the entire interest range shifts upwards.

Closely related to opportunity costs of holding banknotes are **alternative payment media**. In addition to the pressure from existing means of payment (e.g., debit and credit cards), cash faces increasing competition from new payment instruments, such as contactless payment facilities in retail trade, new payment procedures for internet purchases and the use of mobile phones.[8] While new payment opportunities may reduce the use of cash, their overall distribution is still negligible. Moreover, they will also compete with existing non-cash payment procedures. We therefore refrain from including a variable for these innovative means of payment.[9] Deutsche Bundesbank (2015) investigates how payment behaviour in Germany has changed in recent years. This study is based on survey data. According to the study, individuals use cash for 53% of total expenditure (excluding regularly recurring payments such as rent). From 2008 to 2011 this share has fallen from 58% to 53%, but it stayed constant since that time. Debit cards are still the most commonly used cashless payment instrument. Their share in terms of turnover is more than 29%. While cash is still the preferred method of payment for small purchases, cashless payments are mainly used to pay for high-value items. In principle, one would expect a negative impact on currency demand from card payments given that bank and credit cards provide a substitute for cash payments. For example, Amromin and Chakravorti (2009) find evidence that the demand for low-denomination notes in OECD countries decreases with increasing debit card usage. However, payment cards are also used to withdraw money from ATMs and could thus increase currency in circulation. As a result, the effect of cashless payment media on currency demand is ambiguous.

In order to capture cashless payments, we use the volume of card payments (*cards*). However, this measure is only available on an annual basis. For our analysis we convert it to a quarterly frequency using the quadratic (match sum) method. There is one further difficulty with payment card data published by the Eurosystem. The Bundesbank, which publishes the data for Germany in its payment statistics, changed its collecting methodology in 2007. After this date the Bundesbank has collected its data from the issuing banks instead of using the overall data of the payment card schemes (PaySys, 2015). Consequently, there is a sharp decline of reported payment cards volumes for Germany (see Figure 4.11). This decline is not related to actual developments in the market. The poor quality of this data set might be responsible for the result found by Bartzsch *et al.* (2015) that card payments do not influence the demand for German notes. Therefore, we use an alternative time series published by PaySys which is based on national and international (Visa, MasterCard) card schemes. Figure 4.11 shows the difference between the two which amounts to €57 billion in 2013, which is 20% of the market (PaySys, 2015, p. 5).

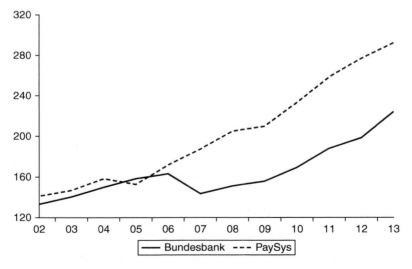

Figure 4.11   Volume of card payments in Germany (€ billion)
Source: Deutsche Bundesbank, PaySys.

Shadow economy transactions are often undertaken in the form of cash due to their anonymity (Schneider, 2002). A rise in the size of the shadow economy should therefore increase the demand for currency. We proxy this influence by taking into account the share of the shadow economy in GDP.[10] However, this variable is not directly observable and can only be estimated with considerable uncertainty. Therefore, we also use a variable that may cause hidden economy transactions. The unemployment rate is expected to have a positive impact on the shadow economy (and thus on currency demand) since a high unemployment rate encourages people to work "underground".

The cumulated net issuance of euro banknotes put into circulation by the Bundesbank ("German" euro banknotes) differs considerably from the domestic holdings of banknotes. Due to large inflows and outflows between countries, net issuance may systematically differ from the demand for cash within the economy. The foreign demand for banknotes issued in Germany can be divided in two groups: first, there is **the demand for German banknotes resulting from residents of other euro-area countries.** This is because German banknotes are perfect substitutes for other euro-area national issuances. In other words, the demand for cash in one euro-area country may be satisfied in part by inflows of cash coming from another member state. The transaction-related part of this foreign demand is taken into account via house prices (*house*) and real private consumption (*diff_pc*) in the euro area without Germany in each case. The former are likely to be a good proxy for the preference for cash payments because real property purchases are often made in cash. The ECB house price indicator for the euro area excluding Germany is chosen as the variable for capturing this effect. **The second category of foreign demand is demand from outside the euro area.** As shown in Section 4.3, a significant portion of the demand for German euro banknotes stems from outside the currency union. In the absence of a variable which directly indicates this demand from many different foreign countries, we proxy it with the euro exchange rate (see also Fischer *et al.*, 2004; Seitz, 1995). An appreciating euro should be associated with a higher attractiveness and thus a higher euro demand from non-euro-area countries. As mentioned in Section 4.3, those euro banknotes in circulation outside the euro area are presumably held, first and foremost, for hoarding purposes, i.e., utilised as a store of value. We use the real effective external value of the euro vis-à-vis the twelve as well as vis-à-vis the twenty most important trading partners (*er12* and *er20*).

It is implausible to assume that the coefficients of the variables determining the demand for banknotes are the same for all denominations.

For example, the transaction motive should be more important for small- and medium-value banknotes. By contrast, store-of-wealth considerations may dominate with respect to high-value banknotes. At the same time, substitution effects may exist between banknotes of similar value. Therefore, we estimate three separate relations, one for small (*small*), one for medium (*medium*) and one for large (*large*) denominations. Our preferred classification is €5–20 for "small" notes, €50–100 for "medium" notes and €200–500 for "large" notes. This classification is chosen because large notes are not distributed by ATMs, which primarily serve to "top up" transaction balances.[11] Moreover, the €50 banknote should be the smallest denomination that is used (amongst other things) for hoarding purposes. We estimate specifications in real terms (*r*). This means that we assume long-run price homogeneity to hold. For the *small* and *medium* categories we choose the price index of domestic cash consumption of households as a price deflator and for the *large* category we use the price index of domestic consumption expenditures of households.[12] The data are quarterly and (if necessary) seasonally adjusted (*sa*). Our sample covers the period from the first quarter of 2002 to the fourth quarter of 2011. In our view, the inclusion of data from 2012 and 2013 would not have a substantial impact on the results. Therefore, we have not updated our dataset. When using interest rates, we work with a semi-log specification. All other variables are in logarithms. The difference operator "d(...)" refers to the first (quarterly) difference. The three cash variables are shown in Figure 4.12.

4.5   Estimating the demand for banknotes

Our empirical approach relies on vector error correction models. We use two kinds of unit root tests: the augmented Dickey-Fuller test (ADF) and the Zivot-Andrews test. In both of these tests the null hypothesis is that the series has a unit root, i.e., is I(1) in levels and I(0) in first differences. We employ the Zivot-Andrews test when we presume structural breaks. For example, owing to the financial crisis there is a break in the intercept at the end of 2008 in *mediumr* and *larger* (see Figure 4.12). Table 4.1 shows the results of the unit root tests for the variables that we employ in our final specifications.

As expected, the value of small-denomination banknotes in circulation (*smallr_sa*), the real effective exchange rates (*er20, er12*), card payments and cash consumption (*ccr_sa*) are unambiguously I(1). The Zivot-Andrews test indicates that the medium and large denominations (*mediumr_sa, larger_sa*) are trend-stationary. However, we assume

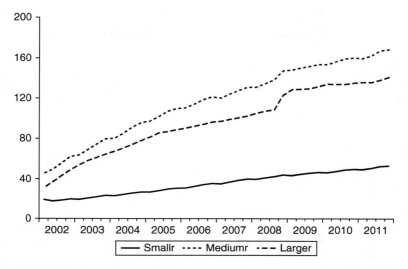

Figure 4.12 Smallr, mediumr and larger value denominations, in real terms (€ billion)
Source: Deutsche Bundesbank.

that they are difference-stationary. Firstly, this is in line with the usual empirical specification. Secondly, the reliability of our unit root tests is impaired owing to the short sample. Moreover, we consider the house price indicator (*house*) and private consumption in the rest of the euro area (*diff_pcr_sa*) to be I(1) instead of I(2) as the tests, which indicate that these series are I(2), are biased owing to the financial crisis.[13]

Owing to the non-stationarity of the time series, the demand for the different denominations is estimated within a vector error correction model (VECM) based on the Johansen (1995, 2000) procedure. This approach seems to be particularly suitable for verifying the long-run equilibrium (cointegration) relationships on which the theoretical considerations are based.[14] The empirical analysis starts with an unrestricted VECM, which takes the following form:

$$dy_t = \mu + \Pi y_{t-1} + \sum_{i=1}^{k-1} \Gamma_i dy_{t-i} + \mathbf{B} x_t + \varepsilon_t, \quad t = 1,...,T, \qquad (4.1)$$

where $\{y_t\}$ represents the vector of the endogenous I(1) variables. $\{\varepsilon_t\}$ denotes the vector of the independently and identically distributed residuals, B is the coefficient matrix of strictly exogenous (non-modelled)

Table 4.1 Unit root tests

	ADF test statistic	Test specification[a]	Zivot-Andrews test statistic	Test specification[b]	Conclusion
smallr_sa	-2.26	C, T, 5			I(1)
d(smallr_sa)	-7.11***	C, 2			
mediumr_sa			-6.50***	C, 2	I(1) instead of trend-stationary
larger_sa			-8.53***	C, 1	I(1) instead of trend-stationary
ccr_sa	-2.66	C, T, 0			I(1)
d(ccr_sa)	-6.97***	C, 0			
int	-1.55	C, T, 6			I(1)
d(int)	-2.90*	C, 6			
er20	-2.87*	C, 0			I(1)
d(er20)	-4.61***	0			
er12	-2.72*	C, 0			I(1)
d(er12)	-4.35***	0			
Cards	0.96	C, 5			I(1)
d(cards)	-3.71***	C, 0			
cards(trend)	-2.02**	0			I(0)
House			-4.17	C and T, 1	I(1) instead of I(2)
d(house)			-3.22	C, 2	
d²(house)			-8.55***	C, 2	
diff_pcr_sa			-3.57	C and T, 1	I(1) instead of I(2)[c]
d(diff_pcr_sa)			-3.72	C, 0	
d²(diff_pcr_sa)			-7.73***	C, 0	

Notes: ***/ **/ *: significant at the 1, 5 and 10% level, respectively. The ADF test refers to the critical values in MacKinnon (1996). The Zivot-Andrews test refers to the critical values in Andrews and Zivot (1992); *cards*(trend), the deviation of *cards* from a Hodrick-Prescott trend. Sample: 2002 Q1 to 2011 Q4; [a] C: intercept; T: linear trend; 0, 1, 2, 3,..., 6: number of lags; lag selection based on (modified) Schwarz information criterion; [b] C: break in intercept; C and T: break in intercept and linear trend; 0, 1, 2: number of lags.

Source: Authors' own calculations.

variables $\{x_t\}$, Γ is the coefficient matrix of the lagged endogenous variables and μ is the vector of constants. The number of cointegration relationships corresponds to the rank of the matrix Π. Granger's representation theorem asserts that if the coefficient matrix Π has reduced rank $r < n$, then there exist (nxr) matrices α (the loading coefficients or speed-of-adjustment parameters) and β (the cointegrating vectors) each with rank r (number of cointegration relations) such that $\Pi = \alpha\beta'$ and $\beta'y_t$ is I(0). The cointegration vectors represent the long-term equilibrium relationships of the system. The loading coefficients denote the importance of these cointegration relationships in the individual equations and the speed of adjustment following deviations from long-term equilibrium.

Given the short sample with only forty (quarterly) observations, the lag order (k) of the system is determined by the minimal lag order that is sufficient to eliminate autocorrelation of the residuals in the VECM. In any case, the chosen cointegration specification assumes an intercept both in the cointegrating equations and in the VAR. In other words, we assume that the level data $\{y_t\}$ have linear trends, but the cointegrating equations have only intercepts.

4.5.1 Structural model for the demand for small-denomination notes

After pretesting, we select small-denomination notes (*smallr_sa*), cash consumption (*ccr_sa*) and the effective exchange rate of the euro vis-à-vis the twenty most important trading partners (*er20*) to enter the cointegration space. These endogenous variables are shown in Figure 4.13. As mentioned above, all of these variables have a stochastic trend, which is a necessary condition for the existence of cointegration relations. Furthermore, we add private consumption in the rest of the euro area (*diff_pcr_sa*) and the value of card payments (*cards*) as exogenous, non-modelled variables to the system of equations. Other potential variables discussed in Section 4.4 are insignificant. In line with Amromin and Chakravorti (2009) we find that the substitution effects with respect to card payments are confined to the demand for small denominations. The interest rate does not influence the demand for these denominations.

The chosen lag order to ensure white noise residuals is two in the VAR in levels, i.e., one in the corresponding VECM. This lag order is between that selected by different lag length information criteria (available upon request).

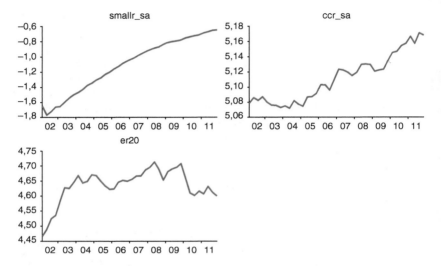

Figure 4.13 Endogenous variables of the VECM for small denomination banknotes
Sources: Deutsche Bundesbank and authors' own calculations.

The number of cointegration vectors is verified by determining the cointegration rank with the trace test and the maximum eigenvalue test (see Table 4.2). These test statistics are subject to a small sample bias, which tends to reject the null of no cointegration too often. Therefore, we corrected them by the factor $(n - mk) / n$, where n is the number of observations, m the number of variables entering the cointegration space and k the number of lags, as suggested by Reimers (1992).[15] However, the critical values of these tests disregard exogenous variables. Therefore, we use the critical values of MacKinnon *et al.* (1999), who suggest a correction according to the number of exogenous I(1) variables. The tests yield unambiguous results. Both the trace test and the maximum eigenvalue test indicate one cointegration relationship.

Table 4.3 displays the estimation results of the VECM. The long-run determinants and the short-run coefficients of the exogenous variables are displayed together with the error correction term. We do not show the equations for the other endogenous variables (real cash consumption and the real effective exchange rate) and the short-run coefficients of the lagged endogenous variables. The signs in the cointegrating equation are as expected: the demand for small banknotes rises when cash consumption and the exchange rate increase. Thus, the small denominations are mainly driven by domestic transactions and foreign demand

Table 4.2 Cointegration rank tests

Number of cointegrating relationships	0		1		2	
	ts	cv	ts	cv	ts	cv
Trace test	45.6*	39.6	16.6	23.6	7.3	11.4
Max-eigenvalue test	28.9*	24.9	9.3	18.4	7.3	14.4

Notes: * Denotes rejection of the hypothesis at the 0.05 level. ts: small sample (Reimers, 1992) as well as exogenous I(1) variables (MacKinnon, *et al.*, 1999) adjusted test statistic; cv: 0.05 level critical value.

Source: Authors' own calculations.

Table 4.3 Estimates and diagnostic test results of the VECM for small denominations

	Cointegrating equation
smallr_sa(-1)	1.00
ccr_sa(-1)	–8.9 (–20.2)
er20(-1)	–3.1 (–15.0)
Constant	61.1
error correction term	–0.17 (–3.9)
constant	0.04 (8.2)
cards	–0.2 (–1.7)
d(*diff_pcr_sa*)	0.004 (4.5)
adj. R^2	0.73
s.e.	0.02
F-statistic	19.0
AIC	–4.9
SC	–4.6
LM (1) [p-value]	19.4 [0.02]
LM (4) [p-value]	4.4 [0.88]
JB [p-value]	1.22 [0.98]

Notes: *t*-statistics in ( ); JB: Jarque-Bera VEC residual joint normality test; LM ( ): VEC residual serial correlation LM Tests of lag ( ); s.e.: standard error of equation; AIC (SC): Akaike (Schwarz) information criterion.

Source: Authors' own calculations.

outside the euro area in the long run. The high coefficient of cash consumption indicates that it was obviously not possible to adequately model certain determinants of cash holdings. The speed-of-adjustment parameter (error correction term) states how much of an existing disequilibrium is reduced within one quarter. Here, about 17% of the imbalance is corrected in one quarter. Cash consumption and the exchange rate are weakly exogenous which means that only cash adjusts to disequlibria. Therefore, the cointegration equation in Table 4.3 can be interpreted as a banknote demand function. While the cointegrating relation catches the demand for small denominations in Germany and outside the euro area, the transaction motive in the rest of the euro area is part of the short-run dynamics. This motive is proxied by the (stationary transformed) seasonally adjusted real private consumption in the rest of the euro area. Its (positive) coefficient is highly significant with a t-value of 4.5. This is in line with the considerable issuance of €5 notes and €10 notes (typical transaction denominations) by the Deutsche Bundesbank. As shown in Figures 4.7 and 4.8, for both of these denominations the cumulated net issuance of the Bundesbank clearly exceeds that of the Eurosystem without Germany. This is evidence that there are significant (net) exports of small-denomination banknotes from Germany to the rest of the euro area. Moreover, the non-cash alternatives in the form of card payments enter the short-run dynamics with a significant negative sign, i.e., a substitution relationship is detected. The stationarity of this variable is generated via calculation of deviation from a trend (estimated by a Hodrick-Prescott filter). This means that only developments

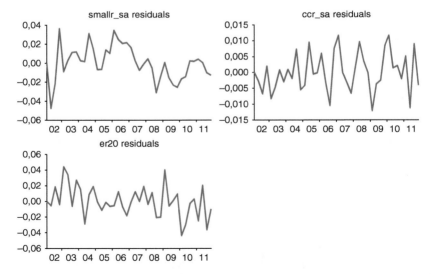

Figure 4.14 Short-run error sequences
Source: Authors' own calculations.

which differ from trend have repercussions on the demand for small banknotes.

The statistical fit of the equation is satisfactory with an adjusted R^2 of 73%. The Jarque Bera test statistic indicates normality of the residuals in the VECM. According to the LM test, the residuals are uncorrelated from lag 2 to 4 with some minor problems at lag 1. Figure 4.14 depicts the short-run error sequences, i.e., the estimated $\{\varepsilon_t\}$ series that equals the residuals in Equation (4.1). By and large, they approximate a white noise process. Figure 4.15 shows the cointegration equation, i.e., the deviations of *smallr_sa* from the long-run relationship. Visual inspection of this long-run error series reveals its theoretical desired property in that the residuals from the long-run equilibrium appear to be stationary. This is also the case in Bartzsch *et al.* (2015), which does not take card payments into account due to data problems. In view of the short sample of only forty quarterly observations, we cannot employ valid tests of parameter stability. However, we have estimated the VECM for alternative samples ending in different quarters of 2011. This procedure suggests no significant changes of the cointegrating equation and the speed-of-adjustment coefficient.

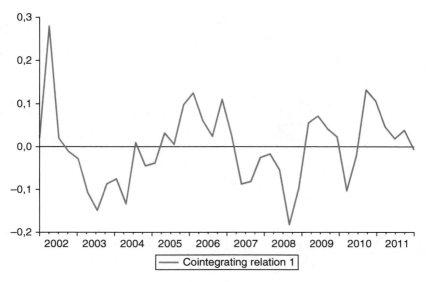

Figure 4.15 Long-run error series

Source: Authors' own calculations.

4.5.2   Structural model for the demand for large-denomination notes

The following variables enter the cointegrating space: large denominations (*larger_sa*), euro-area house prices outside Germany (*house*), the real effective external value of the euro vis-à-vis the twelve most important trading partners (*er12*) and the term structure parameter (*int*). These endogenous variables are shown in Figure 4.16. Furthermore, we add the following strictly exogenous variables to the system of equations: a dummy variable for the onset of the financial crises in the fourth quarter of 2008, *d2008q4*, and a dummy variable for the public debt crisis in the euro area that began in the first quarter of 2010, *d_debt2010q1*. The latter variable should capture the public debt crisis–related increase in the demand for large denominations. Other potential exogenous variables are insignificant.

The lag order (*k*) of the system is again determined by the minimal lag order that is sufficient to eliminate autocorrelation of the residuals in the VECM. The chosen lag order is two for the VAR in levels, i.e., one in the corresponding VECM. This is also the lag order suggested by the Hannan-Quinn information criterion (result available upon request).

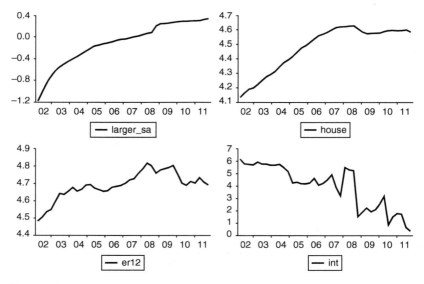

Figure 4.16   Endogenous variables of the VECM for large denomination banknotes
Source: Deutsche Bundesbank and authors' own calculations.

The results of the trace and maximum eigenvalue tests on the number of cointegration vectors are shown in Table 4.4. Again we small-sample adjust the test statistics according to Reimers (1992). Both tests suggest one cointegration relationship. The critical values assume no deterministic exogenous series, and this assumption is violated in our case. However, given the unambiguousness of the test results, we should be on the safe side in restricting the *VECM* to one cointegration relationship.[16]

Table 4.5 displays the estimation results of the VECM. Again we only show the equation for banknotes without the short-run coefficients of the lagged endogenous variables. The signs in the cointegrating equation are as expected: the demand for large-denomination banknotes rises when house prices in the rest of the euro area and the exchange rate increase, and it declines when interest rates increase. It seems that the large-denomination notes in circulation are mainly driven by foreign demand in the long run. The interest rate semi-elasticity is fairly low. If the whole spectrum of yields rises by one percentage point, the value of large denomination banknotes declines by only 0.09 percent. In the case of large denominations, about 50% of the imbalance is corrected in one quarter. While the real effective exchange rate is weakly exogenous, the speed-of-adjustment parameter in the equation for the house price indicator is highly significant and in the equation for interest rates it is marginally significant (*p*-value of 0.051). However, the adjustments of house prices and interest rates to deviations from the cointegrating relation lack a convincing economic explanation, and they hardly affect the equation for big banknote denominations in the system.[17] Therefore, we interpret the latter as a banknote demand equation within a system.

Table 4.4 Cointegration rank tests

Number of cointegrating relationships	0		1		2		3	
	ts	cv	ts	cv	ts	cv	ts	cv
Trace test	68.72*	47.86	23.30	29.80	10.46	15.49	0.35	3.84
Max-eigenvalue test	45.42*	27.58	12.84	21.13	10.10	14.26	0.34	3.84

Notes: * Denotes rejection of the hypothesis at the 0.05 level. ts: small sample adjusted test statistic according to Reimers (1992), cv: 0.05 level critical value.

Source: Authors' own calculations.

Table 4.5   Estimates and diagnostic test results of the VECM for large denominations

	Cointegrating Equation
larger_sa(-1)	1.000
house(-1)	−0.82 (−7.9)
er12(-1)	−2.03 (−10.7)
int(-1)	0.09 (8.8)
constant	12.9
error correction term	−0.48 (−5.0)
constant	−0.02 (−1.4)
d2008q4	0.10 (2.5)
d_debt2010q1	0.03 (1.6)
adj. R^2	0.61
s.e.	0.039
F-statistic	9.79
AIC	−3.47
SC	−3.13
LM (1) [p-value]	21.38 [0.16]
LM (4) [p-value]	20.26 [0.21]
JB [p-value]	28.38 [0.00]

Notes: *t*-statistics in ( ); JB: Jarque-Bera VEC residual joint normality test; LM ( ): VEC residual serial correlation LM Tests of lag ( ); s.e.: standard error of equation; AIC (SC): Akaike (Schwarz) information criterion.

Source: Authors' own calculations.

As mentioned, we also include two crisis variables in the VECM as strictly exogenous variables. The escalation of the global financial crisis after the bankruptcy of Lehman Brothers in September 2008 resulted in a sharp increase in the issuance of German large-denomination notes (Deutsche Bundesbank, 2009, pp. 52f). This is modelled by the dummy variable *d2008q4*. It is an impulse variable that takes the value one in the fourth quarter of 2008 and zero otherwise. In other words, the financial crisis is assumed to have resulted in a *one-time* increase in the *real* demand for large denominations. Economic crises in general go hand in hand with an increase in demand for large banknote denominations. Therefore, we also try to model the repercussions of the European public debt crisis which started at the beginning of 2010. The corresponding dummy variable *d_debt2010q1* is a shift variable. It is equal to one from the first quarter of 2010 to the end of the sample and zero in all other quarters. This corresponds to a continuously increasing *level* of (real) banknote demand. While having the right positive sign, the coefficient of *d_debt2010q1* is only marginally significant. However, the estimated coefficients of the VECM are robust with regard to the inclusion or omission of *d_debt2010q1*. The statistical fit of the system of equations is rather good with an adjusted R^2 of 61%. There is no indication of autocorrelation of residuals up to lag 4. However, the Jarque Bera test statistic indicates non-normality of the residuals in the VECM. As cointegration theory is asymptotically valid under the assumption of independently and identically distributed residuals, this result should not be too serious a problem. Figure 4.17 depicts the short-run error sequences, i.e., the estimated $\{\varepsilon_t\}$ series (residuals) in Equation (4.1). By and large, they approximate a white noise process. Figure 4.18 shows deviations of actual banknote developments from the long-run relationship. This long-run error series also appears to be stationary.

Once again we have estimated the VECM for alternative samples ending in different quarters of 2011 to get an idea of potential instabilities. Visual inspection suggests no significant changes of the cointegrating equation and the speed-of-adjustment coefficient.

4.5.3 A single-equation model for medium denominations

We do not succeed in modelling the medium denominations within a VECM. Therefore, we rely on a single-equation approach for this denomination category.[18] To be more specific, we estimate a banknote demand equation with Dynamic OLS (DOLS). This method generates

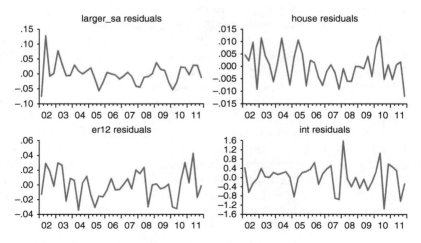

Figure 4.17 Short-run error sequences
Source: Authors' own calculations.

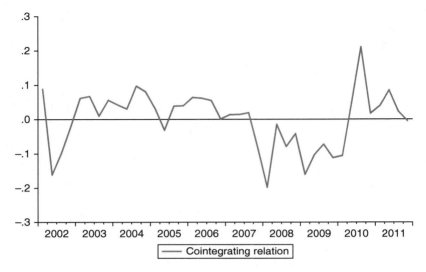

Figure 4.18   Long-run error series
Source: Authors' own calculations.

an asymptotically efficient estimator that eliminates the feedback in the cointegrating system (see, e.g., Saikkonen, 1992; Stock and Watson, 1993). It involves augmenting the cointegrating regression with lags and leads of stationary exogenous variables so that the resulting cointe-grating equation error term is orthogonal to the entire history of the stochastic regressor innovations. In our case, the lags and leads are chosen by the Akaike criterion with a maximum lag (lead) of 4. The computation of the coefficient covariance matrix is done by rescaled OLS. In this procedure, the long-run variance of the DOLS residuals is estimated with the Bartlett kernel and a fixed Newey-West bandwidth of 4.

The cointegration equation is made up of real medium denominations (*mediumr_sa*), cash consumption (*ccr_sa*) and private consumption in the rest of the euro area (*diff_pcr_sa*). Exogenous variables added are the term structure parameter (*int*), the (change in the) unemployment rate (*un*) and a financial crisis dummy variable which is 1 in the fourth quarter of 2007 and zero otherwise (d2007q4). Other variables, especially card payments, do not influence the demand for medium notes. The estimation results are shown in Table 4.6. The transaction variables in Germany and in the rest of the euro area determine the evolution of medium-denomination notes in the long run. In line with theory, the elasticity with respect to domestic transactions is lower than that of small denominations (see Table 4.3). The short-run dynamics are governed by opportunity costs measured by interest rates and the unemployment rate: an increase in the whole spectrum of yields decreases the demand for medium notes whereas rising unemployment leads to higher banknote demand. This is in line with a shadow economic interpretation. The statistical properties of the estimation are satisfactory. Only the Engle-Granger test of cointegration points to some minor stability problems, whereas the Hansen stability test indicates stability of the cointegration relation. Figure 4.19 shows the residuals of the estimated equation.

4.6 Summary and conclusions

In this paper, we analysed the cumulated net issuance of euro banknotes by the Deutsche Bundesbank ("German" euro notes in circulation). The strong growth in German euro notes in contrast to the weak increase in other euro-area countries can be explained as follows. Firstly, the dynamics of euro notes are, to a large extent, driven by demand from outside the euro area, and this demand is predominantly met by Germany. Secondly, Germany is also an important net exporter of euro

Table 4.6 Estimates and diagnostic test statistics of the DOLS equation for medium denominations

Variable	Coefficient
ccr_sa	2.8 (3.2)
diff_pcr_sa	5.0 (11.4)
C	−47.9 (−11.3
int	−0.03 (−2.7)
d(*un*)	1.0 (3.4)
d2007q4	−0.1 (−1.7)
adj. R^2	0.99
s.e.	0.03
long-run variance	0.0009
JB [p-value]	0.49 [0.78]
Hansen [p-value]	0.07 [>0.2]
EG [p-value]	−3.47 [0.13]

Notes: t-statistics in ( ); JB: Jarque-Bera residual normality test; s.e.: standard error of equation; Hansen: Hansen parameter instability cointegration test; EG: Engle-Granger cointegration test with automatic lag selection according to Schwarz criterion.

Source: Authors' own calculations.

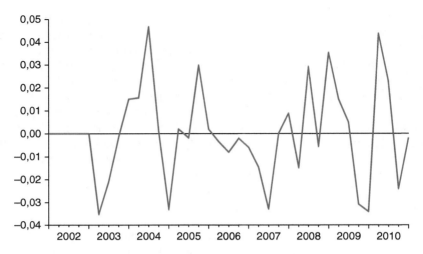

Figure 4.19   The cointegration relation for medium denominations
Source: Authors' own calculations.

notes to other euro-area countries. However, the lion's share of foreign holdings is in non-euro-area countries.

The importance of foreign demand is reflected in the vector error correction models, which we estimate using genuine euro data up to the end of 2011. It seems that the demand for small denominations is mainly driven by domestic transactions and foreign demand from outside the euro area in the long run. Card payments as alternative means of payment influence the short-run dynamics. The transaction motive in the rest of the euro area (without Germany) is also part of the short-term dynamics. This is in line with the fact that the cumulated net issuance of €5 notes and €10 notes by the Deutsche Bundesbank exceeds that of the Eurosystem. The cointegrating equation for the large denominations reveals that the demand for these denominations rises due to foreign demand from other euro-area countries and from outside the euro area, and it declines with increasing interest rates. The effect of the escalation of the global financial crisis after the bankruptcy of the US investment bank Lehman Brothers in September 2008 and the euro area public debt crisis also exert a significant influence. The medium denominations, which could only be modelled within a single-equation approach, are driven by domestic transactions and foreign demand from other euro-area countries in the long run. Interest rates and the unemployment rate are only important in the short run.

Card payments do not exert any influence on the demand for medium and large denominations. Their influence is limited to small denominations. This is in line with the literature. This might also be due to the dominance of other the factors, especially foreign demand, poor data quality and the small sample considered.

With the reservation of the small sample period, the vector error correction models seem to be rather stable. In line with the low or even missing interest rate (semi-)elasticities, we do not expect significant portfolio shifts into cash owing to the currently very low level of interest rates. This is confirmed by financial accounts data on the acquisition of financial assets in Germany (until the end of 2014). By contrast, the declining value of the euro exchange rate since 2014 due to the unconventional monetary policy measures by the Eurosystem should exert a significant negative effect on the demand for banknotes.

Notes

1. Although the results of the indirect approaches are slightly higher than the figures obtained in the direct approaches (see Bartzsch *et al.*, 2011b), the latter are largely confirmed. An update of the estimates in Bartzsch *et al.* (2011b) is presented in Section 4.3.
2. For further information on the stronger growth in the foreign demand for euro banknotes in recent years, see ECB (2014).
3. The percentage share is negative if the cumulated *net* issuance of the respective denomination is negative.
4. These differences also hold for the composition of the value of banknotes put into circulation by denomination, albeit to a lesser degree; see Bartzsch *et al.* (2015).
5. Additional purposes and proxy variables can be found in Seitz and Setzer (2009).
6. In the Baumol-Tobin model (Baumol, 1952; Tobin, 1956), an inclusion of interest rates may also be rationalised by transaction demand, see Alvarez and Lippi (2007) for a modern version of this model.
7. An empirical implementation of Friedman's proposal within a money demand framework can be found in Friedman's and Schwartz (1982) for the US and in Seitz (1998) for Germany.
8. An overview of innovative payment instruments can be found in Deutsche Bundesbank (2012).
9. Generally, a time trend could be used as a crude proxy for the process of financial innovation.
10. We thank Friedrich Schneider for the provision of this time series on shadow economic activities in Germany. Since this time series has a yearly frequency, we converted it to a quarterly frequency using the quadratic (match average) method.

11. For a similar classification scheme to isolate transactional and store-of-wealth roles of currency in a multi-country study, see Amromin and Chakravorti (2009). They select the medium-note category by determining which denomination is prevalently distributed by ATMs. Denominations above this threshold are categorised as "large" while those below this threshold are categorised as "small".
12. Taking the price index of domestic cash consumption of households as a deflator for the large category does not change the results.
13. There is a "bump" in 2008 owing to the financial crisis; see the house price variable in Figure 4.16.
14. Rao (2007) compares our chosen econometric method with others to distinguish between short-term and long-term relationships. He finds that there are often only minor differences in the estimates.
15. An alternative would be to adjust the critical values, see Cheung and Lai (1993). As they use an analogous correction to that of Reimers (1992), the results are in any case qualitatively the same.
16. The sensitivity of the critical values in cointegration tests with respect to the deterministic specification (trend assumption) might be regarded as a benchmark here. See Table 1 on p. 276 in MacKinnon (1991).
17. In our context, it seems quite natural that only banknotes adjust to this deviation and not the other variables.
18. Bartzsch *et al.* (2015) proceed in presenting times series models for these denominations (€50, €100) which are used by the Deutsche Bundesbank within the scope of the annual banknote production planning in the Eurosystem.

Bibliography

Akinci, Ö. (2003), Modeling the demand for currency issued in Turkey, *Central Bank Review*, 3, pp. 1–25.

Alvarez, F.E. & F. Lippi (2007), Financial innovation and the transactions demand for cash, *CEPR Discussion Paper 6472*.

Amromin, G. & S. Chakravorti (2009), Whither loose change? The diminishing demand for small denomination currency, *Journal of Money, Credit and Banking*, 41, pp. 315–335.

Andrews, D.W.K. & E. Zivot (1992), Further evidence on the great crash, the oil price shock and the unit root hypothesis, *Journal of Business and Economic Statistics*, 10, pp. 251–270.

Bartzsch, N., G. Rösl & F. Seitz (2011a), Foreign demand for euro banknotes issued in Germany: Estimation using indirect approaches, *Deutsche Bundesbank Discussion Paper*, Series 1, 21/2011.

Bartzsch, N., G. Rösl & F. Seitz (2011b), Foreign demand for euro banknotes issued in Germany: Estimation using direct approaches, *Deutsche Bundesbank Discussion Paper*, Series 1, 20/2011.

Bartzsch, N., R. Setzer & F. Seitz (2015), The demand for euro banknotes issued in Germany: Structural modelling and forecasting, *MPRA Paper* No. 64949, June.

Baumol, W.J. (1952), The transactions demand for cash: An inventory theoretic approach, *Quarterly Journal of Economics*, 66, pp. 545–556.

Boeschoten, W.C. (1992), Currency use and payments patterns, Kluwer Academic Publishers, Dordrecht.

Briglevics, T. & S. Schuh (2014), U.S. consumer demand for cash in the era of low interest rates and electronic payments, *ECB Working Paper* 1660.

Cheung, Y.-W. & K.S. Lai (1993), Finite-sample sizes of Johansen's likelihood ratio tests for cointegration, *Oxford Bulletin of Economics and Statistics*, 55, pp. 313–328.

Cusbert, T. & T. Rohling (2013), Currency demand during the global financial crisis: Evidence from Australia, Reserve Bank of Australia, *Research Discussion Paper* 2013-01.

Deutsche Bundesbank (1997), Estimating the term structure of interest rates, Monthly Report, October, pp. 61–66.

Deutsche Bundesbank (2009), The development and determinants of euro currency in circulation in Germany, Monthly Report, June, pp. 45–58.

Deutsche Bundesbank (2012), Innovations in payment systems, Monthly Report, September, pp. 47–60.

Deutsche Bundesbank (2015), *Payment behaviour in Germany in 2014 – Third study of the utilisation of cash and cashless payment instruments*, Frankfurt am Main, Germany.

Doyle, B.M. (2000), 'Here, Dollars, Dollars…' – Estimating currency demand and worldwide currency substitution, Board of Governors of the Federal Reserve System, *International Finance Discussion Papers* 657.

European Central Bank (ECB) (2014), *The international role of the euro*, July, Frankfurt am Main, Germany.

Fischer, B., P. Köhler & F. Seitz (2004), The demand for euro area currencies: Past, present and future, *ECB Working Paper* 330.

Friedman, M. (1977), Time perspective in demand for money, *Scandinavian Journal of Economics*, 79, pp. 397–416.

Friedman, M. & A.J. Schwartz (1982), The effect of the term structure of interest rates on the demand for money in the United States, *Journal of Political Economy*, 90(1), pp. 201–212.

Johansen, S. (1995), *Likelihood-based inference in cointegrated vector autoregressive models*, Oxford University Press, Oxford and New York.

Johansen, S. (2000), Modelling of cointegration in the vector autoregressive model, *Economic Modelling*, 17, pp. 359–373.

Khamis, M. & A. Leone (2001), Can currency demand be stable under a financial crisis? The case of Mexico, *IMF Staff Papers* 48, pp. 344–366.

MacKinnon, J.G. (1991), Critical values for cointegration tests, in Engle, R.F. and C.W.J. Granger (eds), *Long-run economic relationships: Readings in cointegration*, Oxford University Press, New York, pp. 267–277.

MacKinnon, J.G. (1996), Numerical distribution functions for unit root and cointegration tests, *Journal of Applied Econometrics*, 11, pp. 601–618.

MacKinnon, J.G., A.A. Haug & L. Michelis (1999), Numerical distribution functions of Likelihood Ratio tests for cointegration, *Journal of Applied Econometrics*, 14, pp. 563–577.

Nachane D.M., A.B. Chakraborty, A.K. Mitra & S. Bordoloi (2013), Modelling currency demand in India: An empirical study, *Reserve Bank of India Discussion Paper* 39.

PaySys (2015), ECB card payment statistics: The missing 792 billions Euro, PaySys Report 02/2015, April, pp. 5–9.

Rao, B.B. (2007), Estimating short and long-run relationships: A guide for the applied economist, *Applied Economics*, 39, pp. 1613–1625.

Reimers, H.-E. (1992), Comparisons of tests for multivariate cointegration, *Statistical Papers*, 33, pp. 335–359.

Saikkonen, P. (1992), Estimation and Testing of Cointegrated Systems by an Autoregressive Approximation, *Econometric Theory*, 8, pp. 1–27.

Schneider, F. (2002), The size and development of the shadow economies of 22 transition and 21 OECD countries, *IZA Discussion Paper* 514.

Seitz, F. (1995), The circulation of Deutsche Mark abroad, *Discussion Paper* 1/95, Economic Research Group of the Deutsche Bundesbank.

Seitz, F. (1998), Geldnachfrage, Zinsen und Zinsstruktur ("Money demand, interest rates and the term structure"), *Konjunkturpolitik – Applied Economics Quarterly*, 44, pp. 256–286.

Seitz, F. & R. Setzer (2009), The demand for German banknotes: Structural modelling and forecasting, *Discussion Paper*, mimeo.

Snellman, J. & J. Vesala (1999), Forecasting the electronification of payments with learning curves: The case of Finland, *Bank of Finland Discussion Paper* 8/99.

Snellman, J., J. Vesala & D. Humphrey (2000), Substitution of noncash payment instruments for cash in Europe, *Bank of Finland Discussion Paper* 1/2000.

Stock, J.H. and M. Watson (1993), A Simple Estimator Of Cointegrating Vectors In Higher Order Integrated Systems, *Econometrica*, 61, pp. 783–820.

Tobin, J. (1956), The interest-elasticity of transactions demand for cash, *Review of Economics and Statistics*, 38, pp. 241–247.

5
Regulating Interchange Fees for Card Payments

Nicole Jonker

5.1 Introduction

The European retail payments market is fragmented. It used to consist of twenty-eight nationally operating payment markets served by national schemes, which were separated from each other by legal and technical barriers. With the unification of the European retail payments market, most of the legal and technical barriers between countries have been removed. National payment instruments for credit transfers and direct debit payments have gradually been replaced by European payment instruments, and since 1 August 2014 there are, in theory, no differences between making payments with these payment instruments within one's own country or to another European country. However, this does not hold yet for card payments, which 'have not reached the same level of harmonisation and integration as credit transfers and direct debits' (European Central Bank (ECB), 2014).[1] According to the ECB, 'substantial efforts are still required in order to achieve a single card payment area', as the card payment market is very complex.

One of the remaining differences between countries concerns the level of interchange fees for card payments. In case of a card transaction, interchange fees are paid by the merchant's bank to the consumer's bank. The level of the interchange fee influences the transaction fees paid by merchants and by consumers. Consequently, it affects consumers' payment habits and merchants' decisions with respect to card acceptance. The European Commission (2007a, 2007c) considers the variation in the level of interchange fees for card payments an important factor for explaining cross-country differences in transaction fees and card usage.

In 1997, European merchants united in EuroCommerce complained about the level of interchange fees for card payments (Börestam and

Schmiedel, 2011). They claimed that banks use interchange fees to extract rents from merchants. Both national competition authorities and the European Commission (Commission) conducted antitrust investigations. In many cases they concluded that the interchange fees were indeed in violation of antitrust legislation.

After years of lawsuits and investigations the Regulation on Interchange Fees for Card-Based Payments (IFR) was published in the *Official Journal of the European Union* (EC, 2015a). Its aim is to lower the cost of payments for merchants and consumers and to remove barriers which hinder the completion of a secure, efficient, competitive and innovative internal EU-wide market for card-based payments, including online and mobile payments. A key element of the IFR is the harmonisation of interchange fee arrangements, which should reduce the cost of card payments for merchants. In addition, it harmonises several business rules related to card payments.

Other public authorities also regulated interchange fees for card payments. The Reserve Bank of Australia (RBA) regulated them in 2003, the Board of Governors of the Federal Reserve Board (FRB) introduced cost-based caps for interchange fees for debit and credit card payments in 2011 as part of the Durbin amendment, and several national interventions had already taken place in and outside Europe, also aiming at limiting the level of interchange fees.

The experiences with interchange fee regulations in these other countries may be useful to assess the possible impact of the IFR on the functioning of the payment card market in the EU. The key question we try to answer is whether the IFR will reduce the fragmentation in the European payment card market and will contribute to an innovative and competitive EU-wide market for card-based payments.

This chapter discusses the way interchange fees have been regulated by several public authorities. In the next section we introduce some conceptual issues regarding interchange fees. Section 5.3 provides a brief overview of the theoretical literature on interchange fees and two-sided markets. Subsequently, Section 5.4 provides an overview of the measures taken by the European Commission and other public authorities to limit the level of interchange fees. Section 5.5 then discusses their similarities and differences. Section 5.6 discusses the impact of the regulatory measures on the payment behaviour of consumers and merchants, with a special focus on the expected impact of IFR on the European payment card market. Section 5.7 concludes.

5.2 Conceptual issues

This section explains the idea underlying the use of interchange fees. It relies heavily on DNB (2007). The example employed for this purpose is that of an interchange fee for a debit card payment. However, the same principle applies for interchange fees used for other non-cash payments such as credit cards, credit transfers or direct debits.

The market for card payments is two-sided in that the payment instrument offered by the card scheme is only sold if two groups of end users (consumers and merchants) are willing to buy it. We explore a four-party payment card system. The four parties consist of the cardholder (the consumer), the consumer's bank (issuing bank), the merchant and the merchant's bank (acquiring bank). Both the consumer's bank and the merchant's bank are affiliated with the debit card scheme. The payment flows involved by a payment card transaction are reflected in Figure 5.1.

To understand interchange fees in the case of debit cards, it is helpful to take a closer look at how non-cash payments are actually processed. We assume that the consumer has a debit card and that the merchant has established a relationship with a bank to accept debit card payments. The consumer makes a purchase for price *p* from a merchant at a point-of-sale. He approves the payment on a payment terminal. The approval triggers an automated authentication and authorisation process by the consumer's bank. Among other things, it checks whether there is sufficient balance on the consumer's bank account. After the checks have

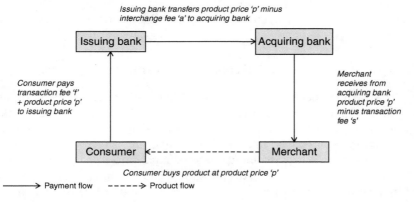

Figure 5.1 Product and payment flows in case of a card payment in a four-party model

been made, the consumer's bank issues an immediate payment guarantee to the merchant. The actual receipt of *p* follows later, after administrative processing by the consumer's bank, the automated clearing house and the merchant's bank.

The consumer's bank can charge the consumer a transaction fee *f* for the debit card payment. The fee can be either positive, zero or even negative in case the bank wants to promote debit card payments. However, most banks do not charge consumers explicit transaction fees for debit card payments, but charge them a periodical fixed fee for a standard payment package, including the current account, online banking services, ATM withdrawals and most non-cash payments.[2] The merchant pays a transaction fee *s* to the merchant's bank. The fee can be either a fixed per transaction fee, a proportion of the purchase's price or a combination of the two. In case of an interchange fee *a* which is usually paid by the merchant's bank to the consumer's bank, the merchant's bank does not only use the merchant's fee to cover its own transaction cost, but also the cost of the interchange fee.

There are several ways to set the level of interchange fees. Banks can negotiate about them bilaterally. However, this is only feasible when there is only a limited number of banks that offer the payment service. If there are many banks involved, the conclusion of bilateral agreements will be a complex and costly process. Instead, the scheme may decide to opt for multilateral agreements where one default fee is agreed upon for all participating banks. Multilateral agreements can be made by banks themselves or by the scheme owner (the company managing the brand and setting the scheme rules). However, multilateral agreements may be in contradiction with competition law. They may be regarded by regulators as a way of price-setting, as they lay a floor under the fees charged by banks to merchants.

5.3   Theory: two-sided markets and interchange fees

The payments card market is a two-sided market, characterised by two different groups of end users ('consumers' and 'merchants') and a platform enabling interaction between these two groups. In the theoretical literature it is assumed that in such a market the two groups of end users are unable to negotiate about the individual prices paid for the jointly bought product (i.e., using the platform to make a card payment for transferring money from the consumer to the merchant). It is the platform which determines the total price and the individual prices paid by the consumer and the merchant.[3] The platform tries to get both consumers and merchants on board by appropriately pricing both sides of the market. Typically, the distribution ratio applied to this end is of influence on the volume of payment card transactions, for in two-sided markets not only the *price level* is decisive, but also the *price structure*, the distribution of the total price $s + f$ between the two end users. Interchange fees paid by one bank to the other bank involved in the card payment can be employed to modulate the price structure for end users.

In a seminal paper, Baxter (1983) provides the rationale for the usage of interchange fees in two-sided markets. The underlying idea is as follows: the consumer and merchant must reach an agreement on the use of a specific payment product which they jointly buy (i.e., cash or debit card payment). So the choice for a specific payment product reflects the preference of two parties instead of just one individual party. Both the consumer and the merchant weigh the marginal costs and benefits of various payment products. If one of them does not agree with payment by debit card, this decision will be induced by the negative outcome of the individual cost-benefit analysis. If the other party prefers to conclude the transaction by means of a debit card, it follows that the outcome of his/her cost-benefit analysis was positive in the sense that the marginal benefits outweighed the marginal cost. Such a situation presents opportunities to modulate the conditions for the other party. A positive cost-benefit outcome of one party in a transaction may be used to influence the outcome of the other party. What happens in such a case is that some part of the balance of the best-off party (with debit card payments, usually the merchant) is transferred, so to speak, to the worst-off party (consumer), so that either party benefits from a card payment. This is only possible, however, if the platform makes the conditions f more attractive for the consumer, for example by lowering its fees or improving its services. Indeed, the merchant has no relationship with the issuing bank and the consumer has no relationship with the acquiring bank. The platform which represents both the issuing and the acquiring bank can make arrangements between issuing and acquiring banks associated with the platform, such as concerning the mutual payment of interchange fees which the receiving bank employs to make the conditions more attractive for its end users.

In Baxter's model, usage of an interchange fee leads to the socially optimal usage of card transactions. However, this result critically depends on the complete pass through of the interchange fee to end users and the inability of merchants to pass through the merchant's transaction fee to consumers by surcharging debit card usage (Gans and King, 2003). Note that in Baxter's model the interchange fee could go to either the issuing bank or the acquiring bank. In later years, it was often assumed that the interchange fee was paid by the acquiring bank to the issuing bank because merchants were considered to be relatively less price-elastic compared to consumers and because the costs associated with a card payment for issuing banks were higher than for acquiring banks.

Baxter's model has been enriched by many economists; see for example Verdier (2011) for an overview. Rochet and Tirole (2002) relaxed the assumption concerning non-competitive behaviour among merchants. Merchants who face competition may accept cards even when acquiring fees exceed merchant benefits. They do so in order to attract customers from competitors or to avoid losing customers to card-accepting competitors. In such a market, the profit maximising interchange fee for issuing banks may be higher than the socially optimal interchange fee, leading to the overprovision of card services. Vickers (2005) described this outcome as the 'must take cards' concern. This expression was adopted later on by Rochet and Tirole (2011) when they introduced an interchange fee based on what they call the 'Tourist Test' or 'avoided-cost test' as an alternative benchmark for the issuer's cost for a card payment that is sometimes used by competition authorities but which is not the socially optimal one according to the theoretical literature.[4] They show that under certain conditions the interchange fee chosen by issuers may indeed exceed the short-term socially optimal level. This affects market efficiency because, if the interchange fee is set too high, the acquiring fee will be set too high as well. Even merchants who face competition and accept card payments may be inclined to turn them down for non-repeat customers ('tourists') as the risk that such a customer will go to another card-accepting merchant is likely to be rather small. By accepting cash instead, these merchants reduce their operating costs. However, from a social welfare perspective in which both marginal cost and marginal benefits of card usage for society are taken into account, it would have been better if these non-repeat customers had used their card. Rochet and Tirole propose an alternative benchmark for regulatory intervention, which is based on the merchant's avoided costs if a cash payment is replaced by a card payment. The acquiring fee passes the Tourist Test if and only if accepting the card for a payment does not increase the merchant's net operating cost compared to cash acceptance. This benchmark is appealing as merchants who accept cards will not have an incentive to steer 'non-repeat customers' towards cash. This benchmark is legitimate if one's aim is to maximise short-term total user surplus.

The Tourist Test benchmark received quite some attention. Bolt *et al.* (2013) and Górka (2014) estimated benchmarks for the Netherlands and Poland respectively using merchants' cost data. Their results differ, indicating that the level of the benchmark depends on local market conditions. Zenger (2011) shows that the benchmark is allocatively equivalent with a benchmark based on perfectly surcharging more costly means of payment by merchants. Leinonen (2011) doubts that interchange fees based on the Tourist Test will promote card usage and enhance cost efficiency because multilateral interchange fees (MIFs) based on the Tourist Test'will result in both banks and merchants being indifferent between cash and cards and thereby delay the realisation of the cost benefits of increased debit card usage'. Bolt *et al.* (2013) go even a step further. According to them, a straightforward application of the Tourist Test methodology may not yield a suitable benchmark for interchange fee regulation in the long run. They show that in markets where debit card usage is increasing and cash usage is declining the benchmark may increase over time, and may even exceed banks' total cost for a debit card transaction. If banks pass on the increasing interchange fee to merchants in the merchant service fee, merchants may be discouraged to stimulate card usage or to invest in a more efficient card payment infrastructure as their benefits will be neutralised by the interchange fee.

Instead of highlighting the 'must take' argument which Rochet and Tirole incorporated in their theoretical model, Korsgaard (2014) questions the two-sidedness of the payment card market. He argues that the payment card market is actually a one-sided market because consumers usually only pay periodical fees which do not depend on card usage. Under the assumption that from the two groups of end users only the merchants face marginal cost, Korsgaard's theoretical model shows that the socially optimal interchange fee only depends on the difference in marginal costs of producing card and cash payments by banks. As the banks' marginal cost of a card payment is often close to that of a cash payment, the optimal interchange fee is likely to be close to zero. It can even become negative if the marginal cost of a card payment is below the marginal cost of a cash payment. In the latter case, acquiring banks receive interchange fees for card payments, which they can use to lower the transaction fees for merchants.

Korsgaard's model predicts that card usage decreases with the level of the interchange fee. If a social planner wants to improve the efficiency of the payment system, the planner will need to stimulate card acceptance by merchants by setting a low or even negative interchange fee, based on the marginal cost of banks. His model provides an explanation of why card usage is relatively high in countries with no or low inter-change fee levels for debit card payments.

5.4   Regulation of interchange fees

5.4.1   International comparison of card usage and interchange fees

There are large discrepancies in payment habits at the point of sale between citizens of different EU countries, as illustrated by Figure 5.2 on card usage. Despite these differences, Bagnall *et al.* (2015) find some universal factors that drive cash and card usage, such as demographic factors, transaction sizes and venue, in their cross-country comparison study.

However, these factors are not sufficient to explain all variation in observed payment patterns. Other factors such as differences in access to banking services for consumers, differences in card acceptance by merchants, differences in the payment instruments offered and the pricing policies used by banks and card schemes may also be important. The way card schemes and banks set interchange fees for card transactions is of influence on the pricing policies employed by issuing and acquiring banks for use of retail payment instruments. It is often argued that high interchange fees would stimulate card usage by consumers. However, in Europe, there is no evidence for this claim. Figure 5.3 shows that countries with the highest card usage are also characterised as the countries with the lowest interchange fee levels, pointing out that high interchange fees are not necessary to stimulate card usage among

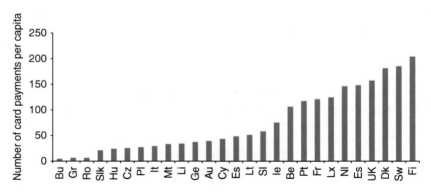

Figure 5.2   Large differences in payment card usage within the EU, 2011

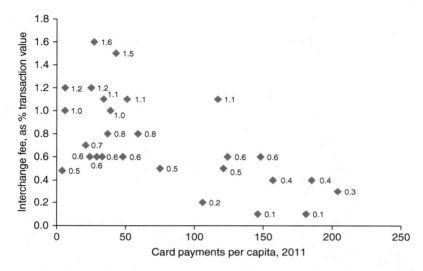

Figure 5.3 High card usage goes together with low interchange fees in the EU, 2011

consumers; see also Korsgaard (2014). Table 5.1 lists the EU countries according to the average level of the interchange fees for debit and credit card transactions in 2011.

According to the Sectoral Inquiry on Retail Banking conducted by the Commission in 2007 (European Commission, 2007a), European banks and international card companies passed on just a quarter of the total sum of interchange fees for debit and credit card payments to consumers in 2004–2005. The inquiry reveals that card issuing alone without interchange fee generated positive profits for issuing banks in 2004 in twenty EU Member States. It also shows that acquiring banks affiliated with debit card networks with low (or even zero) interchange fees charge merchants relatively lower transaction fees, which may stimulate card acceptance among merchants.

A comparison of card usage and the average interchange fee level in the EU with those of countries of comparable wealth level on different continents also does not point at a clearly positive relationship between interchange fee level and card usage. The number of card transactions (debit and credit) per capita in the EU was 74 in 2010. The average interchange fee for card transactions was 0.5% of the transaction value (debit card transactions: 0.4% of the transaction value, credit card payments: 0.8% of the transaction value). In Australia, Canada and the USA, card

Table 5.1   EU countries by average interchange fee for debit and credit card payments, 2011[a]

Rank	Country	Avg. interchange fee (in %)	Rank	Country	Avg. interchange fee (in %)
1	Denmark	0.09	15	Spain	0.63
2	Netherlands	0.15	16	Slovakia	0.70
3	Belgium	0.25	17	Slovenia	0.82
4	Finland	0.26	18	Germany	0.83
5	Sweden	0.42	19	Estonia	0.95
6	Latvia	0.43	20	Austria	1.00
7	United Kingdom	0.44	21	Greece	1.03
8	Bulgaria	0.48	22	Lichtenstein	1.05
9	France	0.52	23	Lithuania	1.05
10	Ireland	0.52	24	Portugal	1.11
11	Luxembourg	0.57	25	Romania	1.16
12	Hungary	0.58	26	Czech Republic	1.17
13	Italy	0.60	27	Cyprus	1.50
14	Malta	0.61	28	Poland	1.61

Note: [a] Iceland, avg. interchange fee rate between 0.45 and 0.78%; Norway, avg. interchange fee between 0.44 and 1.13%

Source: European Commission (2013)

Table 5.2   No relationship between card usage and interchange fees between the three continents

Region	Year	Number of card payments per capita	Interchange fee as share of transaction value (in %)
EU	2011	74	0.5
Australia	2014	210	+/−0.2
Canada	2014	215	+/−0.9
Japan	2012	70	High
USA	2014	249	+/−1.0

Sources: BIS (2014), European Commission (2013) and Hayashi and Maniff (2014).

usage is almost three times higher than in the EU, but interchange fees are not always higher. In Australia interchange fees are on average 2.5 times lower than in the EU. On top of that, card usage in Japan is with on average 70 card payments per capita lower than in the EU, whereas interchange fees are on average higher than in the US, according to anecdotal information.

5.4.2 Regulation of interchange fees

Public authorities worldwide have taken regulatory measures to reform the payment cards market. In this section the measures taken by the EU in 2015 are discussed and compared with regulatory measures taken earlier by the Commission, Spain, Poland, Australia and the US.

5.4.2.1 Regulatory measures in the EU

The Interchange Fee Regulation for Card-based Payment Transactions in the EU, 2015

On 19 May 2015, the final text of the Regulation on Interchange Fees for Card-based Payment Transaction was published in the *Official Journal of the European Union* (EC, 2015a). The IFR applies to card transactions where both the issuing and the acquiring bank are located in the EU. Its aim is to foster an EU-wide market for payments for consumers and businesses. It is intended to provide payment service providers legal clarity and a level playing field for offering EU-wide payment services and to promote efficiency and innovation in the payment cards market at the point of sale and in e-commerce. The Commission identified the use of multilateral interchange fees in four-party card schemes as one of the most important barriers to achieve an integrated EU-wide market. In addition, it identified several business rules imposed by card schemes on merchants that limit the market power of merchants.

The core of the regulation is the setting of caps for interchange fees of debit and credit card transactions made by consumers with cards issued by four-party schemes. The levels of these caps were calculated according to the Tourist Test methodology, using merchants' cost data for cash, debit card and credit card payments for Belgium (Banque Nationale de Belgique, 2005), the Netherlands (Brits and Winder, 2005) and Sweden (Bergman *et al.*, 2007).[5,6] The caps entered into force on 9 December 2015, six months after the entry into force of the IFR on 8 June 2015. There are different caps for debit and credit card transactions:

- Interchange fees for cross-border debit cards payments in the EU are capped at 0.2% of the transaction value.
- For domestic debit card payments Member States may either define an ad valorem cap (default) or impose a fixed per transaction cap (Member State option). The ad valorem cap is 0.2% of the transaction value, and the fixed per transaction cap is five eurocents, provided that the sum of interchange fees does not exceed 0.2% of the annual transaction value of the domestic debit card transactions within each payment card scheme.

- EU Member States may also apply two other options. Firstly, they may impose lower caps for domestic card payments. Secondly, during a transition phase of five years they may allow banks and card schemes to apply a weighted average interchange fee of no more than the equivalent of 0.2% of the annual average transaction value of all domestic debit card transactions.
- Interchange fees for credit card payments are capped at 0.3% of the transaction value. This holds for both domestic and cross-border payments. For domestic credit card transactions Member States may define a lower per transaction interchange fee cap.

The caps do not apply to transactions with commercial payment cards or payment cards issued by three-party schemes or to cash withdrawals. Other articles of the IFR which cover business rules also apply to commercial payment cards and payment cards issued by three-party schemes in order to ensure a level playing field with four-party schemes.[7] The article on licensing specifically aims at improving cross-border competition in the European payment card market. It prohibits any territorial restrictions that card schemes may impose on issuers and acquirers who want to offer payment services to consumers or businesses on a cross-border basis.

Apart from the no-steering rule which has come into force as of 8 June 2015, and the rules on licensing and the provision of information to payees which have come into force on December 2015, all these regulatory measures shall come into force on 9 June 2016, one year after the entry into force of the IFR.

Visa's cross border interchange fees for card payments, 2002

Before the adoption of the IFR, the Commission had several rulings regarding the multilateral interchange fees for cross-border card payments in the EU set by card networks MasterCard and Visa. Below a brief summary is provided on some key rulings, highlighting the Commission's changing view on which factors should be taken into account when determining the appropriate level of multilateral interchange fees that contributes best to end users' welfare. Extensive information on all the rulings can be found on the website of the Commission. Rulings of the Commission have often been used by national competition authorities when assessing the agreements made in their jurisdiction; see for instance the discussion of the interchange fee regulation in Spain in this chapter.

In September 2000, the Commission formally objected to the MIFs set by Visa. The way the MIFs were set by Visa was not transparent.

After discussions between the Commission and Visa and consultation of interested parties, Visa submitted a reform package to the Commission. Subsequently, the Commission announced on 24 July 2002 that it granted Visa's multilateral interchange fees for cross-border debit and credit card payments an exemption under Article 81 (3) of the EU Treaty until 31 December 2007, under the condition that Visa implemented several organisational changes. According to the Commission, the multilateral interchange fees set by Visa restricted competition between banks, but it also concluded that they can enhance technical and economic progress, if the levels of the interchange fee were set in a reasonable and equitable manner. Noteworthy is that in 2002 the Commission's attitude towards interchange fees was still fairly positive, whereas from 2007 onwards that was not the case anymore for the cross-border interchange fees set by MasterCard (European Commission, 2007b) and Visa (European Commission, 2010).

The reform package included a stepwise reduction of the weighted average MIF level for deferred debit and credit card payments to 0.7% of the transaction value in December 2007. An important element of the reforms was that the cap for credit card payments could also become lower than 0.7%, depending on the outcome of a cost study among issuing banks on the cost they made for specific services. These services were the cost for transaction processing, the payment guarantee and the free funding period. For debit card transactions Visa had to introduce immediately a flat-rate cap for the interchange fees of EUR 0.28. The Commission considered debit and credit card services relevant and beneficial for the card-accepting merchants. Furthermore, this package included a first step to make interchange fees more transparent to end users by allowing member banks to inform merchants about the level of the interchange fees and its three main components, at their request. Visa had to inform merchants of this possibility.

Rulings by the Commission on interchange fees are closely followed by national competition authorities in the EU, when assessing interchange fees of card payments of domestic card networks. In the remainder of this chapter a brief discussion follows of the reforms on interchange fees in Spain and Poland. The reforms in Spain are inspired by the Visa case in 2002, whereas the Polish reform follows the Commission's stance in the MasterCard case in 2007–2009 and the recently introduced IFR.

Interchange fee regulation in Spain, 1999

Experiences in Spain with lowering interchange fees are very interesting as they may provide insight into the potential impact of interchange fees on the functioning of the payment cards market in countries that can be characterised by low card acceptance by merchants and high interchange fees.

Cash usage was relatively high in Spain and card usage very low, compared to similar countries with respect to size and geographical location, like France, Germany and Portugal (Carbó Valverde *et al.*, 2003). One of the reasons was the very low card acceptance by Spanish merchants, caused by high multilateral interchange fees for debit and credit card and the accompanying high transaction fees for merchants. The Spanish government intervened in the Spanish cards market in order to stimulate card adoption by merchants and card use by consumers. Bolt and Chakravorti (2011) gives an overview and discussion of the several measures taken since the late 1990s by the Spanish Government related to the setting of interchange fees, and Carbó Valverde *et al.* (2010) provide empirical evidence of the impact of the reforms using bank level data from 1997 to 2007.

Negotiations with the payment networks in Spain and merchant associations to reform interchange fee arrangements for debit and credit card payments and implementation of revised interchange fees were conducted by the Ministry of Industry, Tourism and Trade, together with the Spanish antitrust authority Tribunal de Defensa de la Competencia (TDC). Below a summary is given on the timing and measures taken to reform the interchange fees for card payments.

- May 1999 – An agreement was reached between the three payment networks and merchant associations to reduce the maximum level of multilateral interchange fees for debit and credit card payments from 3.5% to 2.75% of the transaction value from 1 July 2002 onwards. Note that the same cap applied to the interchange fees for debit card and credit card payments. This agreement was approved by the TDC on 26 April 2000.
- December 2005 – Payment networks and merchant associations agreed on a timetable in which the maximum level of interchange fees and transaction fees for merchants for debit card transactions and credit card transactions were further reduced stepwise. An important element of the agreement was that interchange fees for debit card payments were no longer equal to the ones for credit card payments. The maximum level of the interchange fee for credit card payments was reduced from 1.40% of the transaction value in 2006 to 0.35% in 2009. For debit card payments, the maximum level of the interchange fee for debit card payments was reduced from EUR 0.53 in 2006 to EUR 0.35 in 2009.

The agreement was the result of several actions of the TDC and the Spanish government. In December 2003 the TDC announced that the payment networks were no longer authorised to set multilateral interchange fees for domestic card payments. The decision was made after an examination by the TDC of how interchange fees were determined by the payment networks. The TDC had received a request from the Spanish government to conduct this examination, following an approval of the Commission on 24 July 2002 regarding the methodology used by Visa to set multilateral interchange fees. In April 2005 the TDC published a resolution requiring card networks to base the maximum level of the interchange fee on issuers' cost for transaction processing and for the risk of fraud. From 2009 onwards, payment networks were required to audit the operation cost for debit and credit card payments.[8]

Carbó Valverde *et al.* (2010) provide empirical evidence of the influence of the government-induced interchange fee reduction on the performance of the payments card market. They find strong evidence that the lowering of interchange fees led to an increased acceptance of payment cards by merchants and higher card usage by consumers, starting from a situation with very low card acceptance by merchants. Their findings hold for both debit cards and credit cards. Regarding bank revenues for card transactions, they show that the increase in the number of cards transactions offset the lower per transaction revenue. Revenues from the issuing side increased, while revenues from the acquiring side remained fairly stable.

Interchange fee regulation in Poland, 2014

Interchange fees have also been capped in Poland, after years of debate and antitrust cases about the appropriate level of interchange fees for debit and credit card payments. The Office of Competition and Consumer Protection in Poland started antitrust proceedings in 2001, after having received complaints by the Polish Organisation of Trade and Distribution (NBP, 2012). The level of the interchange fee used to be jointly set by banks who were members of Visa Poland or Europay/MasterCard Poland.

On 19 September 2013 the Polish Parliament adopted an amendment to the Act on Payment Services in which interchange fees for domestic debit and credit card transactions were capped at 0.5% of the transaction value. The act came into force on 1 January 2014, and issuers and acquirers of card payments were given a six-month adjustment period in which they could implement the new legislation. However, already on 28 November 2014 a new Amendment was adopted implying a further lowering of the maximum fee level to 0.2% for domestic debit card transactions and 0.3% for domestic credit card transactions (Czarnecki, 2015). The newest caps came into force on 29 January 2015. Prior to the introduction of caps, in 2013, the average interchange fees were quite high in Poland (domestic debit card payments: 1.65% of the transaction value, domestic credit card payments: 1.50% of the transaction value), compared to the average levels in the EU (average MIF debit card: 0.25%, average MIF credit card 0.87%). Between 2011 and 2013 Visa and MasterCard lowered the interchange fees of most types of debit and credit card payments. However, in 2013 they were still at least twice as high as the cap of 0.5% that came into force in 2014 (Górka, 2014).

In addition, the legislation also imposes a maximum fee for new card issuers during their first three years of operation. Furthermore, it aims at increasing transparency by requiring issuing banks to provide information about the methodology used to determine the interchange fee level.

As the regulatory measures have only been recently implemented, no hard conclusions can be drawn yet about their impact on the card usage and the functioning of the cards market. It seems likely that they will lead to significantly lower revenues for issuing banks. Furthermore, there is some indication that in 2014 merchants' card acceptance grew strongly (Górka, 2015).

5.4.2.2 Regulatory measures in Australia and in the United States

Australia, from 2003 onwards

In the early 2000s, the Reserve Bank of Australia (RBA) conducted several consultations together with the Australian Competition and Consumer Commission (ACCC) on the functioning of the Australian payment cards market, following the recommendations made in the 1996–1997 Inquiry on the functioning of the Financial System (Financial System Inquiry, 1997). The RBA and the ACCC concluded in their joint study (RBA and ACCC, 2000) that the card systems exercised market power and had arrangements which weakened the efficiency and competition of the Australian payment system. In particular, they indicated that the following three factors impeded the efficiency of the retail payment system: the collective setting of interchange fees of credit card payments, the 'no surcharge' rules which prevent merchants to pass on costs of credit card usage to customers and the high entry criteria to the credit card market. The RBA intervened in the card payment market through two series of reforms and by enforcing more transparency on the cost and fee structure on card payments. The reforms have been reviewed or are under review of the Payments Systems Board regarding their effectiveness. The first series of reforms was announced by the RBA in August 2002 and was focused on the credit cards market (RBA, 2002). The reforms consisted of the following three (legislative) measures:

- January 2003 – Standard on merchant pricing. This measure removed the restrictions imposed by four-party credit card companies on merchants to surcharge customers for credit card usage.
- July 2003 – Standard on interchange fees. The Standard set an interchange fee benchmark for each card scheme, based on the average cost of the issuers in the scheme.
- February 2004 – Access Regimes. The measure was intended to reduce the entry barrier to the credit card schemes for non-financial institutions. It involved the creation of a special class of institutions which could only be engaged in credit card payments.

The second wave of reforms was published in April 2006 and was focussed on the debit card market. The aim of these reforms was to promote the electronic funds transfer at point of sale (EFTPOS) system because it was more cost efficient than the international debit and credit card systems. However, at that time, for financial institutions it was more attractive to encourage consumers to use the international debit and credit card systems due to the high interchange fees for issuers. The measures include:

- July 2006 – Standards to Visa debit interchange fees, Visa's 'honour all cards' and 'no surcharge' rules. The aim of the Standard on interchange fees was to decrease the differences in interchange fee levels between payments in the EFTPOS system and payments in the international debit and credit card system. The interchange fees of debit card payments with the Visa or the Maestro system fell from around 44 cents to 12 cents paid to the issuing bank, whereas interchange fees for the EFTPOS system were reduced to 4–5 cents, paid to the acquiring bank. In addition, from January 2007 onwards, card companies were no longer allowed to impose the 'honour all cards' rule on merchants who accepted debit card payments to also accept the scheme's credit card payments and vice versa.
- 1 January 2010 – Revised standard interchange fees EFTPOS. Subsequently, a scheme was created, dubbed ePal, to govern the EFTPOS system. The scheme narrowed down the differences between interchange fees even further, by introducing a weighted average

cap of 12 cents for multilateral interchange fees to be paid to the issuing bank, as was already the case for the international debit card systems.

- July 2013 – Standard for bilateral interchange fees. Bilateral interchange fees were regulated, such as the ones used by ePal, making them more consistent with the multilateral interchange fees for EFTPOS debit card payments and debit card payments with international schemes.

In 2007/8, the Board reviewed the reforms from 2002–2003. In September 2008 the Board published its conclusions: the reforms improved the price signals in the card payment system; they had increased price transparency, and entry barriers to access to the card schemes had lowered (RBA, 2008). So, overall, the reforms had enhanced the competitiveness of the card payment market. However, it also recommended that there was room for further improvement on the transparency by publishing average interchange fees and scheme fees.

In 2015 the RBA provided an overview of the developments in the Australian cards market and the impact of the reforms on its functioning (RBA, 2015). Overall, there are indications that the reforms have influenced consumers' payment behaviour, as the growth rates in card usage of different types of payment cards changed after the reforms. Before the reforms credit card usage grew more strongly than debit card usage. After the reforms, the opposite was the case.

Regarding interchange fees for credit card payments made with MasterCard or Visa, the weighted-average interchange fees rates have declined below the average pre-reform levels. A remarkable development in the business model applied by these two schemes is that they increased the number of categories for interchange fees, leading to a widening in the range of interchange fees, from below 0.70 percentage points prior to the reforms to 1.80 percentage points in 2013. For interchange fees for Visa and Maestro debit card payments similar developments have taken place. The reduction of interchange fees for credit card payments was passed on to merchants – and to some extent to consumers. According to an annual survey by the RBA on bank fees, annual fees for credit card payments appeared to have risen around the time of the reforms, but seem to have remained stable afterwards and probably even declined in real terms. The reward programs have become less generous, at least for the 'basic' credit card programs. Merchants enjoyed a significant reduction in merchant transaction fees for credit card payments. They have fallen by 0.63 percentage points, which is more than the average reduction in interchange fees. The fall was not only due to reductions in the merchant fees for Visa and MasterCard credit card payments, but also due to declining merchant fees in three-party credit card schemes, which were not affected by the reform in interchange fees.

Regarding debit card payments, no signs have been found that the interchange fee reforms have led to higher bank fees for consumers. Debit card payments are usually not separately priced to consumers, but consumers pay a periodical fee for a standard payment package, including several payment and account services. However, the merchant transaction fees for EFTPOS transactions have increased by approximately 12 cents since their interchange fees have been regulated (initially interchange fees were paid to the acquiring bank and after the reform they were paid to the issuing bank). Still, merchant fees for EFTPOS transactions are lower than the fees for debit card payments of Visa or MasterCard. Overall, the RBA estimates that since November 2003 the reforms led to a reduction in fees paid by merchants of approximately 13 billion Australian dollars.

The RBA also removed some restricting business rules, such as the ban on the imposition of the 'no steering rule' in 2003. One of the aims was to make consumers more cost conscious and to stimulate them to use cost-efficient means of payment. Over time, the share of merchants which surcharged one or more card schemes increased. At the end of 2007, around 23% of the very large merchants surcharged card payments, as did about 10% of the small merchants (Chakravorti, 2010). The level of the surcharge seems to be positively correlated with the merchant transaction fee, and credit card payments are more likely to be surcharged than debit card payments, which are less costly to merchants. Results from a consumer survey held in 2010 commissioned by the RBA revealed that consumers indeed became more aware of the costs associated with credit card usage and became cost sensitive. When faced with a surcharge for credit card usage, half of the consumers opt for a free alternative such as the debit card or cash. So surcharging contributed to the efficiency of the Australian payment system. However, there are also signals that in a small number of cases, mainly in the taxi and airline industry, merchants apply excessive surcharges. Therefore, in May 2012, the Board decided to allow card schemes to limit surcharges to a reasonable level of card acceptance for merchants (RBA, 2015).

The United States, 2011

In the United States there have been years of conflicts and lawsuits between merchants, banks and card networks about the existence and the appropriate level of interchange fees for card payments. The Durbin Amendment to the Dodd-Frank Wall Street Reform and Consumer Protection Act was an attempt to solve this problem. It has given the Board of Governors of the Federal Reserve System the mandate to regulate interchange fees for debit card payments. The Act was adopted by the Senate on 15 July 2010. The Board published on 16 December 2010 its proposal to regulate interchange fees. It included a cap on interchange fees for debit card payments of 12 dollar cents. The cap was based on issuers' per transaction cost for the authorisation, clearing and settling of the payment, including the per transaction processing fees paid to the network. However, after strong protest from interested parties arguing that lower interchange fees would lead to higher consumer fees, on 29 June 2011 the Board published Regulation II, in which interchange fees were capped at 21 dollar cents plus 0.05 percentage points of the transaction value.[9] The higher value reflects the usage of a broader definition of allowable cost than in the initial proposal. The new cap came into force on 1 October 2011. Financial institutions with assets below USD 10 billion are exempted from the regulation. Prior to the reform in 2009, the average interchange fee was 23 dollar cents for a PIN-based debit card payment and 56 dollar cents for a signature-based debit card payment. The reform led to an overall reduction of the interchange fee levels of about 45% for a typical debit card payment of USD 38 (Federal Reserve Board, 2011).

The Durbin amendment also intends to improve the efficiency of the card payment market and the competition therein. It forbids card networks to prohibit merchants from offering customers a discount for debit card usage instead of the credit card. Furthermore, it allows merchants to set a lower bound below which they do not need to accept credit card payments. These measures intend to promote usage of the more cost-effective debit card at the expense of the credit card. In addition, the regulation prescribes that issuing banks put at least two unaffiliated card networks on a debit card, and that merchants can subsequently choose the card network. This article intends to promote competition in card acquiring and to reduce costs for merchants as they may direct debit card payments to less costly networks.

The regulation in the US was recently implemented, so thus far there is limited evidence about its overall impact on the card payments market. Hayashi (2012) focuses on first effects of the amendment on networks and banks. She concludes that the intervention seems to have the intended impact on the payment card industry. It has raised competition among card networks, resulting in shrinking transaction fees for merchants. However, large card networks and banks seem to seek for ways to compensate for their lower revenues. Card networks have introduced fixed monthly fees charged to merchants, and banks have introduced new consumer fees for debit cards and current accounts. Hayashi (2013) shows that the initial industry responses may have different effects for different groups of merchants and consumers. Although many merchants benefit from lower fees for debit card transactions, some turn out to be paying higher transaction fees. It also seems to be the case that competition among PIN debit networks has increased as some merchants make active use of the control they now have on transaction routing.

Kay *et al.* (2014) examine the impact of the regulation of interchange fees in the US on banks' profitability. They find that banks that fall within the scope of the regulation lost nearly USD 14 billion annually, or 4% of their core non-interest income. They did not completely offset this reduction in revenues through higher debit card volumes or higher credit card volumes. There is also no evidence indicating that banks reduced their operational costs. However, they find that regulated banks increased the consumers' periodical payment package fee. These higher fees compensated about 30% of the lost interchange fee revenues. However, although consumer fees were raised, the number of bank accounts grew, as well as the number of debit card payments.

5.5   Comparing different ways to regulate interchange fees for card payments

This section discusses the similarities and differences between the approaches followed by public authorities to regulate interchange fees for card payments and their impact on the functioning of the payment card market. Table 5.3 provides a summary of the reforms.

5.5.1   Similarities

Interchange fees are often reformed in a stepwise manner (see for example Australia, the EU and Spain). Later reforms are stricter than the earlier ones with respect to the maximum level of the interchange fee for debit and credit card transactions. There are two explanations for this. First, regulators may wish to assess the impact of a reform on the behaviour of consumers and merchants. According to the mainstream theoretical literature and the payment card industry, reducing interchange fees may discourage consumers from using payment cards. However, recent research casts some doubts on these results. If after a reduction in

Table 5.3 Overview of different regulatory approaches

Country	Entry into force	Scope: type of card	Jurisdiction	Approach interchange fees	Other business rules?	Impact banks' revenues	Impact consumers	Impact merchants	Impact card usage
Australia	2003–2004	Credit card	Domestic	Benchmark avg. MIF; avg. issuers' cost: 0.5%;	No-steering; Lowering entry barriers;	Not known	Increase periodical fee and decrease rewards	Decrease merchant fees	Increased usage of debit cards
	2006–2007	Debit card	Domestic	Benchmarks for international debit systems and for the domestic EFTPOS system	Ban imposition HAC-rule and no surcharge rule;	Not known			
	2010	Debit card	Domestic	Benchmark avg. MIF: 12 cents to issuer		Not known			
	2012–2014	Debit card	Domestic	Avg. IF debit EFTPOS flowing to issuer	Amendments framework entry barriers; Limit surcharges to reasonable cost card acceptance	Not known			
United States	2011	Debit card	Domestic	Issuers' cost specific services debit card transactions	Less restrictions WRT network routing Providing discounts debit card usage and usage lower bound for credit card usage.	Reduction core noninterest income 4%	Increase periodical fee	Not known	No evidence of reduced growth debit card usage
European Union	2002	Debit + credit card	Cross-border	Issuers' cost for specific services Cap debit card:28 eurocent Cap credit card: 0.7%	More transparency	Not known	Not known	Not known	Not known

Country	Year	Card type	Geographic scope	Regulated cost / caps	Additional measures	Effect				
	2009	Debit + credit card	Cross-border and in some Member States: domestic	Merchants' cost for specific services; Cap debit card: 0.2% Cap credit card: 0.3%	No HAC; Surcharging allowed; More transparency	Not known	Not known	Not known	Not known	Not knwon
	2015	Debit + credit card	Cross-border and domestic	Merchants' cost for cash and card payments; Cap debit card: 0.2% or 5 eurocent; Cap credit card: 0.3%	No HAC; Co-badging; No fee blending; More transparency; Licensing; No steering; Separation card scheme and processing	Not known	Not known	Not known	Not known	Not known
Spain	2002	Debit + credit card	Domestic	Debit + credit card: 2.75%;		Revenues issuing banks increased and acquiring banks stabilised	Higher annual fees credit card	Lower merchant fees and higher card adoption both debit and credit cards	Debit and credit card usage increased	
	2006	Debit + credit card	Domestic	Issuers' cost specific services: Debit card: 1.40%; Credit card: 53 eurocent;						
	2009	Debit + credit card	Domestic	Cap interchange fee: Debit card: 0.35%; Credit card: 35 eurocent		Not known	Not known	Not known	Not known	
Poland	2014	Debit + credit card	Domestic	Debit + credit card: 0.5%;	Cap new issuers; More transparency	Revenues issuing banks decreased	Not known	Lower MSC and higher card acceptance	Not known	
	2015			Debit card: 0.2%; Credit card: 0.3%		Not known	Not known			

interchange fees, card acceptance and card usage increases, there may be room for regulators to introduce further reductions. Second, it may be the case that banks and card networks attempt to circumvent regulatory measures, and stricter rules are necessary to correct for that.

Another similarity is that the maximum level of an interchange fee is often estimated using a benchmark, which is calculated using an objective method. For credit card payments the maximum interchange fee is expressed as a share of the transaction value, whereas for debit card payments the cap is often a fixed per transaction fee or a combination of a fixed fee and an ad valorem component.

A final similarity is that most regulators do not only set limits to interchange fees, but they also attempt to improve the competitiveness of the payment card market by removing restricting business rules imposed by card companies on merchants.

5.5.2 Differences

There are also differences in the way interchange fees have been regulated in different jurisdictions. First of all, the way the maximum level of interchange fees is determined differs. In the early regulations, no benchmark was used to set the maximum level of the interchange fee. In later regulations issuers' costs have often been used to set a benchmark. Regulators specified which services issuers were allowed to include in their cost calculations. The advantage of this approach is that it is an objective method, which provides other stakeholders clarity about which factors influence the level of the interchange fee and to what extent. Disadvantages of this method are that according to the economic literature, it does not yield the socially optimal interchange fee because it only takes into account part of the cost of one side of the market, ignoring the marginal costs made by acquiring banks and marginal benefits for consumers and merchants. Another disadvantage of a cost-based methodology may be that it does not stimulate issuing banks to enhance the efficiency of authorising and processing card payment transactions. However, this may be solved by setting the interchange fee at the cost level of efficient issuers.

The Commission switched from using issuers' cost to merchants' cost for setting a benchmark, based on the Tourist Test. The advantage of this method over using issuers' cost as a benchmark is that it will make card payments as costly to merchants as cash payments. Contrary to benchmarks based on issuers' cost, benchmarks based on the Tourist Test yield interchange fees that maximise welfare of consumers and merchants in the short run. However, this method also has caveats, as pointed out by

Bolt *et al.* (2013). It discourages merchants to invest in the efficiency of card payments, and a straightforward application of the Tourist Test methodology may yield rising interchange fees in certain markets.[10]

Another difference concerns the scope of the regulations. In Australia, the first series of reforms in 2002–2004 focused on credit card payments. It was only in the second series that debit card payments also fell within the scope of the regulations. In the US, the Durbin Amendment focuses on debit card payments, whereas elsewhere credit card payments are also regulated.

A final distinction concerns the jurisdiction of the regulation. Most regulations focus on domestic payments as they are results of decisions of national public authorities. However, until 2015 the regulations of the Commission were aimed at cross-border card payments. It is only in 2015 that the Commission's Regulation covers all card transactions in the EU. Specific elements of the Regulation are that it promotes competition between payment service providers at a European level.

5.6 Assessing the impact of regulations on the payment card market

5.6.1 Impact of earlier regulation

Most reforms have recently come into force, so little data is available yet to assess their impact on the functioning of the payment card market. However, Australia and Spain had already reformed the payment card market in the early 2000s. The impact of the reforms have been assessed by the RBA (2008, 2015) and by Carbó Valverde *et al.* (2010). Furthermore, Hayashi (2012, 2013) and Kay *et al.* (2014) examined the first effects of the impact of the Durbin Amendment on the US banking industry.

Overall, the findings indicate that regulating interchange fees for debit and credit card payments contributes to the efficiency of the retail payment system. Interchange fees for debit and credit card payments have been reduced, and acquiring banks have passed the reductions on to merchants by lowering merchant transaction fees for card payments. The growth in card usage did not slow down due to the reforms. In Spain card acceptance by merchants increased and so did card usage by consumers. Furthermore, in Australia, debit card usage increased at a higher rate than before the reforms, whereas the opposite was true for credit card payments. In addition, the RBA did not find any evidence that the innovative power of the Australian payment card industry suffered from the reforms.

Despite warnings from the payment card industry, no evidence was found in Australia and Spain that consumers had to pay higher annual payment package fees due to the regulation of interchange fees for debit card payments. However, there is some evidence that issuing banks in the US raised deposit fees for consumers in order to compensate for declining revenues. In Spain, bank revenues out of card payments did not deteriorate due to the reforms, as the lower per transaction revenue was offset by the increase in the number of card transactions.

Finally, some evidence was found that card holder fees for credit cards went up somewhat or that issuers offered less generous reward programs for credit card payments. However, these increases in annual consumer fees did not seem to lead to a reduction in the number of current accounts or credit cards issued.

5.6.2   Expected impact of the IFR on the card payment market in the EU

Experiences with reforms in Australia and Spain indicate that it is to be expected that the IFR will lead to higher card acceptance among merchants and higher domestic card usage by consumers in countries where the interchange fees used to be higher than the recently introduced caps. In that respect, it seems likely that the differences in card usage between EU countries will narrow. Especially, debit card usage may grow more strongly, as issuers may retrench their reward programs for credit card payments. This will enhance the efficiency of the retail payment system, as debit card payments are among the most cost efficient means of payment at the point of sale in the EU (Schmiedel *et al.*, 2013). How quickly these changes will take place is hard to predict, as payment habits change only gradually.

It is also hard to predict how effective the IFR will be in influencing consumers' payment behaviour when they are abroad. Consumers will only use their payment cards outside their home country, if they are quite certain about card acceptance. It is therefore key that the payment card industry together with merchants seeks for ways to improve (cross-border) card acceptance, for instance, through promoting the acceptance of major card schemes, so that consumers can use their debit cards anywhere in the EU.

A related issue is cross-border competition in the EU-wide payment card market. According to the IFR's article on licensing, it is up to individual banks to decide whether they want to offer services to consumers and businesses outside their country; scheme rules should not prohibit them anymore from doing so. So, banks are in the lead with respect to supplying their card services to merchants and consumers across the border. However, it seems to be the case that MasterCard's scheme rules still limit acquiring banks' possibilities to do so. The European Commission (2015b) sent a Statement of Objections to MasterCard on 9 July 2015, outlining its preliminary view that MasterCard's scheme rules still restrict cross-border competition between acquiring banks. The main problem seems to be that scheme rules prevent merchants located in a country with high interchange fees to benefit from lower interchange fees and transaction fees offered by acquiring banks located in other Member States. Maybe, issues like this are just temporary. If not, additional reforms may be necessary to ensure that scheme rules do not hamper cross-border acquiring. However, it may also be a signal that banks themselves are not eager to engage in cross-border acquiring and compete with banks located in other Member States. If that is the case, further reforms may not be effective either.

Increased competition and innovation may also come from newcomers in the market, including non-banks. The IFR may indeed lower the entry barriers for new payment service providers. Entry cost may go down as the harmonisation of business rules enlarges the market from twenty-eight individual Member States to the entire EU, leading to economies of scale and higher potential revenues. The overall reduction of interchange fees may lower entry barriers even further as it ensures a more even level playing field between existing players and newcomers. With lower interchange fees, these newcomers will need to offer less generous fees to issuing banks than before the reform. The barrier to enter the market may become even lower with the adoption of Payment Services Directive 2 (PSD2). Under PSD2, payment instrument issuers have the right to get confirmation on the availability of funds on the current account from account servicing payment service providers. Moreover, payment initiation service providers may initiate transactions from an account held at another payment service provider, under strict security conditions.[11] This may make newcomers less dependent on cooperation with existing players to offer their services. On the other hand, the overall reduction of interchange fees may make the European market less attractive for new payment service providers due to lower profit margins at the acquiring side. There is some anecdotal information, that because of that reason, certain non-banks that offer payment services in the US are reluctant to offer their services in the EU as well.

5.7   Concluding remarks

The European Commission published on 19 May 2015 the Regulation on Interchange Fees for Card-based Payment Transactions in the *Official Journal of the European Union* (EC, 2015a). The aim of the regulation is to lower the cost of payments for merchants and consumers and to remove barriers which hinder the completion of a secure, efficient, competitive and innovative internal EU-wide market for card-based payments, including online and mobile payments.

Based on experiences with regulations in other countries, it is to be expected that the IFR will indeed lead to a less fragmented European payment card market. For most Member States the caps imply a significant reduction of the level of the interchange fees for domestic card payments, leading to higher card acceptance by merchants and card usage by consumers. Whether consumers when in other Member States will use their payment cards as often as in their own country depends on the acceptance of different card schemes throughout the EU. At the moment, there are still discrepancies between card acceptance at home and abroad. It is therefore key that the payment card industry together with merchants continues to seek for ways to improve (cross-border) card acceptance.

With respect to improving cross-border competition in the EU-wide payment card market, further legislation to promote cross-border acquiring may be necessary. Currently, one scheme employs scheme rules that prohibit banks located in countries with low interchange fees to use this low fee for the provision of acquiring services to merchants located in Member States with higher interchange fees. With respect to making the payment market more competitive at the EU level, lowering entry barriers for newcomers may also be a good way to boost competition. The IFR already provides some of the necessary conditions. Together with the upcoming adoption of Payment Services Directive 2 (PSD2), which allows third-party providers to offer their services directly to consumers and have access to their payment accounts under strict security conditions, newcomers may be less dependent on the willingness to cooperate of incumbents to provide their payment services to European consumers and businesses.

Notes

1. The Single Euro Payments Area (SEPA) is an initiative of the European banking industry. Its aim is that all electronic payments across the euro area, either by credit card, debit card, credit transfer or direct debit, are as easy as domestic payments within one country are now. The credit transfers and direct debits

are regulated under the SEPA Regulation (EC 260/2012). Card payments do not fall within the scope of this regulation. The SEPA Regulation marked 1 February 2014 as the point at which all credit transfers and direct debits in euro would be made under the same technical standards and conditions for end users. However, an Amendment was made to introduce an additional transition period of six months – until 1 August 2014.

2. For credit card payments, issuing banks often reward cardholders for every credit card transaction made by means of a loyalty program or by giving discounts ('cash back').

3. In practice, some merchants may be able to negotiate about the level of the transaction fee with the acquiring banks or card scheme. This holds especially for large merchants with market power.

4. See for example, the European Commission (2002, 2007) for cross-border debit and credit payments in the European Union, the Reserve Bank of Australia (2002), the Board of Governors of the Federal Reserve Bank in the United States (2011) as part of the Durbin amendment.

5. The caps of 0.2% of the transaction value for debit cards and 0.3% of the transaction value for credit cards were estimated by MasterCard, using information on merchants' cost for cash and card transactions published by the Dutch, Belgian and Swedish central banks (see Brits and Winder, 2005; Banque Nationale de Belgique, 2005; Bergman *et al.*, 2007) and following the Tourist Test methodology. MasterCard (2009) published these caps in April 2009 when it announced a number of undertakings as a reaction on the Commission's ruling in December 2007 that MasterCard's cross-border interchange fees for debit card and credit card payments in the EU were in breach of EC Treaty rules on restrictive agreements. The package of undertakings was the result of extensive talks between MasterCard and the Commission on MasterCard's compliance with the antitrust legislation.

6. The European Commission published on 18 March 2015 a study on merchants' costs of processing cash and card payments. This study was carried out together with Deloitte Consulting. Cost data from large merchants in ten EU countries were collected in order to deliver updated benchmarks for the Tourist Test. For large merchants the analysis found that Tourist Test benchmarks stay well below the benchmarks applied in the IFR. The Commission expects that these results will play a role in on-going and competition proceedings. Results are available via this site: http://ec.europa.eu/competition/sectors/financial_services/enforcement_En.html.

7. Next to interchange fees and licensing the IFR covers the following business rules. Co-badging: Card schemes may no longer impose scheme rules which hinder or prevent issuers from co-badging two or more different payment brands or applications on a payment card or equivalent payment device. Unblending: Acquirers shall offer and charge merchants transaction fees individually specified for different categories and different brands of payment cards with different interchange fee levels unless the merchants request the acquirer to charge him blended fees. In addition, acquirers shall provide merchants reports with individually specified information on the amount of the transaction fees paid, interchange fees and scheme fees applicable with respect to each category and brand of payment cards, unless the merchant informs the acquirer that he has different preferences. Honour all cards rule: Card schemes

are not allowed to oblige merchants to accept all card payments within the framework of the payment card scheme if the merchant decides to accept one type of payment card. No-steering rule: Card schemes and acquiring banks are not allowed to impose restrictions on merchants who want to promote certain means of payment, or to inform consumers about the level of interchange fees or the level of the merchant's transaction fees. Separation of card scheme and processing activities: Payment card schemes and processing entities shall be independent in terms of accounting, organisation and decision-making processes; shall not present prices for payment card scheme and processing activities in a bundled manner; and shall not cross-subsidise such activities.

8. It is unclear whether information on issuers' cost for card transactions was used after 2009 to set the level of multilateral interchange fees for debit and credit card payments.
9. If the issuer invests in fraud prevention, issuers may receive a 1 cent higher interchange fee.
10. According to Bolt *et al.* (2013) adjustments should be made to the theoretical model to account for specific market characteristics and to only consider cost categories reflecting merchant's marginal costs. Layne-Farrar (2013) goes even a step further, and also includes merchants' marginal benefits of card payments as well when applying the Tourist Test to US merchant data.
11. Newcomers that want to provide payment initiation services would be required to become licensed under the PSD2 before they offer their services within the EU.

Bibliography

Bagnall, J., D. Bounie, K. Huynh, A. Kosse, T. Schmidt, S. Schuh and H. Stix (2015), Consumer cash usage: A cross-country comparison with payment diary survey data, forthcoming in the *International Journal of Central Banking*.

Banque Nationale de Belgique (2005), Costs, advantages and disadvantages of different payment methods, December.

Baxter, W.P. (1983), Bank interchange of transactional paper: Legal perspectives, *Journal of Law and Economics*, 26(3), 541–588.

Bergman, M., G. Guibourg and B. Segendorf (2007), The costs of paying – private and social costs of cash and card, *Sveriges Rikskank Working paper Series* 212.

Bank for International Settlements (BIS) (2014), Statistics on payment, clearing and settlement systems in the CPMI countries – Figures for 2013, available at https://www.bis.org/cpmi/publ/d124.htm.

Bolt, W. and S. Chakravorti (2011), Pricing in retail payment systems: A public policy perspective on pricing of payment cards, *DNB Working Paper* 331.

Bolt, W., N. Jonker and M.A. Plooij (2013), Tourist test or tourist trap? Unintended consequences of debit card interchange fee regulation. *DNB Working Paper* 405.

Börestam, A. and H. Schmiedel (2011), Interchange fees in card payments, *ECB Occasional Paper Series*, No. 131.

Brits, H. and C. Winder (2005), Payments are no free lunch, *DNB Occasional Study* 3(2).

Carbó Valverde, S., D. Humphrey and R. López del Paso (2003), The falling share of cash payments in Spain, *Moneda y Crédito*, 2017, 167–190.

Carbó Valverde, S., S. Chakravorti and F. Rodrigues Fernandez (2010), Regulating two-sided markets: An empirical investigation, Revised version of *Working Paper* 2009-11, Federal Reserve Bank of Chicago.

Chakravorti, S. (2010), Externalities in payment card networks: Theory and evidence, *Review of Network Economics*, 9(2), 1–28.

Czarnecki, J. (2015), New statutory reduction of interchange fees: Important regulations also for acquirers, *New Technologies Newsletter*, March-April.

De Nederlandsche Bank (DNB) (2007), Interchange fees and the unification of the European payment market, *DNB Quarterly Bulletin*, December 2007.

European Commission (2007a), Report on the Retail Banking Sector Inquiry, *Commission Staff working document.* available at http://ec.europa.eu/competition/sectors/financial_services/inquiries/sec_2007_106.pdf.

European Commission (2007b), Antitrust: Commission prohibits MasterCard's intra-EEA multilateral interchange fees, Press release, available via http://europa.eu/rapid/press-release_IP-07-1959_en.htm?locale=fr.

European Commission (2007c), Antitrust: Commission prohibits MasterCard's intra-EEA multilateral interchange fees- frequently asked questions, memo, available via http://ec.europa.eu/competition/antitrust/cases/dec_docs/34579/34579_2265_6.pdf.

European Commission (2010), Antitrust: Commission makes Visa Europe's commitments to cut interbank fees for debit cards legally binding, Press release, available via http://europa.eu/rapid/press-release_IP-10-1684_en.htm?locale=en.

European Commission ((2012), Regulation (EU) no 260/2012 of the European Parliament and of the Council of 14 March 2012 on establishing technical and business requirements for credit transfers and direct debits in euro and amending Regulation (EC) No 924/2009, *Official Journal of the European Union*, 14 March 2012.

European Commission (2013), Summary of the impact assessment, *Commission Staff Working Document*, SWD(2013) 289.

European Commission (2015a), Regulation (EU) 2015/751 of the European Parliament and of the Council of 29 April 2015 on interchange fees for card-based payment transactions, *Official Journal of the European Union*, 19 May 2015.

European Commission (2015b), Antitrust: Commission sends Statement of Objections to MasterCard on cross-border rules and inter-regional interchange fees, Press release, available via http://europa.eu/rapid/press-release_IP-15-5323_en.htm.

European Commission (2015c), Antitrust: Commission prohibits MasterCard's intra EEA multilateral interchange fees – Frequently asked questions, available via http://europa.eu/rapid/press-release_IP-15-5323_en.htm

European Central Bank (ECB) (2014), Card payments in Europe . A renewed focus on SEPA for Cards, available via http://www.ecb.europa.eu/pub/pdf/other/cardpaymineu_renfoconsepaforcards201404en.pdf

Federal Reserve Board, (2011), 2009 interchange fee revenue, covered issuer costs and covered issuer and merchant fraud losses related to debit card transactions, *Federal Reserve Board paper*, 5 March.

Financial System Inquiry (1997), Financial system inquiry final report (S. Wallis chair), March, available at http://fsi.treasury.gov.au/content/FinalReport.asp.

Gans, J.S. and S.P. King (2003), The neutrality of the interchange fees in payment systems, *The B.E. Journal of Economic Analysis and Politics*, 3(1), 1–18.

Górka, J. (2014), Merchant indifference test application – A case for revising interchange fee level in Poland, in: *The Usage, Costs and Benefits of Cash – Revisited, Conference Volume International Cash Conference 2014*, Deutsche Bundesbank.

Górka, J. (2015), Transformując rynek płatności – Polska w awangardzie europejskiej (Transforming payments market – Poland in the European vanguard) given at the Third International Congress Cashless Payments in Warsaw, 15 March 2015.

Hayashi, F. (2012), The new debit card regulations: Initial effects on networks and banks, *Economic Review*, Fourth Quarter 2012, 79–115, Federal Reserve Bank of Kansas City.

Hayashi, F. (2013), The new debit card regulations: Effects on merchants, consumers, and payments system efficiency, *Economic Review*, First Quarter 2013, 89–117, Federal Reserve Bank of Kansas City.

Hayashi, F. and J. Maniff (2014), Public authority involvement in payment card markets: Various countries – August 2014 update, Federal Reserve Bank of Kansas City.

Kay, B., M.D. Manuszak and C.M. Vojtech (2014), Bank profitability and debit card interchange regulation: Bank responses to the Durbin Amendment, Working paper.

Korsgaard, S. (2014), Paying for payments: Free payments and optimal interchange fees, *ECB Working Paper Series*, No. 1682, June 2014.

Layne-Farrar, A. (2013), Assessing the Durbin's Amendment's debit card interchange fee cap: An application of the 'tourist test' to US retailer data, *Review of Network Economics*, 12(2), 157–182.

Leinonen, H. (2011), Debit card interchange fees generally lead to cash-promoting cross-subsidisation, Bank of Finland *Discussion Research Papers*, No. 3(2011).

MasterCard (2009), MasterCard Europe reaches interim arrangement with European Commission on cross-border interchange fees, press release, accessible via https://www.mastercard.com/us/company/en/newsroom/european_commission_announcement.html.

National Bank of Poland (NBP) (2012), Analysis of the functioning of the interchange fee in cashless transactions on the Polish market, January 2012.

Reserve Bank of Australia (RBA) and Australian Competition and Consumer Commission (ACCC), (2000), Debit and creditcard schemes in Australia. A study of interchange fees and access, October 2000. Accessible via http://www.rba.gov.au/payments-system/resources/publications/payments-au/interchg-fees-study.pdf

Reserve Bank of Australia (RBA) (2002), IV Final Reforms and Regulation Impact Statement, August 2002, accessible via http://www.rba.gov.au/payments-system/reforms/cc-schemes/final-reforms/complete-stmt.pdf

Reserve Bank of Australia (RBA) (2008), Reform of Australia's payments system: Conclusions of the 2007/08 review, September 2015.

Reserve Bank of Australia (RBA) (2015), Review of card payments regulation, Issues paper, March 2015.

Rochet, J.-C. and J. Tirole (2002), Cooperation among competitors: some economics of payment card associations, *RAND journal of economics*, 33(4), 549–570.

Rochet, J.-C. and J. Tirole (2011), Must-take cards: Merchant discounts and avoided costs, *Journal of the European Economic Association*, 9(3), 462–495.

Schmiedel, H., G. Kostova and W. Ruttenberg (2013), The social and private costs of retail payment instruments: A European perspective, *Journal of Financial Market Infrastructure*, September 2013.

Verdier, M. (2011), Interchange fees in payment card systems, A survey of the literature, *Journal of Economic Surveys*, 35(10), 273–297.

Vickers, J. (2005), Public policy and the invisible price: Competition law, regulation and the interchange fee, *Proceedings of a Conference on Interchange Fees in Credit and Debit Card Industries*, Federal Reserve Bank of Kansas City, Santa Fe, NM, 231–247.

Zenger, H. (2011), Perfect surcharging and the tourist test interchange fee, *Journal of Banking and Finance*, 35(10), 2544–2546.

6
IBANs or IPANs? Creating a Level Playing Field between Bank and Non-Bank Payment Service Providers

Jakub Górka

6.1 Introducing the problem

The intention of the European legislative bodies, which is enshrined in different legal acts, such as the Payment Services Directive and the second Electronic Money Directive, is to boost competition and innovation on the payments market by creating new categories of payment service providers, i.e., payment institutions (PIs) and electronic money institutions (EMIs). Traditionally, banks operating current accounts of consumers and companies used to be major payment service providers (PSPs), which as a group faced only marginal competition in the payments business at the front end. However with the advent of new laws on payments in Europe and the rising willingness of customers to use innovative services of non-banks, questions need to be posed about the level playing field between old and new players.

Despite the fact that banks are not keen on PIs and EMIs, provided that new PSPs do not provide ancillary payment services but threaten banks' core payments business, it seems right to say that new entrants should have equal status with incumbents in the area of payments.

Currently PIs and EMIs are not fully independent of banks which, being well-entrenched players, are the more powerful group of payment service providers, with legally guaranteed privileges that are not available to new payment service providers. It is necessary to verify how to remedy this problem and make new players fully independent of banks. If non-banks are to operate on equal basis with banks, a few issues need to be addressed.

This chapter is organised as follows. Section 6.2 indicates potential benefits of the Single Euro Payments Area (SEPA) and the regulators' approach towards integration of the retail payments market in the European Union. Section 6.3 focuses exclusively on new PSPs. Section 6.4 shows how the path from IBANs (International Bank Account Number) to IPANs (International Payment Account Number) is being paved. Section 6.5 deals with the issue of PSPs' access to payment systems and to central banks' infrastructure and includes a short theoretical risk assessment. Section 6.6 investigates the issue of access of Third Party Providers to bank accounts and takes a look at mobile wallets. Section 6.7 concludes.

6.2 The SEPA and the approach of regulators

The payments industry finds itself in a state of flux. It is shaped by demand because consumers and businesses require services tailored to their needs, which adapt to social and economic context and must change quickly due to progress in technology. It is also shaped by supply because payment solution providers, in the pursuit of profit, attempt to cater to customers' satisfaction by inventing new products and services.

The new payments landscape emerges from the game of supply and demand, but, as the 2014 Nobel Prize Laureate in economic sciences Jean Tirole says, sometimes positive changes need coordination and support from regulators who set up an adequate legal framework and are able to reduce or eliminate market failures (2014). In the European Union (EU) the coordination takes place at the pan-European level, where laws are passed after the consultation process involving the Council of the European Union (representing Member States), the European Parliament and the European Commission (EC), which is often *spiritus rector* that prepares draft legal acts, as in the case of the Payment Services Directive (PSD), the Interchange Fee Regulation (IF Reg) and the Electronic Money Directive (EMD).

The Single Euro Payments Area project (SEPA) is grounded on the premise that there should be no distinction between cross-border and domestic electronic retail payments as well as cash payments, if the Single Euro Cash Area project (SECA) is included. The stress is, however, put on e-payments because cash is perceived as costly and not matching the vision of the advanced economy, where most processes become automated and digitised. Therefore we see a pan-European regulators' push for the end-to-end Straight Through Processing (STP), allowing all transactions to be processed seamlessly and entirely electronically through the whole payments cycle without any manual intervention or redundant actions. The STP could result in high cost savings and fewer failures in handling of transactions, as its advocates put it.

According to the PricewaterhouseCoopers (PwC) analysis of sixteen EU countries representing 97% of the EU euro-denominated transaction values, all SEPA benefits, once fully embraced, could bring reduction of annual costs by €21.9 billion across all stakeholders as a result of efficient processing and streamlined bank account infrastructure, reduction of nine billion bank accounts and up to €227 billion in released liquidity and credit lines due to cash pooling and more efficient clearing (2014). PwC correctly mentions additional benefits which could be realised from adoption of e-invoicing and the extended use of the XML ISO 20022 standard. Erik Nooteboom notices that the SEPA strengthens the position of consumers and businesses (2014).

Facilitating electronic payments and invoicing is part of the first pillar of the Digital Agenda – achieving the Digital Single Market. The Digital Agenda itself forms one of the seven pillars of the Europe 2020 Strategy, which is designed to accelerate the growth of the European Union by making better use of the potential of Information and Communication Technologies (ICTs). The Digital Single Market should put an end to fragmentation of Member States' markets, bringing down barriers to easy cross-border access to digital content, completing the SEPA and raising the level of protection in cyberspace. The actions will, among others, include digitalising industry, unlocking the benefits of e-services and advancing digital skills, developing interoperability and standards in areas such as the Internet of Things, cybersecurity, big data and cloud computing (European Commission, 2015).

Before adopting in July 2013 proposals for the IF Reg and the PSD2, the European Commission, aiming to directly address major obstacles on the way to the integrated European retail payments market, initiated broad public consultation by publishing on 11 January 2012 the Green Paper "Towards an Integrated European Market for Card, Internet and Mobile Payments" (European Commission, 2012). The consultation involved a wide range of stakeholders – not only the government structures which work with the EC as part of the Payments Committee, and not only the Payment Systems Market Expert Group (PSMEG), representing supply and demand sides of the market and assisting the Commission in drafting legal acts and initiatives on payment systems, but also all other interested parties from the European Union. The Commission received more than 300 written contributions to the Green Paper (their full text and the summary report are published on the EC's website), which should be seen as a satisfactory response for such a complex matter. The Green Paper addressed following areas of concern:

• market fragmentation, market access and market entry for existing and new service providers;
• payment security and data protection;
• transparent and efficient pricing of payment services;
• technical standardisation;
• interoperability between service providers; and
• governance of SEPA.

The EC in the Green Paper analysed many issues within all areas of concern. With regard to the first one, which directly relates to increasing competition (see the list above), it was indicated that, in contrast to banks, payment institutions and e-money institutions do not have direct access to clearing and settlement systems, because only credit institutions and investment firms, under art. 2(b) of the Settlement Finality Directive, may participate in designated settlement systems. Owing to this fact, non-bank payment service providers are unable to compete on equal footing with banks because they have to use the services of banks to settle payments. Besides, it was emphasised that banks as keepers of bank accounts can deny access to the information on the availability of funds, which would be requested by non-bank entities, even when acting on behalf of bank accounts' owners.

The so-called account information services (AIS) and payment initiation services (PIS) will be covered by the revised Payment Services Directive (PSD2), for which the compromise has been reached on 5 May 2015 (the compromise final version was published on 2 June and the one referred to in this chapter was adopted by the European Parliament on 8 October). The PSD2 will replace the existing Payment Services Directive which has been in place since 2007 (effectively later since it needed some time to be transposed into national legislations).

European officials perpetually call for more competition in the payments market and equal treatment of all payment service providers. Lately Andrus Ansip, the Vice-President of the European Commission responsible for developing the Single Digital Market said (2015): "The revised directive, known as PSD2...will include Third Party Payment Providers, which were not covered until now, and make them supervised payment institutions...By increasing competition between existing and new providers, it will give people a wider and better choice of payment systems."

Yves Mersch, Member of the Executive Board of the European Central Bank put the issue in an even more straightforward manner (2015): "the emergence of new payment services and payment service providers requires a level playing field for newcomers and for long-established players, as well as an appropriate level of protection for the payment service users."

6.3   Emergence of new categories of PSPs

Historically, the legal foundation for establishing electronic money institutions (EMIs) was laid down much earlier than for payment institutions (PIs). The European Parliament and the Council adopted the first Electronic Money Directive (EMD1) in 2000, while the second Electronic Money Directive (EMD2), repealing the first one, was adopted in 2009.

In Europe a debate about issuing electronic money and its impact on the stability of the monetary system took place in the 1990s. Electronic money, according to art. 2(2) of the EMD2 "means electronically, including magnetically, stored monetary value as represented by a claim on the issuer which is issued on receipt of funds for the purpose of making payment transactions, and which is accepted by a natural or legal person other than the electronic money issuer." Electronic money is classified as the third type of money next to cash and deposit money (Bleyen *et al.*, 2010). At first, prospects for a fast take-off of e-money seemed to be promising, although it had to tackle typical problems of networks goods by overcoming the chicken-and-egg deadlock (Van Hove, 1999). Malte Krueger (2002), analysing the position of the European Commission and the European Central Bank, underlined that regulators were dubious about the idea that only banks should be allowed to issue e-money, hence, in order to stimulate competition and e-money product innovations, the EMD1 introduced a new class of financial intermediaries – the EMIs, which – being subject to an adequate level of prudential supervision – could have benefited from lighter regulatory regime than banks – e.g., the initial capital of €1 mln, no reserve requirement at the central bank. In the EMD2 the initial capital threshold was set even lower at €350 th., and EMIs were no longer considered credit institutions. EMIs are not allowed to take deposits and grant credits, unless from their own funds, but can offer payment services listed in the PSD.

The PSD, which backs implementation of SEPA, established another category of PSPs – payment institutions. They can, like EMIs, benefit from the single passporting in the European Union and in fact many already have. According to the PSD-Annex, PIs are allowed to provide and execute the following payment services throughout the EU:

- cash deposits/withdrawals and operations required for operating a payment account;
- execution of payment transactions (credit transfers, direct debits, card and card-based payments), also covered by a credit granted for a maximum of twelve months if the credit is closely linked to a payment service provided;
- issuing and/or acquiring of payment instruments; and
- money remittance.

The PSD2 adds to this list two additional payment services – payment initiation services (PIS) and account information services (AIS), which similarly to issuing of payment instruments do not involve taking possession of payment service users' funds. As defined in art. 4 (15 and 16) of the PSD2, PIS "means a service to initiate a payment order at the request of the payment service user with respect to a payment account held at another payment service provider" and AIS "means an online service to provide consolidated information on one or more payment accounts held by the payment service user with either another payment service provider or with more than one payment service provider."

PIs need to be licensed fulfilling a number of criteria. Depending on the type of payment services to be provided PI must ensure initial capital from €20 th. to €125 th. and on-going capital calculated according to one of three methods set out in art. 8 of the PSD and determined by the competent authority in a Member State. PIs are obliged to safeguard funds received from payment service users either by ring fencing those funds or by covering them with an insurance policy or another equally strong guarantee from an insurance company or a credit institution. Typically the second option is much more expensive, and PIs prefer to separate funds of users from other types of funds and deposit them at a credit institution or invest in low-risk liquid assets as defined by national competent authorities. Thus, in case of a PI's insolvency, fund owners should be able to recover their holdings. Besides PIs must comply with Anti-Money Laundering and Counter-Terrorism Financing (AML/CTF) legislation and abide by all the rules set out to protect payers and payees in a proper manner, in title III of the PSD on transparency of conditions and information requirements for payment services. According to art. 16 of the PSD, PIs are also permitted to perform activities closely related to payment services, such as ensuring the execution of payment transactions, foreign exchange services, safekeeping activities, and the storage and processing of data. Also, consistent with the PSD philosophy, different entities, e.g. mobile operators or merchants, can become hybrid payment institutions by starting to provide payment services next to running their core business. All PIs are regulated. Their credibility is increased by the fact that they are subject to a supervisory and prudential regime proportionate to the financial and operational risks which are narrower than those arising from the activities of banks.

Janina Harasim aptly pointed out that new PSPs brought value added on the retail payments market because they were innovative, flexible, often rich in experience from other fields of economic activities (not always financial) and ready to offer services at a lower cost than banks (2013, pp. 96–99). Payment initiation services, for example, evolved in e-commerce in response to the need to offer a cheaper alternative to payment cards for consumers and merchants, providing the latter with the payment confirmation/guarantee, which incentivised vendors to prepare shipments of goods without undue delay.

EMIs and PIs are very similar in many aspects. However, PIs are usually not allowed to issue electronic money, although there are countries which, using the national option, granted PIs operating within their own territory the right to issue e-money. This is the case in Poland, where PIs can issue e-money, provided that the outstanding e-money value will not exceed €5 mln (art. 73a(4) of the Polish Act on Payment Services). Until recently, however, in the official statistics of the Polish central bank or the Financial Supervision Authority in Poland there was no e-money in circulation, although some pre-paid products from Poland would most probably qualify as e-money in other Member States. According to preliminary results of a study (VVA Europe, 2015) on the EMD2 impact, commissioned to VVA Europe by the European Commission, pan-European guidance on classifying products and services as e-money is needed, in particular highlighting the differences between payment accounts and e-money accounts. The study also mentions that the value and number of e-money transactions in Europe are steadily increasing although the existing data is not complete. As of July 2014 there were 177 EMIs in the EU with more licenses under way, but 27% of all of them had by that time been issued in the United Kingdom and 21% in Denmark (see Figure 6.1 and the note below). The majority of EMIs obtained their license since 2011, so it seems that the new Electronic Money Directive was supportive in this respect.

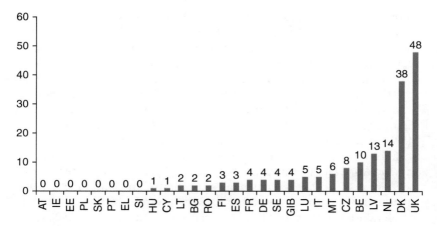

Figure 6.1 Number of EMIs per country in the EU, 2014
Note: The number of EMIs in Denmark seems to be overestimated.
Source: VVA Europe (2015).

Leo Van Hove and other specialists in the field once felt very enthusiastic about the widespread adoption of e-money, which is cheap in terms of societal costs (2008). Admittedly, this product category is today developing but in a different shape than it was envisaged in the past. Proprietary systems of electronic purses, such as Avant in Finland, Proton in Belgium or Mulibanco Electronic Purse in Portugal, did not succeed or have seen only limited success in Europe. However, there are a lot of other payment services offered by a growing number of payment institutions which meet the demand of consumers and businesses.

For every payment service listed in the PSD-Annex, PIs need an authorisation from a competent body. According to the study by London Economics, *iff* and PaySys, which served the European Commission as basis for evaluating the impact of the PSD, in 2012 the largest number of authorisations were issued for money remittance (40% of the total), the second most common type of authorisation was acquiring/issuing of payment instruments (19% of the total), and the third was execution of payment transactions including transfer of funds to a payment account (15% of the total) (2013, p. 33). At that time as much as 40% of all PIs (224 out of 568 in the EU) were registered in the United Kingdom. This shows that what also played an important role, apart from the development stage of the retail payments market in the UK, was regulatory divergences and effects of arbitrage between jurisdictions. Also, the PSD provided an option to waive some PSD provisions for so-called small payments institutions dealing exclusively with money remittance business. Under art. 26 of PSD a waiver applied when the total amount of payment transactions executed by this entity did not exceed €3 mln per month, with some permissible variance across countries – in Poland the threshold was set significantly lower at €0.5 mln. According to the London Economics, *iff* and PaySys study, about 2,200 small payment institutions were registered in Europe by late August 2012, out of which 45% were in Poland and 44% in the UK (2013, p. 39).

Since 2012 the number of authorised and small payment institutions has increased rapidly throughout the EU, e.g., in Poland in December 2014 there were 27 authorised payment institutions and 1,356 small payment institutions, whereas in December 2012 there were only three PIs and 1,122 small PIs (data from the Polish Financial Supervision Authority, 2015).

The study by London Economics *et al.* (2013) presented a useful typology of activities undertaken by PIs, such as money remittance, foreign exchange broking, card acquiring, card schemes, internet payment service provision, other services (operating ATM networks, renting POS devices, proving IT solutions, etc.), card issuing, credit provisioning, other financial and business services provision and telecoms payment services.

What is evidently missing from this list is operating payment accounts. Under art. 4(14) of the PSD1 and art. 4(12) of the PSD2 "'payment account' means an account held in the name of one or more payment service users which is used for the execution of payment transactions". In principle such accounts should offer full functionality, including the possibility to execute credit transfers, direct debits and card payments. Bank payment accounts, beyond all shadow of doubt, facilitate all of those operations, unlike different electronic/digital/mobile wallets of PIs and EMIs. Today e-wallets are typically prepaid accounts available online via electronic or mobile channels, possibly with an option to link a payment card or much less frequently other payment instruments. Services such as PayPal, Google Wallet (or AndroidPay), ApplePay, SamsungPay, PayU or native applications of smaller providers, e.g., offering ticketing and parking services such as SkyCash, mPay or moBilet in Poland, are examples of e-wallets. Some of them, like PayPal, naming but one, have large merchant and consumer bases. PayPal is useful in e-commerce in B2C and P2P domains but it has limitations. It cannot substitute for bank accounts entirely. PayPal took advantage of e-mail addresses, which may mimic the system of bank account numbers, but in fact PayPal accounts form a closed environment and are not compatible with bank accounts at the same layer. A PayPal user cannot initiate a SEPA credit transfer to someone else's bank account.

In order to put non-bank PSPs on equal footing with banks, three issues intertwine:

1. One is an option to have a right to assign their own IBANs to accounts of payment service users.
2. Two is a possibility to directly access payment systems, also designated, on fair and objectively defined terms.
3. Three is a right to open accounts at central banks which operate designated payment systems.

6.4   From IBANs to IPANs

IBAN, which stands for International Bank Account Number, facilitates identifying bank account numbers in an easy and machine-readable form. According to the SWIFT IBAN Registry, as of June 2015, sixty-six countries worldwide, including all twenty-eight Member States of the European Union, were using the IBAN numbering system. IBAN enables communication and processing of cross-border as well as domestic transactions. It is designed in a way to allow validation of the information provided by calculating the check digits, so the probability of making a mistake while typing in an IBAN is low. IBAN can be of use in an electronic or a paper environment, in the latter case typically by adding blank spaces between every four characters.

The IBAN structure is subject to the international ISO 13616-1 standard of 2007 (with later amendments), while ISO 13616-2 defines roles and responsibilities of the registration authority – the SWIFT.

According to ISO 13616-1 the format of the IBAN shall be:

2!a2!n30c

where:

- The first two letters (2!a) should always be a two-character country code, as defined in ISO 3166-1 (e.g., FI for Finland, DE for Germany).
- The third and fourth characters (2!n) shall be the check digits.
- The remaining part should consist of up to thirty alphanumeric characters (30c) for a BBAN (Basic Bank Account Number), which has a fixed length per country and, included within it, a bank identifier with a fixed position and length per country.

The exact structure of IBAN is country specific, but it can have a maximum of thirty-four characters. Table 6.1 comprises examples of IBAN for selected countries.

In developing ISO 13616-1 for numbering bank accounts, the technical committee in charge agreed it was not necessary to develop one single method for identifying the account in each country. It recognised the need to retain, where possible, the current national identification system, which required some adjustments but in principle could have been kept. As a result, the IBAN structure is flexible, although it follows common rules. IBANs differ from country to country. In some of them the IBAN length is 16 characters, in others IBANs can be 28 characters long (see Table 6.1). The number must be fixed for a country. The inner structure of an IBAN is defined nationally by competent authorities, e.g., in Costa Rica, bank identifier does not include branch specification in the BBAN (Basic Bank Account Number), whereas in Italy it does. Table 6.2 below presents Poland's specific IBAN structure.

A bank identifier, as named in ISO 13616-1, is also called a business unit sort code in Poland. Those codes, based on the Ordinance No. 15/2010 of the President of Narodowy Bank Polski of 15 July 2010, are assigned by the Polish central bank as requested by a given bank. It can decide as to whether it will number their branches or other business units (such as bank departments) within the first eight digits of the Basic Bank Account Number. In practice many bank branches have not been numbered in Poland yet because banks, operating on a single centralised IT system, did not always deem it appropriate. In such a case those bank branches are not included in the registry of Narodowy Bank Polski, operated by the Payment System Department. According to the NBP official website, there are three times more bank business units which have not been granted separate sort codes than those which are listed in NBP registers (NBP, 2015).

Table 6.1   IBAN examples per country (selection)

Country	IBAN length	IBAN example
Belgium	16	BE68539007547034
Finland	18	FI2112345600000785
Germany	22	DE89370400440532013000
Netherlands	18	NL91ABNA0417164300
Poland	28	PL61109010140000071219812874

Source: SWIFT Registry (2015).

Table 6.2 The IBAN structure in Poland

top	National Bank Account Number (BBAN + check digits)																								
P	L	2	5	1	0	6	0	1	0	2	8	2	2	7	7	2	7	1	4	3	8	5	7	4	1
Country code		Check digits		Bank code*								Account number													
				Bank identifier/Sort code																					
IBAN (International Bank Account Number)																									

Note: *Four digits for cooperative banks, three digits for other banks.

Source: Narodowy Bank Polski (National Bank of Poland) (2015).

The last sixteen digits of IBANs in Poland are used as numbers that identify clients' bank accounts at given banks, which assign them according to their own numbering system. Checksums of entire IBANs must obviously be validated according to the standard. In Poland IBAN is determined by adding PL in front of the NRB – domestic account number.

Based on ISO 13616, a Polish norm for numbering domestic account numbers was developed. The Polish norm PN-F-01102 of December 2012 defines elements and principles of creating NRBs, that is, National Bank Account Numbers (BBAN + two check digits). Its scope is not restricted to banks but broadens to encompass payment service providers including credit unions, payment institutions and electronic money institutions.

However, the norm is more of a technical character and, according to Polish law, the central bank is authorised to grant sort codes only to banks and not to non-bank PSPs. In order to widen its competencies, a new law amending the Polish Act on Payment Services must be passed. As of June 2015 there was a proposal in place. The Polish Ministry of Finance had started the legal procedure already back in 2014 in order to enable non-bank PSPs to assign their own IBANs to clients, but then the proposal was left in limbo.

There is no need to replicate the same patterns across all European countries; nevertheless, the Polish example shows that PIs' and EMIs' rights to assign IBAN can encounter hurdles. In order to verify as to what extent it was still a problem in SEPA countries, I conducted a survey among Member States in May/June 2015 by distributing electronically a short questionnaire through the Polish Ministry of Finance to national payment experts or contacting directly competent authorities in Member States. The query consisted of three questions with an option to give comments. The first and most important question was: "Are there in your country non-bank payment service providers (PSPs), such as payment institutions and electronic money institutions, authorised to issue their own International Bank/Payment Account Numbers (IBANs/IPANs) and assign them to accounts of payment service users (PSUs) on a similar basis as banks do?" If the answer was "yes", respondents were asked to provide the underlying legal basis and the authority responsible for assigning bank identifiers / sort codes.

The response rate was 60%. This means that eighteen out of thirty countries (twenty-eight EU countries + Switzerland and Norway) answered to the query within the two-month period (see the results in Table 6.3).

Table 6.3 Information on issuance of IBANs (June 2015)

Country	Issuing authority for bank identifiers / sort codes	PIs and EMIs allowed to assign IBANs?
Austria	Oesterreichische Nationalbank	Not answered to the query
Belgium	Secretatiaat van de Interbancaire Overeenkomsten/Secrétariat des Accords Interbancaires (managed by the central bank)	Yes
Bulgaria	Bulgarian National Bank	No
Croatia	Croatian National Bank	No
Cyprus	Central Bank of Cyprus	Not answered to the query
Czech Republic	Česká národní banka / Czech National Bank	Yes
Denmark	The Danish Bankers Association	Yes
Estonia	Estonian Banking Association	No
Finland	The Federation of Finnish Financial Services	Yes
France	ACPR (Banking Supervisor)	Yes
Germany	Deutsche Bundesbank	Yes
Greece	Bank of Greece	Not answered to the query
Hungary	Magyar Nemzeti Bank (The Central Bank of Hungary)	Yes
Ireland	Banking & Payments Federation Ireland	Not answered to the query
Italy	Banca d'Italia	Yes
Latvia	SWIFT	Not answered to the query
Lithuania	Lietuvos Bankas (Bank of Lithuania)	Yes
Luxembourg	The Luxembourg Bankers' Association	Not answered to the query
Malta	Central Bank of Malta	Not answered to the query
Netherlands	Dutch Payment Association	Yes
Norway	Finance Norway	Yes
Poland	Narodowy Bank Polski	No
Portugal	Banco de Portugal	Not answered to the query
Romania	SWIFT	Not answered to the query
Slovakia	National Bank of Slovakia	Not answered to the query
Slovenia	National Bank of Slovenia	Yes

Continued

Table 6.3 Continued

Country	Issuing authority for bank identifiers / sort codes	PIs and EMIs allowed to assign IBANs?
Spain	Banco de España	Yes
Sweden	Swedish Bankers' Association	No
Switzerland	SIX Interbank Clearing (in accordance with the Swiss National Bank)	Not answered to the query
United Kingdom	Payments Council	Not answered to the query

Source: Own survey and the ECB website (SEPA countries).

Depending on the country, a different authority can be responsible for providing bank identifiers (the first component of IBAN). It is most typically the central bank (in seventeen cases), but also an industry (payment or bank) association (in nine cases), the supervisory authority (in one case), the clearing house (in one case) or SWIFT (in two cases) (see Table 6.3). Sometimes Business Identifier Codes (BICs) issued by SWIFT are used as bank identifiers, like in Latvia, Romania, the Netherlands and in the United Kingdom. Then PSPs derive IBANs from BICs according to the ISO 13616-1 country-specific format. Often, unlike in Poland, the process of assigning bank identifiers is not governed by any particular law but is based on self-regulation.

Likewise, several Member States, such as e.g. Finland, Germany, Lithuania, Norway and Spain, indicated that the right to grant sort codes to banks, PIs and EMIs is a matter of self-regulation. Most of the eighteen countries responded that currently non-bank PSPs can be allocated their sort codes and subsequently these new market entrants can assign IBANs to accounts of PSUs. However, in five Member States surveyed – Bulgaria, Croatia, Estonia, Poland and Sweden – it was not possible, although in Estonia and Poland it is bound to change. According to the draft amendment to the Polish Act on Payment Services, the central bank will have the power to assign sort codes to non-bank PSPs, apart from assigning numbers to banks, and in Estonia the Financial Supervision Authority will be in charge. Norway, where the Norwegian Banking Association (Finance Norway) is responsible for assigning sort codes, did not give straightforward answer, stating that they had never been approached by a PI in this respect but if they were, the outcome would probably be a positive one.

A few countries, which responded to the query, noted that the right to assign IBANs by PIs and EMIs stems directly from the Payment Services Directive, but is not so relevant as long as non-bank PSPs cannot participate in designated payment systems. In Belgium non-bank PSPs may issue their own IBANs, but in practice very few do so because they prefer to organise their payment flows using accounts kept in commercial banks. As a consequence, they have indirect access to interbank payment systems similar to that of other bank customers. In Finland, according to the survey results, other PSPs like smaller banks and PIs are mostly operating based on a correspondent bank agreement with one clearing bank. They can then use some common accounts for all their customer transactions within the correspondent bank's IBAN series. They can also get a sub-series of IBAN numbers within the IBAN series of the correspondent bank. In both cases they would use the clearing bank's BIC. Norway commented that the real issue is not whether non-banks are assigned bank identifiers, but for which services non-banks are able to use them. And this is conditioned by the direct participation in the Norwegian Interbank Clearing System (NICS).

Survey results confirm the hypothesis that three issues intertwine here: the right to assign own IBANs, the possibility to directly access payment systems and the right to open accounts at the central bank. For designated and often also for other systemically important payment systems, it is not possible to get direct access without maintaining an account at a central bank, where the settlement occurs.

We can presume with high probability that in many of the countries whose representatives did not respond to the query PIs and EMIs are theoretically allowed to get their IBANs, but it may be of little use to them since they are not able to access designated payment systems. Such non-bank PSPs focus on other payment services, not on offering payment accounts with fully reachable credit transfers and direct debits, which is however guaranteed by banks. The Business Identifier Code (BIC), can be assigned not only to banks, but also to clearing houses and even to non-financial institutions (SWIFT, 2015). Therefore, in countries where IBANs incorporate BICs as bank identifiers and there is no other authority than SWIFT to assign sort codes, it is most probable that PIs and EMIs are technically able to create their own IBANs.

It seems that the right to have its own sort code and allocate IBANs to payment accounts of PSUs by non-bank PSPs is of lesser value without direct access to major payment systems, but it gives the latter one advantage. PIs and EMIs become less dependent on their bank PSPs, which operate their account and subaccounts of their clients. Non-bank

PSPs can then freely change their servicing bank PSPs. The migration to another bank becomes less difficult. The existing IBAN series of a non-bank PSP just need to be cross-linked to the IBAN series of technical accounts at a new servicing bank, but from the perspective of a PSU nothing changes. He or she has the same account number and can preload their e-wallet with funds exactly the same way they have been doing so far. In addition, if a PI decides to offer its client a credit transfer or a direct debit, a payee will see in the transfer details it was initiated at the PI and not at the PI servicing bank. This strengthens the relationship between a PI and a PSU, not to mention that banks face new competition in this area. Obviously benefits increase when a PI can access a payment system on equal basis with banks (see the next section).

Linking IBANs with mobile phone numbers opens new possibilities to develop P2P mobile payments (e.g., based on SEPA credit transfers) and increase mobile wallets' functionality, regardless of whether these services are offered by PIs and EMIs or banks (see Section 6.6).

The significance of IBAN in Europe is rising. According to the so-called SEPA end-date Regulation (EU) No 260/2012, IBAN should be the sole number required to identify a payment account. Therefore from 1 February 2016 (from 1 November 2016 for non-euro Member States) onwards, payers and payees will not have to use any additional code, such as a BIC (SWIFT) code, for cross-border credit transfers and direct debits in euro. The "IBAN only" rule will come into effect.

Finally, it is worth considering whether in the SEPA area it is not justified to refer to IBANs as IPANs since the offering of payment accounts is not anymore restricted to banks only. Besides, this new terminology has already been incorporated in the law (see Payment Services Directive): we talk about payment accounts, not bank accounts. According to the so-called Payment Account Directive (PAD) passed in July 2014, every European citizen should have a right to open and use a payment account with basic features. PAD objectives are: to raise the level of financial inclusion and enhance consumer protection and competition on the market by easier switching of payment accounts (also cross-border) and more transparency and comparability of fees. After PAD implementation, which should happen within two years of its publication date, such accounts will be offered, for technical reasons, by credit institutions, but the objectives of the Directive could be better achieved if PIs and EMIs were also able to offer such services, especially if these non-bank PSPs, due to their specificity, would be less willing to sell other products, such as, e.g., credits, which are not considered a basic payment account feature.

6.5   Access to payment systems and to central banks' infrastructure

Recital 16 of the PSD envisages that it is crucial for any PSP to access the services of payment system technical infrastructures in order to process payments and transfer money efficiently. Art. 28 of the PSD, and in the PSD2 art. 35, stipulates that it falls under the responsibility of Member States to ensure that "the rules on access of authorised or registered payment service providers that are legal persons to payment systems shall be objective, non-discriminatory and proportionate and that those rules do not inhibit access more than is necessary to safeguard against specific risks such as settlement risk, operational risk and business risk and to protect the financial and operational stability of the payment system." According to this law, operators of payment systems are not allowed to discriminate between different PSPs, neither on the basis of participation nor on their rights and obligations in the system. However, paragraph 2 of this provision leaves designated payment systems and closed loop systems out of the PSD2 scope. Luckily, it also says that

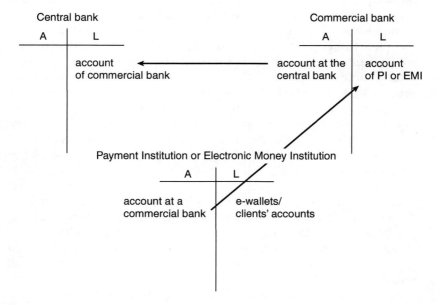

Figure 6.2   Current *modus operandi* of PIs and EMIs
Source: Own concept.

authorised and registered PSPs (such as PIs or EMIs) can demand that direct participants pass through their payment orders in an objective, proportionate and non-discriminatory manner. Thus new provisions will guarantee indirect assess. In addition, art. 36 of the PSD2 ensures that PIs will have an access to credit institutions, which cannot refuse to open accounts for PIs and hinder PIs' activity.

As Figure 6.2 clearly depicts, PIs and EMIs are in a subordinate position vis-a-vis a competitor group – commercial banks. Their payment orders, to enter payment systems, must be processed through a commercial bank. There is a potential room to exert power on PIs and EMIs in terms of timely execution of payments or imposing additional conditions which may even be labelled by banks as objective and necessary. Besides, banks may monitor the entire payment flow generated by a PI or an EMI, thus being able to become aware of competitors' type of activity and even learn about their customers. Moreover, pricing remains an issue, although it cannot be negated that also direct access to payment systems entails costs.

According to feedback from the EC's consultation on the Green Paper "Towards an Integrated European Market for Card, Internet and Mobile Payments (2012), there was no consensus among stakeholders on whether non-direct access to clearing and settlement is problematic to non-bank PSPs. Most banks stated that indirect access for PIs and EMIs was sufficient and beneficial in terms of reduced costs and risks, whereas most non-bank PSPs disagreed and shared an opinion that indirect access generated higher costs, complexity and more lengthy processes. Most retailers and consumers were in favour of direct access of non-bank PSPs, indicating the need for openness and non-discrimination. Some stakeholders made suggestions to amend the Settlement Finality Directive (SFD) accordingly; however, the majority pointed out the need to ensure that direct access of PIs and EMIs does not raise operational and liquidity risks (London Economics *et al.*, 2013, p. 215).

In its impact assessment accompanying the proposal for revising the Payment Services Directive, the EC considered three options regarding access of PIs and EMIs to designated payment systems: option of no policy change, option to allow PIs to participate directly in designated payment systems and an intermediate option to establish objective and transparent rules for PIs to access indirectly designated payment systems (European Commission, 2013, pp. 263–264). As it was presented at the beginning of this section, the EC adopted the intermediate option, which will lead to easier access for non-bank PSPs to major payment systems, although it will not make incumbents and new entrants exactly equal in this respect.

Concerning access to other payment systems, such as, e.g., card payment systems, PIs and EMIs have already benefited from provisions laid down in the Payment Services Directive 2007/64/EC. It appears that in four-party schemes the possibility to issue and acquire card payment transactions and provide ancillary services under the same conditions as banks brought value added to schemes, merchants and cardholders and did not give rise to higher risk.

It is, however, understandable that in terms of systemically important payment systems all risks should be scrutinised adequately before new entrants are permitted to directly access the designated infrastructure.

Central banks can have concerns about risks associated with PIs and EMIs because these new PSPs do not meet the same prudential and solvency supervision requirements and risk management policies as banks.

Besides, commercial banks, which are granted the right to open accounts at the central bank, are subject to reserve requirement. When facing liquidity problems, they can incur short-term loans on the inter-bank market or an intra-day credit directly at the central bank. These facilities are not available to PIs and EMIs at the moment. However, PIs and EMIs differ from credit institutions. According to recital 34 of the PSD2, the spectrum of PIs' activities is much narrower than the spectrum of credit institutions because PIs are specialised payment service providers which are not allowed to accept deposits and they can only use funds received from users to deliver payment services. Likewise, according to recital 13 of the EMD2, the issuance of electronic money is not deposit taking activity. Both PIs and EMIs cannot create money through lending. They do not use a money multiplier and are not subject to reserve requirements. Therefore their supervisory regime should be lighter and aligned more closely to the attendant financial and operational risks. Indeed, the initial and on-going capital requirements for non-bank PSPs are less stringent than for banks. However, PIs and EMIs must comply with a set of rules that ensure sound and prudent management (see Section 6.3). Before being granted an authorisation, but also in the course of conducting business, non-bank PSPs have to prove to the supervisory authority that their internal arrangements – including risk policy management, contingency planning, organisational structure, system of internal control and external audits, etc. – are robust.

PIs and EMIs have much more limited investment capabilities than banks, and they are obligated to maintain much higher liquidity.

Pursuant to art. 10 of the PSD2 and art. 7 of the EMD2, PIs and EMIs must fulfil rigid safeguarding requirements. They should ring fence funds or e-money received from users. These funds can be deposited at a credit institution or invested in secure low-risk assets, such as Treasury bills or bonds issued or guaranteed by public authorities. A catalogue of low-risk assets is defined by competent authorities of Member States.

In Poland as of December 2014, PIs had at their disposal about €100 mln in liquid assets out of which 96% was money held at a current account in banks, 1% was cash and 3% secure assets with a maturity date of up to seven days (Polish Financial Supervision Authority, 2015).

According to art. 10 par. 1a of the PSD2, assets backed by users' funds should be protected against claims of PIs' other creditors, in particular in the event of insolvency. As it was mentioned earlier (Section 6.3) PIs do not need to ring fence funds if those funds are covered by an insurance policy or a comparable guarantee. However, high costs deter PIs from such arrangements, and they prefer not to commingle funds of users with other types of funds.

Risk management in a payment system consists in its continuous monitoring and in using adequate security measures. Central banks operating designated payment systems must take into account a list of associated risks, such as credit, legal, operational, liquidity, settlement and systemic risk (Górka, 2013, pp. 21–22). Those types of risks are interdependent.

Non-bank PSPs do not have a long track record, and there is hardly any empirical research about their risk activity. For this reason most central banks in the EU are reluctant to open accounts to PIs and EMIs and permit them to access large-value payment systems whose smooth and uninterrupted functioning is vital to financial stability.

On the other hand, as it was presented, the risk profile of PIs and EMIs is well defined in the legal framework. Their assets, directly linked to users' funds transferable on demand, are liquid and in practice separated from other types of funds. In order to mitigate the liquidity and settlement risk in the payment system, central banks can freely require securing adequate amount of liquidity, proportionate to the level of PIs' and EMIs' obligations against their creditors. Using a prepaid model, where funds would be deposited by non-bank PSPs to accounts maintained at the central banks in advance, could well address credit, liquidity and settlement risks.

Enabling access of non-bank PSPs would, on the one hand, lead to transferring these types of risks to PIs and EMIs but, on the other hand, would force them to make technical and legal investments necessary to link to the designated payment systems. Obviously, it should be left to the discretion of PIs and EMIs whether they would apply for a direct participation in large-value payment systems and bear related costs or organise the payment flow as smaller banks or credit unions through bigger players. It also depends on the type of payment services rendered. For the time being, for many non-bank PSPs the lack of direct access to major payment systems seems not to pose a problem. However, it can quickly change, in particular when PIs and EMIs are willing to offer payment accounts with full functionality or engage in instant payments. Therefore, although indirect access to designated payment systems warranted by art. 35 par. 2 of the PSD2 is a step in a good direction, in the longer run it seems questionable to discriminate between different categories of PSPs at all.

6.6   Access to bank accounts and the development of mobile wallets

Another issue, slightly different in nature than access to payment systems but also important in fostering competition and innovation on the payments market in the EU, is access to customers' payment accounts at banks (XS2A).

Opening up banks to the so-called Third Party Providers (TPPs) has been the most debated topic of the revised PSD. Until the very last moment before the compromise on the PSD2 in May 2015 was reached, hot discussions between stakeholders and regulators had taken place. In the opinion of the EC, a legal vacuum for payment initiation services (PIS) and account information services (AIS – see the definitions in Section 6.3) must have been filled, since both types of services were present on the market but they were not covered by any legal rules governing rights and obligations between TPPs, account servicing banks and users. PIS and AIS were recognised as beneficial to the market. Credit transfers initiated on behalf of clients by non-bank PIS providers (such as Sofort, Trustly, SafetyPay, DT-Online and Citadel) served as a cheaper alternative to cards payments for internet merchants and provided them with a payment guarantee (European Commission, 2013, pp. 137 and 224). Interestingly enough, banks, based on contractual agreements, also engaged in this business (e.g., iDEAL in the Netherlands, giropay in Germany, eps in Austria, MyBank in Italy and PostFinance in Switzerland). AIS, on the other hand, allow consumers to collect and consolidate information from different bank accounts in one single place, helping them to manage personal finances. There are also other services that could be built on top of AIS; e.g., banks and non-bank lending institutions began to use information retrieved from customers' different bank accounts to rate their creditworthiness. AIS can contribute to many big/rich data services enabling different businesses to analyse massive datasets, linking financial and non-financial information.

Not surprisingly, representatives of the banking sector expressed concerns about the activity of non-bank TPPs in respect to a number of areas. Javier Santamaria, the chair of the European Payments Council, found sharing login and transaction credentials of account holders with a TPP unsecure, unless relying on a strong customer authentication and based on a redirection model through a standardised open European interface (not yet existing). Also, he regarded as problematic that account servicing banks would be the first "port of call" held liable in situations of unauthorised transactions executed with the involvement of TPPs. Moreover, he pointed out that TPPs should not have access to the payment infrastructure of banks and to the data of their clients without financial compensation to banks (Santamaria, 2014).

Harry Leinonen noted that TPPs involved in payment initiation services emerged due to a lack of standardised t+0 e-payment solutions (2015). His recommendation to support faster/instant payments and require, in the future, $t + 0$ delivery instead of $t + 1$ for credit transfers as a legal obligation for PSPs is worth considering.

After extensive consultations, the revised PSD took shape. Legislators addressed areas of abovementioned concerns, taking into account positions of all payment stakeholders. In light of the PSD2, the mandate for PIS and AIS activity must come from an explicit consent of account holders. Art. 66 and art. 67 set out rules on access to payment accounts for PIS and AIS services respectively. Briefly put, PIS providers shall:

- not hold users' funds in connection with the provision of PIS,
- keep personal credentials of account holders secure and not accessible to third parties,
- authenticate themselves to an account servicing PSP (usually a bank) every time a payment is initiated,
- not store sensitive data of PSUs and request from them any other data than those necessary to provide PIS,
- not use, access and store any data for purposes other than the provision of PIS, and
- not modify any transaction feature (especially the amount or the recipient).

Account servicing PSPs shall, on their part:

- securely communicate with PIS providers,
- make available all information on transaction initiation to the PIS provider immediately after the receipt of the payment order, and
- not discriminate payment orders transmitted by PIS providers (in particular in terms of timing, priority and charges).

Legislators acknowledged that security of electronic payments is of fundamental importance and all relevant security measures should be taken to protect PSUs and prevent risk of fraud, including phishing (see recitals 93–96 of the PSD2). Therefore, pursuant to art. 98, strong customer authentication would be required when the payer accesses his or her payment account or initiates a payment transaction. Such a strong customer authentication should even include elements dynamically linking the transaction to a specific amount and a specific payee (strong transaction authorisation) with a possible lighter regime for low-risk payments (such as, e.g., low-value mobile payments), to be further defined in the standard developed by the European Banking Authority as set out in art. 98 (regulatory technical standards on authentication and communication).

According to art. 73 par. 2 of the PSD2, indeed, an account servicing PSP liable for refunding losses to users will be the first port of call. However, in a situation where a PIS provider is liable for the unauthorised payment transaction, it shall immediately compensate the account servicing PSP for the losses incurred, and the burden of proof that a payment transaction was appropriately authenticated will be on a PIS provider.

PIS and AIS will not depend on the existence of a contractual relationship between TPPs and account servicing banks, and the PSD2 will not, for the provision of those types of services, define any particular business model, whether based on direct or indirect access (see recitals 30 and 93 and art. 66 and 67). It is clear that legislators did not put banks at the centre of these provisions, but rather account holders as the owners of funds and personal data, to whom a decision should be left about the choice of a trustworthy PSP. The lack of contractual arrangements will make it more difficult for banks to charge TPPs, but they will be free to charge customers, e.g., for executing credit transfers. The question of whether it is justified to charge twice for the same service was already raised when discussing new provisions on the pan-European forum. The current operational models will be in place before, pursuant to recital

93 and art. 98 of the PSD2, the European Banking Authority specifies the requirements for common and open standards of communication between TPPs, account servicing PSPs, payers, payees and, possibly, other PSPs.

Some time ago, Michael Salmony (2014) proposed a concept of an Open Standard Interface for Controlled Access to Payment Services (CAPS), linking the regulators' vision with the interests of account servicing PSPs and TPPs. In his opinion, open access to bank accounts could unlock the potential of the new services rendered by TPPs, but it can simultaneously bring benefits to banks in the form of new revenue streams. Salmony called for developing a safe infrastructure, where access to accounts based on contracts (signed with contract aggregators) would be granted in a limited way depending on a service type, where fees – attractive for all parties – would be determined by market forces and where consumers would remain in control, giving permission to exploit their payments account data to chosen service providers.

A similar concept has been introduced by the Euro Banking Association (not to be confused with the European Banking Authority), whose Working Group on Electronic and Alternative Payments issued, in May 2015, an opinion paper on Digital Customer Services Interface (DCSI) which could be defined as a pan-European application programming interface (API) facilitating access of TPPs to bank accounts but at the same time giving possible access to customers (and their data) via TPPs to banks. API is a technology allowing software applications to communicate without human intervention. An API specifies the mechanism to connect to software, what data and functionality is available and a set of rules (standardisation) that other software applications have to follow to access data and functionality (Euro Banking Association, 2015, p. 9). As Mounaim Cortet and Douwe Lycklama from Innopay note, APIs are nothing new. Google, Facebook and Twitter offer APIs to external parties, and PayPal is a prominent example of a PSP who used an API functionality to enhance its business and build an entire ecosystem of firms and services while being itself at the core of this ecosystem. However, XS2A disrupts the banking sector and requires adapting their business and operating models to new conditions, where dis- and re-intermediation processes triggered by TPPs take place (Cortet and Lycklama, 2015).

The DCSI concept aims to bridge the gap between fintech challengers with banks not only in the payments area but also in other areas, such as, e.g., digital identity. Payment account attributes could be reused to validate identity on other websites. The DCSI concept develops technical and business layers, with internal fees, like charge-per-request collected for TPPs using account servicing banks' Know-Your Customer/ AML expertise (Euro Banking Association, 2015, p. 18).

The future will show whether the Euro Banking Association's initiative to create the DSCI will manage to get sufficient support in the financial sector and outside of it – between merchants and consumers, as well as whether this concept will fit in with the approach of the European Banking Authority, which will be responsible for setting requirements for common and open standards of communication between TPPs, banks and PSUs, as set out in the PSD2.

Brett King noticed: "the unhinging of the bank account from the bank spells massive disruption for the financial services industry. It means that eventually the bank account will just be a value store commodity" (2013, p. 32).

The revolution brought about by the electronic/mobile wallets development is gaining momentum. Non-bank PSPs worldwide strive to deliver improved user experience by facilitating seamless one-click/ one tap instant payments in physical, e-, m- and finally in universal commerce. Until recently, one of the major barriers to the growth of mobile payments initiated with cloud-based electronic wallets has been the problem of accessing the liquidity kept at bank accounts by transferring funds using a different payment instrument than a card of an international scheme (see Figure 6.3). However, with the push from regulators in Europe, who bring overlay services provided by TPPs into the scope of the PSD2, and with the possible development

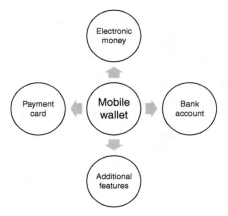

Figure 6.3   Functionality of mobile wallets
Source: Own concept.

of APIs to payment accounts at banks, this setback may soon cease to exist. Digital wallets, just as their physical counterparts, can also be equipped with additional features, such as loyalty cards, tickets, coupons or electronic receipts. Besides, just as in traditional wallets, users can store value in mobile wallets by keeping a positive balance of funds, electronic money or even private currencies – e.g., bitcoins (see Figure 6.3).

Mobile wallets can be provided by both bank and non-bank PSPs. However, it seems that non-bank players are more active in this area, like Google, Apple, Samsung, PayPal, PayU, or iPay, to name but a few. Banks, in cooperation with Visa and MasterCard, launch V.me by Visa or MasterPass wallets linked to payment cards. Banks also create mobile payment solutions designed for easy P2P transfers and C2B mobile payments, such as Blik in Poland, MobilePay in Denmark or Paym in the UK, which are connected to users' bank accounts.

Nevertheless, in general, banks are slow to innovate, because of heavy regulatory burden, legacy systems and complicated interbank agreements (King, 2013, p. 345). PIs and EMIs, on the other hand, are not entangled into high-risk deposit-lending or investment activities characteristic for banks. They can be agile and innovative.

Such companies as Amazon, Google, Apple and Facebook mastered building relationships with consumers. They all know how to leverage their business with information used as capital. This is the reason why banks worry about competition from them (Skinner, 2014, p. 104). Building a context around payments and shaping a positive user experience is key.

Jürgen Bott and Udo Milkau asked an accurate question in the context discussed in this section: *mobile wallets and current accounts: friends or foes?* (2014). According to the presented view the answer is: friends. Mobile wallets, defined more broadly as innovative ways to exchange payments, and current accounts, as a secure and stable platform for liquidity provided by banks as highly trusted partners, can coexist and collaborate, provided that non-bank and bank PSPs operate in a well governed environment with clear rules set by regulators (Bott and Milkau, 2014, pp. 297–298).

The payments ecosystem becomes more complex. In the payment chain there is space for many companies. Chris Skinner predicts: "In the near term, you might be buying an Apple download using a Zynga credit through an O2 wallet backed by a PayPal payment which is on a Visa card issued by a bank" (2014, p. 50).

6.7 Conclusions

PIs and EMIs are new payment service providers and special purpose financial institutions which have much to offer to consumers and companies. It is argued in this chapter that new entrants ought to be placed on equal footing with banks in order to fully exploit all opportunities.

First, they need to have the right to assign their own IBANs (IPANs) to accounts of payment service users. As the survey conducted between Member States revealed, this option is not yet available in all SEPA countries.

Second, they need to have the right to directly access payment systems, also designated ones, on fair and objectively defined terms. The position of PIs and EMIs considerably improved after adoption of the first PSD. They gained fair access to payment systems, like those of international card organisations, but still are not allowed to become direct participants of large-value or other systemically important payment systems.

Third, they need to be granted the right to open accounts at central banks. This will eventually make them independent of banks and facilitate settlement in the central bank's money.

The modalities of those three intertwining issues have been discussed in more detail throughout the chapter. Creating a de facto level playing field between bank and non-bank PSPs is a multistage process, and there are systemic and mental obstacles to be overcome. However, in the longer time horizon, there seems to be little justification for discrimination between PSPs. The approach towards all of them should be unified and purely risk based. The risk area needs to be further researched, also empirically.

The PSD2 reduces another hindrance impeding competition and innovation on the payments market in the EU because it opens up banks, i.e., it gives TPPs access to bank accounts which constitute a reservoir of liquidity. Thus, electronic and mobile wallets offered by PIs and EMIs will gain a new dimension and deliver greater functionality to users. It will not happen immediately. The value of such services will grow gradually, hopefully fostered by development of an open interface (API) to all of the EU's 7,000 banks across all countries.

It should be hoped that the revised PSD will fuel innovation among smaller non-bank PSPs, not just giant companies such as Google. Facilitating access to information and liquidity stored at bank accounts will certainly lower barriers to entry. PIs and EMIs will be able to offer other payment services than provided until recently, including the basic one – operating a payment account. Addressing the three major issues discussed in this chapter and providing access to information and liquidity stored at bank accounts will help transform mobile wallets into fully fledged payment accounts. This can have diverse consequences, one of which might be a gradual substitution of card payments with SEPA credit transfers and SEPA direct debit serving as basic payment instruments for money transfers, including instant payments (their rollout on a pan-European scale is presently much desired). The second consequence might be an enhanced market status of PIs and EMIs. They can become more trusted parties, and this also generates obligations.

Note

I would like to thank Paweł Łysakowski from Narodowy Bank Polski (National Bank of Poland) for sharing his knowledge and providing me with information on IBAN and Pierre-Yves Esclapez from the European Commission for his valuable remarks on P2P mobile payments and the VVA study on electronic money institutions. I am also indebted to Paweł Bułgaryn from the Polish Ministry of Finance and Tomasz Krawczyk from the Polish Ministry of Foreign Affairs for distributing my questionnaire on IBANs/IPANs to national payments experts in SEPA countries.

References

Ansip, A. 2015. "Keynote speech: Retail payments in the Digital Single Market", ECB and Suomen Pankki conference, *Getting the balance right: innovation, trust and regulation in retail payments*. Helsinki, 4 June, https://ec.europa.eu/commission/2014–2019/ansip/announcements/speech-vice-president-ansip-ecbsuomen-pankki-conference-helsinki-getting-balance-right-innovation_en date accessed 15 June 2015.

Bleyen, V.-A., Van Hove, L., and Hartmann, M. 2010. "Classifying payment instruments: A Matryoshka approach", *Communications & Strategies*, Vol. 1, No. 79, 73–94.

Bott, J., and Milkau, U. 2014. "Mobile wallets and current accounts: Friends or foes?", *Journal of Payments Strategy & Systems*, Vol. 8, No. 3, 289–299.

Cortet, M., and Lycklama, D. 2015. "PSD2 'Access to Account' (XS2A): Time to get real about banking API business strategies", *Innopay Blog, Payments Article*, 10.06.   https://www.innopay.com/blog/psd2-access-to-account-xs2a-time-to-get-real-about-banking-api-business-strategies/ date accessed 30 June 2015.

Electronic Money Directive (EMD). Directive 2000/46/EC of the European Parliament and of the Council of 18 September 2000 on the taking up, pursuit of and prudential supervision of the business of electronic money institutions. In: Official Journal of the European Communities of 27 October, L 275.

Electronic Money Directive 2 (EMD2). Directive 2009/110/EC of the European Parliament and of the Council of 16 September 2009 on the taking up, pursuit and prudential supervision of the business of electronic money institutions amending Directives 2005/60/EC and 2006/48/EC and repealing Directive 2000/46/EC. In: Official Journal of the European Communities of 10 October, OJ L 267.

Euro Banking Association, Working Group on Electronic and Alternative Payments. 2015. "Opinion paper on Digital Customer Services Interface (DCSI)", Version 1.0, 11 May.

European Commission. 2012. "Green Paper: Towards an integrated European market for card, internet and mobile payments", 11 January, Brussels.

European Commission. 2013. "Impact assessment accompanying the proposal for revising the Payment Services Directive" http://eur-lex.europa.eu/legal-content/EN/TXT/?uri=CELEX:52013SC0288 date accessed 25 June 2015.

European Commission. 2015. "Communication from the Commission of 19 May 2010 to the European Parliament, the Council, the European Economic and Social Committee and the Committee of the Regions – A Digital Agenda for Europe [COM(2010) 245 final – Not published in the Official Journal]" https://ec.europa.eu/digital-agenda/en/our-goals/pillar-i-digital-single-market http://europa.eu/legislation_summaries/information_society/strategies/si0016_en.htm http://ec.europa.eu/priorities/digital-single-market/, date accessed 25 May 2015.

Górka, J. 2013. *Efektywność instrumentów płatniczych w Polsce (Efficiency of payment instruments in Poland)*, Warsaw: Publishing House of the Faculty of Management, University of Warsaw. http://jgorka.pl/wp-content/uploads/e-book-Efektywno%C5%9B%C4%87-instrument%C3%B3w-p%C5%82atniczych-w-Polsce-J.G%C3%B3rka-2013.pdf. DOI: 10.7172/978-83-63962-30-2.

Harasim, J. 2013. *Współczesny rynek płatności detalicznych – specyfika, regulacje, innowacje (Contemporary retail payments market – specificity, regulations and innovations)*. Katowice: Publishing House of the Economic University in Katowice.

Interchange Fee Regulation (IF/MIF Reg), Regulation (EU) 2015/751 of the European Parliament and of the Council of 29 April 2015 on interchange fees for card-based payment transactions, In: Official Journal of the European Union of 19 May, OJ L 123.

International Organization for Standardization (ISO). 2007. "ISO 13616-1, Part 1: Structure of the IBAN and ISO 13616-2, Part 2: Role and responsibilities of the Registration Authority", with later amendments.

King, B. 2013. *Bank 3.0: why banking is no longer somewhere you go, but something you do.* Singapore: Marshall Cavendish Business.

Krueger, M. 2002. E-money regulation in the EU. In Pringle, R., and Robinson, M. (eds), *E-Money and Payment Systems Review*, London: Central Banking, pp. 239–251.

Leinonen, H. 2015. "Regulatory interventions in retail payments – why? – when? – how?". Presentation, *IIIrd International Congress on Non-Cash Payments*, Warsaw, 18 March, http://en.kongresplatnosci.pl/#prezentacje date accessed 30 June 2015.

London Economics and *iff* in association with PaySys. (2013). "Study on the impact of Directive 2007/64/EC on payment services in the internal market and on the application of Regulation (EC) NO 924/2009 on cross-border payments in the Community", February, http://ec.europa.eu/finance/payments/docs/framework/130724_study-impact-psd_en.pdf date accessed 25 June 2015.

Mersch, Y. 2015. "Introductory speech", ECB and Suomen Pankki conference, *Getting the balance right: innovation, trust and regulation in retail payments.* Helsinki, 4 June, https://www.ecb.europa.eu/press/key/date/2015/html/ sp150604.en.html date accessed 15 June 2015.

Narodowy Bank Polski (NBP). 2010. Ordinance No. 15/2010 of the President of Narodowy Bank Polski of 15 July 2010 on the method of numbering banks and bank accounts, NBP Official Journal No. 9/2010, item 9.

Narodowy Bank Polski (NBP). 2015. "Banks in Poland, register of bank codes – FAQs" http://www.nbp.pl/homen.aspx?f=/en/banki_w_polsce/ewidencja/pytania_ odpowiedzi_en.html, date accessed 27 May 2015.

Nooteboom, E. 2014. "Taking the SEPA journey: From fragmentation to EU-wide payments". *Journal of Payments Strategy & Systems*, Vol. 8, No. 4, 339–342.

Payment Account Directive (PAD). Directive 2014/92/EU of the European Parliament and of the Council of 23 July 2014 on the comparability of fees related to payment accounts, payment account switching and access to payment accounts with basic features. In: Official Journal of the European Union of 28 August, L 257/214.

Payment Services Directive (PSD). Directive 2007/64/EC of the European Parliament and of the Council of 13 November 2007 on payment services in the internal market amending Directives 97/7/EC, 2002/65/EC, 2005/60/EC and 2006/48/EC and repealing Directive 97/5/EC. In: Official Journal of the European Communities of 5 December, OJ L 319.

Payment Services Directive 2 (PSD2). Version adopted by the European Parliament for a Directive of the European Parliament and the Council on payment services in the internal market and amending Directives 2002/65/EC, 2013/36/ EU and 2009/110/EC and repealing Directive 2007/64/EC COM(2013)547, 8 October 2015.

Polish Act on Payment Services of 19 August 2011. Dz.U. 2011 Nr 100 poz. 1175.

Polish Financial Supervision Authority (KNF). 2015. Register of Payment Institutions. Quarterly Information, www.knf.gov.pl, date accessed 27 June 2015.

Polski Komitet Normalizacyjny (PKN, Polish Standardisation Committee), Polish Norm PN-F-01102 on IBAN, Bankowość i pokrewne usługi finansowe. Numer rachunku bankowego (NRB). Elementy i zasady tworzenia. December 2012.

PricewaterhouseCoopers (PwC). 2014. "Economic analysis of SEPA, benefits and opportunities ready to be unlocked by stakeholders", *Report*, 16 January.

Salmony, M. 2014. "The concept of an open standard interface for Controlled Access to Payment Services (CAPS). A commentary: Access to accounts – why banks should embrace an open future". *EPC Newsletter*, Issue 21, January.

Santamaria, J. 2014. "The emergence of new payment service providers and their impact on the regulatory and market environment". *Journal of Payments Strategy & Systems*, Vol. 8, No. 4, 407–414.

SEPA end-date Regulation. Regulation (EU) No. 260/2012 of the European Parliament and of the Council of 14 March 2012 establishing technical and business requirements for credit transfers and direct debits in euro and amending Regulation (EC) No. 924/2009. OJ L 94.

Settlement Finality Directive (SFD). Directive 2009/44/EC of the European Parliament and of the Council of 6 May 2009 amending Directive 98/26/EC on settlement finality in payment and securities settlement systems and Directive 2002/47/EC on financial collateral arrangements as regards linked systems and credit claims. In: Official Journal of the European Communities of 10 June, OJ L 146.

Skinner, C. 2014. *Digital bank: Strategies to launch or become a digital bank*, Singapore: Marshall Cavendish Business.

SWIFT. 2015. "SWIFT Directories Factsheet" http://www.swift.com/solutions/ factsheet_downloads/SWIFT_Directories_factsheet.pdf, date accessed 25 June 2015.

Van Hove, L. 1999. "Electronic money and the network externalities theory: lessons for real life". *Netnomics*, Vol. 1, No. 2, 137–171.

Van Hove, L. 2008. "On the war on cash and its spoils". *International Journal of Electronic Banking*, Vol. 1, 36–45.

VVA Europe. 2015. "Study on the impact of Directive 2009/110/EC on the taking up, pursuit and prudential supervision of the business of electronic money institutions". Presentation, *Payment Systems Expert Group meeting at the European Commission*, 28 April 2015.

Tirole, J. 2014. "Market failures and public policy", *Nobel Prize Lecture*, Stockholm University, 8 December.

7
Mobile Payments: The Second Wave

Malte Krueger

7.1 "M-payments": an elusive concept

When addressing the issue of m-payments, it is difficult to come up with a proper definition. The term remains as opaque as ever. As a consequence, "m-payments" refers to very different types of payments that only have in common that the mobile phone is used somewhere in the payment process. The mobile phone is used as:

- a plastic body,
- an identifier (using the SIM),
- a communication channel,
- a computer and
- a payment terminal.

Mobile phones are used for payments in the mobile Internet, they are used for proximity payments at the POS and they are used for P2P payments.

Thus, one and the same thing may sometimes be labelled as "m-payment" and sometimes as "e-payment". For instance, take someone who enters the Internet, initiates a purchase on the Amazon website and selects direct debit as payment option. If a laptop is used, the transaction is labelled "e-payment"; if a smart phone is used, it is labelled "m-payments". If someone uses a Near Field Communication (NFC) enabled credit card at the POS, he makes a "card payment"; if he uses an iPhone connected to the same underlying card account, it is an "m-payment". Or what about those chip cards that can be glued to the plastic body of a mobile phone? If such a device is used should the transaction be labelled as "m-payment" or "card payment"?

So, often there is no clear dividing line between m-payments and other types of payment. At the same time, the types of payment that are principally regarded as "m-payments" differ substantially. An "m-payment" could be a credit transfer initiated from a mobile phone, a transfer of e-money, a payment via the mobile Internet, a payment at the POS – using NFC or the camera of the phone and a QR code. Arguably, it could also be a payment where the mobile phone is used as a payment terminal. This fuzziness of the term makes it difficult to come up with generalisations.

7.2 The first m-payment wave

Currently, we are witnessing the second mobile payment wave. The first wave roughly went in parallel with the dotcom boom. The dotcom crash in the year 2000 also marked the end for many m-payment initiatives. Subsequently, it took more than ten years for m-payments to recover. Today, m-payments are, once again, grabbing the headlines and attracting a lot of investment. Given the boom-and-bust history of m-payments, it is instructive to consider what lessons can be drawn from past failures.

The first m-payment boom was driven by three related developments:

- the ongoing spread of mobile telephony,
- the expected expansion of m-commerce and
- the dotcom boom.

Principally, m-payments can be used for m-commerce, e-commerce and in the real world. In the real world, it is the pure number of mobile phones that makes them a promising payment device. In 2002, the number of mobile users passed the one billion mark. Moreover, the market was confident (with reason) that ultimately almost universal coverage could be reached. Phone-based chip cards already outnumbered payment cards with chips. According to EuroSmart, an industry body, in 2000 the chip card industry shipped 370 million micro-processor cards to the telecoms industry and 120 million to the banking industry.[1] Given that in some areas of the world almost everybody would own a mobile phone equipped with a chip, some observers doubted that a separate card-based e-purse would still be required for making payments.

The spread of mobile phones also held big promise for the future of m-commerce. Indeed, the industry was highly optimistic. While mobile phones were mostly used for voice traffic, SMS (Short Message Service) had caught on with surprising speed and operators were hoping that MMS (Multimedia Message Service) would become equally popular. The main bottleneck consisted of limited bandwidth of the mobile networks. However, as the huge amounts paid for 3G licenses showed, the mobile operators were prepared to invest heavily to change this. The UK auction in 2000 raised £22.5 billion (EUR 38.3 billion),[2] and the German auction even yielded EUR 50.8 billion. Such high bids were made possible by the dotcom boom that pushed up the value of mobile operators and made it easy for them to raise large sums of fresh capital. Not surprisingly, the dotcom crash also marked the end for many m-payment projects.[3] Capital became scarce and many projects were postponed or silently closed down. However, as the subsequent development showed, other factors, as well, were at work. These impediments were to make m-payments a niche product for almost ten years.

The mobile Internet was a big promise, but initially, mobile operators could not deliver. Data transmission was slow and hand-sets were too primitive. The first rollouts (remember WAP?) were a complete disaster, and even subsequent developments did not spark enthusiasm. Thus, at the POS, m-payments did not deliver, and on the mobile Internet there still was no market. In spite of all the hype, the technology was not yet ready to offer customers a breath-taking experience. With hindsight, we can say that mobile phones were not yet powerful enough to replace PCs and laptops as platforms for handling all kinds of interesting content. Moreover, bandwidth remained a problem.

Similarly, the use of mobile phones for POS payments was cumbersome and slow and could not convince potential users. Contactless was not (yet) an issue. Consider the example of Paybox: Founded in 1999, Paybox (50% owned by Deutsche Bank) launched a much hyped m-payment service in five European markets. It was usable at the POS on the Internet and for P2P payments. However, the number of users (consumers and merchants) remained limited. When looking the steps of a Paybox transaction at the POS, it becomes clear why:

1. Consumer provides merchant with his mobile phone number (or Paybox number).
2. Merchant transfers the number and the amount payable to Paybox.
3. Paybox calls you on your mobile phone and quotes the amount and the merchant.
4. Consumer authorises the payment with the Paybox PIN and confirms pressing hash.

Wonderful – isn't it? Somehow, users were not convinced, and when the dotcom boom burst, Deutsche Bank pulled the plug. Much has changed since 2000, and therefore, from a technological point of view the m-payment's future looks much brighter now than ten years ago.

The only model of the first m-payment wave that has survived and continues to thrive is operator billing. Paying for ring tones and other digital goods that can be downloaded directly on the mobile phone has been a huge success. The foremost customers are youngsters who often do not have a bank account or a credit card. So, operator billing is the only way they can make a payment. This billing service has been a huge success for mobile operators, and it is expected that billing volumes will continue to grow well into the future (Hernandez, 2014). This part of the m-payment business has somewhat remained in obscurity. Other ventures received much more attention. However, whatever else the mobile operators tried in m-payments was far less successful. Finally, the dotcom crash reduced the appetite for new pilots, and the whole m-payment topic ceased to draw public attention.

7.3 The second m-payment wave: technology

7.3.1 The rise of NFC

For quite some time contactless payments – using Near Field Communication (NFC) – have been a big issue. Contactless has not only sparked hopes that cards may finally win the "war on cash". NFC has also been one of the drivers of a second m-payment wave.[4] The reasons are straight-forward. First, payment applications can also be stored on a mobile phone and, second, an increasing number of mobile phones have been equipped with NFC. Thus, a phone can perform the same functions as a card. Moreover, a phone can provide additional functions, in particular, a mobile phone equipped with the necessary software (app) may allow a user to communicate with the card (to carry out balance enquires, view transactions data, etc.).

So far, implementation has been restricted by the lack of contactless acceptance points. With the spread of NFC terminals, this obstacle is losing significance. In the US, Apple Pay has been a big success, so far (see below), in spite of a limited availability of NFC terminals. However, one should not forget that NFC has been introduced to make card payments faster and more convenient, and it may still be the case that cards, rather than mobile phones, will be used primarily at NFC terminals (Judt and Viola, 2013).

For the moment, NFC is the most widely used technology for contactless payments. But it should not be forgotten that there are other technologies, such as Bluetooth and QR Code, that can be transmitted with the help of the mobile phone's camera or even additional devices using Magnetic Secure Transmission (MST) technology that allows mobile phones to communicate with the old generation of terminals (see www.looppay.com).

7.3.2   Host card emulation

The spread of NFC has given a big push to mPOS. But some impediments have remained. The standard mPOS model basically mimics the payment card. Instead of storing payment data on a chip card, they are stored on a secure element (SE) within the phone. That could be either the SIM card (model 1), an embedded SE of the phone (model 2) or a micro SD card (model 3). The first model requires banks to co-operate with mobile network operators (MNOs). This has been a conflict-prone issue in the early 2000s, and the same is true today. Moreover, since the customers of a bank are using different MNOs, a bank would have to deal with all MNOs in a particular country. The second model is currently used in co-operation with Apple. This model seems to work well but comes at a price for the banks. The third model is costly because banks would have to provide customers with the card – implying extra costs of the micro SD card and for its safe delivery.

Host Card Emulation (HCE) gets around these problems.[5] With the availability of phones with an NFC interface directly connected to the operating system (OS) of the phone, HCE can be used to side-step the necessity of an SE in the phone by "putting the SE in the cloud". This has been made possible by the 2014 version of Android (Android KitKat 4.4). Mobile phone holders may download a payment app that will store the payment credentials and manage the communication with contactless terminals. For payment terminals, the phone looks just like a contactless smart card.

Obviously, storing credentials in the SE is more secure than storing them in the unprotected memory of the phone. Permanent payment credentials would not be safe enough in the phone's memory. Thus, HCE requires an adjustment of the security architecture. Use of tokens would be a possibility. In order to be able to carry out a transaction even if the phone is offline, a new token would have to be stored on the phone ahead of the transaction.

Both card schemes, Visa and MasterCard have strongly endorsed tokenisation. Therefore, it does not come as a surprise that both card schemes have also been quick to endorse HCE.[6] While HCE may be a way to cut out MNOs, it involves a new player that may also be difficult to deal with, the providers of mobile operating systems, in particular Google, the provider of Android. Android is mostly free and open source. Still, Google is a powerful player with vast resources and its own ambitions in the world of payments. HCE would make the card industry less dependent on MNOs but more dependent on the providers of mobile operating systems. Moreover, the position of wallet providers such as Google, Amazon and PayPal may be strengthened.

The success of HCE at the POS cannot be taken for granted because HCE may have its drawbacks in terms of user experience. Since permanent payment credentials cannot be safely stored on the phone, payments can only be carried out if a token has been stored in advance. Therefore, whenever connectivity is a problem, payment may temporarily be impossible. Moreover, even if Android currently is the clear market leader, full market coverage would require that other mobile OS providers would also be on board. Thus, HCE would have to be working well with different operating systems, each potentially out in the market with various releases. Making sure that the result will be robust and convenient for users may be quite a challenge.

In Europe, the emergence of hub TSMs (Trusted Service Managers) may make it easier for MNOs and banks to co-operate. In Poland, MasterCard-owned Trevica (http://www.trevica.pl/) allows banks to upload payment applications to the phones of various MNOs. This model is currently exported to other European countries (see MasterCard, 2014b). Thus, the SIM-based approach is also advancing.

Contactless will succeed if it is fast and convenient. Maybe HCE-based mobile payments will be able to deliver. But given the complexities of the processes involved, one wonders whether this model is suited for payments made by "tap" or "wave". In the end, the winning model of contactless m-payments may be the reduced size plastic card glued to the back of the phone.[7]

7.3.3 The spread of smart phones and the rise of the mobile Internet

The payment requirements of e-commerce have been met to an astonishing degree by existing payment systems. In some cases, existing systems were used without any change (paper check, cash on demand, credit transfer). In other cases, there were smaller modifications (credit card or debit payment without signature). Finally, there are cases of more complex adaptations to the Internet (Verified by Visa, SecureCode and the integrated online credit transfer). The strong performance of existing payment systems has made it difficult for innovative newcomers to enter the market.

The same may happen in the world of m-commerce. After all, the payment environment is not so radically different from the e-payment environment. Nevertheless, there has been a big push to develop mobile wallets that are meant to store all kinds of payment credentials plus loyalty coupons, tickets, etc. In fact, there are so many offers that a "War of the Wallets" (Seyedi, 2015) has been diagnosed.

It is still too early to predict the outcome. However, it should not be forgotten that in e-payments, one particular provider gained a large slice of the market: PayPal. Looking at German m-payment figures, PayPal may be about to replicate this success in m-payments.

7.4   The second m-payment wave: some success stories

7.4.1   M-Pesa

It is not quite right to put M-Pesa into the second wave. In a way, M-Pesa and similar schemes appearing in Africa are a development in their own right. However, after the burst of the first m-payment wave, M-Pesa has been continuously used as a showcase and as a kind of benchmark for other markets. In particular, policy makers in industrialised countries, most notably Europe, used M-Pesa as a proof that there is gap in the payment system and that something needs to be done to promote m-payments.

So what is M-Pesa, a joint venture of Vodafone and African mobile operator Safaricom, all about? Two things are essential. First, M-Pesa has been rising in a country where most people do not have a bank account. Second, the success of M-Pesa is based not only on an m-payment technology but also on a network of agents that allow customers to convert cash into mobile money and vice versa.

In a way, M-Pesa has converted prepaid mobile accounts into rudimentary bank accounts. Most importantly, is has provided the unbanked with the ability to perform something like a credit transfer. M-Pesa was launched in 2007 in Kenya and subsequently expanded to Tanzania (2008), Fiji (2010), South Africa (2010), the Democratic Republic of the Congo (2012), India (2013), Mozambique (2013), Egypt (2013), Lesotho (2013) and Romania (2014).

Kenya is the showcase for M-Pesa. Safaricom, Vodafone's partner in Kenya, derives almost 20% of its revenue from M-Pesa. There are nineteen million customers, of which thirteen million are active on a monthly basis. The service is made accessible by an agent network of 81,025. Moreover, there are 122,000 registered merchants, of which 20% were actively using M-Pesa in 2014 (Safaricom 2015, p. 10 and p. 42).

It cannot be disputed that M-Pesa is providing a hugely beneficial service for its users. It is frequently overlooked that M-Pesa only works because there is a large agent network that allows users to convert cash into M-Pesa funds (e-money) and vice versa. Thus, the notion that systems like M-Pesa allow countries like Kenya to jump straight into the a cashless m-payment world is only 50% correct. The key benefit of M-Pesa has been to allow users to send and receive cash in a convenient way. As Figure 7.1 shows, there is a large net transfer from the city to district and rural areas.

To make this possible, there must be a corresponding flow of cash on the wholesale side of the business. Either large agents themselves have to transport cash to rural areas, or the banks who serve agents have to do this.

Meanwhile, M-Pesa does not only offer mP2P and mPOS but it is also venturing into other payment services, usually provided by banks: "salary disbursements, utility payments, airtime purchase and cashless distribution for companies such as Coca Cola, Unilever, East African Breweries Ltd, British American Tobacco, Nation Media, Standard Group etc." (Safaricom 2014, p. 42).

In markets with a developed banking system, fund transfers and the service of providing cash and accepting cash deposits are provided by the banking system. Off and on, banks are doing a pretty good job, and

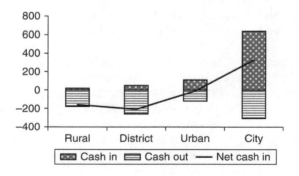

Figure 7.1 Average daily values of client transactions in Kenyan Shilling '000
Source: Based on Eijkman *et al.* (2010), p. 236.

there seems to be little scope for new contenders. Therefore, the notion that countries like Kenya are "ahead" and other regions like the European Union have to "catch up" is also completely misplaced. Rather, M-Pesa shows how the mobile phone, the prepaid accounts of the phone users and the agent networks that were initially built to sell prepaid airtime can be used to create a rudimentary banking system, providing huge benefits to the formerly unbanked.

7.4.2   Apple

Combining the mobile phone and NFC has been a topic for a number of years, already. (Remember the Visa pilot during the London Olympics?) But the topic really took off only with Apple's launch of "Apple Pay" in the US in October 2014 (Apple, 2014). Apple Pay allows its users to make contactless payments at the POS. It works on the iPhone 6 and the Apple Watch. Moreover, it is compatible with the iPhone 5, iPhone 5c and iPhone 5s.

Apple Pay relies on an NFC antenna and a secure embedded chip (secure element). Its Passbook software allows users to store multiple payment cards on the secure element alongside loyalty cards, boarding passes, coupons, etc. When using an iPhone the user can rely on Apple's Touch ID for authentication. However, when using the Apple Watch, this security feature is not available; users simply have to double-click.

Like other initiatives, Apple Pay tries to replace the plastic card at the physical POS. But Apple will not be involved in the payment flow and will not track customer transactions. Thus, for the moment it acts more like a technical service provider. It is noteworthy, however, that Apple does not simply put a toe into the water. Rather it takes a determined step, partnering with the main card schemes, American Express, MasterCard and Visa, and most of the large bank card issuers in the US (including Bank of America, Capital One Bank, Chase, Citi and Wells Fargo).

Apple's move has been heralded as "New Era at Cash Register" (Isaac, 2014). But what exactly is going to change? If Apple (and other contenders) were successful, cards would be replaced to some extent by smartphones. But that does not mean that the traditional players of the large four-party card schemes will also be replaced. For the moment, Apple relies on these players to deliver its payment service. Apple itself provides a wallet that contains card credentials that can be used for payments. Unlike PayPal, Apple is not integrated into the payment flow. Apple does not provide e-money or payment accounts. In this sense, the Apple wallet is more like a "container" whereas the PayPal wallet includes PayPal branded payment services. This matters from a business point of view. Apple does not pose a threat to financial institutions, yet.

There is a hitch, however. If press reports are to be believed, Apple receives a hefty fee of 0.15% for providing "container services" (or "wallet services") (Fiveash, 2014). The mere fact that Apple has been able to negotiate such a high fee already shows its strong position vis-á-vis the banks. If Apple Pay were to become a success and a significant share of consumers were to use it, Apple's service as a kind of gatekeeper would be even more valuable. The banks would be more and more dependent on Apple. So far, banks have always tried to avoid such a position of dependency. In the past, this has been a major stepping-stone in joint projects between mobile operators and banks. Banks were hesitant to put payment applications on operator-controlled SIM cards. In partic-ular, they did not like the idea of having to pay operators for using the SIM. Now, in the end, this is the model they have agreed upon with Apple. Maybe in the future there will be a similar deal with Google.[8] But will the banks be happier and less dependent with these two giants as partners than they would be with the operators?

It is still too early to predict how well Apple Pay will be doing. Current performance seems to be promising. Market research found that Apple Pay has surpassed PayPal as a mobile payment instrument in the US (see 451 Research, 2015). However, a lot will depend on the success of EMV (the Europay, MasterCard and Visa technical standard) implementation in the US. With the installation of new chip-enabled card terminals the NFC-capability is likely to spread significantly.[9]

According to Paypers (2015), in early spring 2015 Apple Pay was accepted at 700,000 merchant locations equipped with NFC termi-nals. Even if these acceptance figures sound impressive, success is not a foregone conclusion. Given that the large card payment processor and acquirer First Data alone serves 3.9 million merchant locations in the US, 700,000 locations is not much more than a drop in the bucket. Thus, a significant replacement of cards by mobile phones seems a long way off. Worse, in spite of the customary user friendliness of Apple prod-ucts, customers may be disgruntled by the lack of acceptance points and finally quit using m-payments.

Apple Pay is expected to be rolled out in other countries, as well. Looking at Europe, things may be more difficult for Apple. Even though parts of Europe are ahead of the US in terms of EMV implementation, regulation may prove to be an obstacle. First, the EU has just passed a regulation of interchange fees that sets a maximum of 0.3% for credit card transactions. Given such a low value, it seems highly unlikely that European banks would be prepared to offer the same 0.15% that the US banks reportedly are paying.[10] So, the question is whether Apple would be prepared to settle for substantially less. If not, it would have to convince merchants (the beneficiaries of low interchange fees) to contribute.

The EU also regulates payment service providers more tightly. The new PSD2 has introduced "payment initiation" as a service that will be regulated in the future.[11] When drawing up the PSD2 draft version, regulators had services in mind that allow payers to initiate a credit transfer and immediately send a confirmation to the merchant – so-called "online banking based e-payment" solutions (OBeP). However, Apple provides a very similar service with Apple Pay. Apple helps card holders to access their card account and initiate a payment transaction. The issuer of the card even relies on Apple to authenticate the owner of the card account. The need to get a payment institution license may be a show-stopper for Apple.

Apart from regulation, another important factor that may make it more difficult for Apple to extract fees from other market players is the lower market share of Apple phones in Europe, where Android is the clear market leader.

Apple basically offers part of its base of dedicated Apple users as potential m-payment customers (the shaded area in Figure 7.2). What do the banks have to gain? They are providing an extra service to their customers that will make it easier for them to retain existing customers and gain new ones. Partnering with Apple allows them to limit the required investment and to profit from Apple's strong brand. As noted above, this comes at a price. Issuing banks pay a transaction fee to Apple, and they are becoming dependent on Apple.

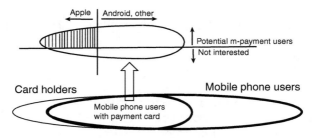

Figure 7.2 What Apple has to offer to card issuers

Meanwhile Google shows that it is unwilling to leave the m-payment field to Apple. Google has bought "Softcard", the payment joint venture of US mobile operators, and has announced that it will offer an Android-based solution, "Android Pay," similar to Apple Pay (Paypers, 2015).

Overall, one may wonder what has prompted Apple to enter the payment arena. In a way, the move into payment is reminiscent of Apple's bold move into selling music over iTunes. When Apple started its iTunes service, it also had only a limited customer base to sell to. Still, it was able to extract favourable conditions from the music industry. At a reasonable price, Apple was able to offer legal music downloads at unparalleled ease of use. The rest is history. Apple ventured into selling apps and became the most expensive brand in the world. Will the same magic work in the field of payments? Probably not. The reason is simple. The payment industry has done a better job in its own field of expertise than the music industry. In spite of frequent allegations to the contrary, there are no huge gaps in the payments field. Payment cards (and cash) are working well at the POS, and they are getting more convenient. Actually, Apple is piggybacking on the industry's current move towards contactless.

But whatever the future brings for Apple Pay, its start has been promising and it shows how one determined player may shake things up.

7.4.3 Square

Like fifteen years ago, the mobile phone is predominantly seen as a consumer device and correspondingly as a potential replacement of the payment card. Less noticed are developments on the acquiring side of the market. The mobile phone is increasingly used as a low-cost payment terminal for POS payments. The best-known example is Square, a US company. But the idea to use smart phones as payment terminals has also been adopted by other players: established acquirers or new upstarts. In some cases, the use of a smart phone as payment terminal does not even require additional hardware. Apart from the mobile phone and an acceptance contract, merchants only need to download a payment application. But often, as also in the case of Square, the phone is converted into a simple form of POS terminal via a card reader that is connected to the phone. In the US, the business model based on the mobile phone (with an attached card reader) used as a mobile card terminal ("m-terminal") has become an impressive success (see also PaySys Consultancy, 2011). Square, the American PSP that has pioneered this model, is serving three million customers (individuals and businesses) (see www.squareup.com). In August 2012, Square could even win Starbucks with its 7,000 stores in the United States. Currently, the company is processing $10 billion in transactions. A recent financing operation valued Square at almost $3.3 billion (Guynn, 2013).

Like PayPal, Square is another example of the successful use of the subacquiring model. Square allows merchants to accept credit cards without entering into an explicit contract with an acquirer. Only under certain conditions do merchants have to enter into a contractual relationship with the acquirer with whom Square works (Paymentech).

In Europe, the Square business model has been copied by a number of companies such as Adyen, iZettel, SumUp, Payleven and Streetpay. These companies are expanding fast and are active on an international basis. Apart from these newcomers, established PSPs are also offering apps that allow merchants to accept card payments via smartphones (to name just a few examples, in Germany: B+S, ConCardis and TeleCash; in Spain: Euro6000).

It is yet too early to draw any conclusions. But current developments show that there may be a strong business case for m-payments in a segment that went mostly unnoticed: the merchant side of the market. If merchants do not have to buy expensive terminals, and if they can carry out software updates by themselves, card acceptance becomes much cheaper. Consequently, the range of potential card acceptors becomes much larger than it used to be. This is good news for merchants, cardholders, schemes and issuers. For PSPs on the acquiring side, the implications may be less favourable. Renting and servicing terminals may become a shrinking business segment. But, there are still some important issues to be addressed.

First and foremost, there is the security issue. Payment terminals are sophisticated pieces of hardware and software that do not come cheap. But there is a good reason for that: security. We have all learned that a flexible and intelligent device like the PC that is capable of running new programs is very convenient. But we also learned that convenience comes at a cost. Intelligent machines can get infected and do things we do not want them to do. The smarter mobile phones get and the more they are used for payments the bigger the danger becomes that they also will be infected by malign viruses. Given this threat, it remains to be seen whether the smartphone will become a payment terminal used beyond the segment of small traders with a low payment volumes.

It is still open whether the Square business model can be implemented one-to-one in Europe. Europe is an EMV area. So, card-present transactions should be chip and PIN. Moreover, EMV will not provide any benefits in terms of safety if sensitive payment data can be typed in on any smartphone. Thus, it is not surprising that Visa insists that card readers come with a secure keyboard for typing in the PIN. Chip card readers with a secure PIN pad – that does not sound like a cheap solution. But Square, iZettle and others seem to have found ways to provide cheap terminals that are chip-capable. Thus, the model may thrive even in an EMV world.

Meanwhile, Square has been moving into another field that is a traditional banking turf: credit (Square, 2015). Access to payment data seems to give Square the ability to offer its customers credit at competitive rates. If this should prove to be successful, banks should start to feel threatened.

7.5 Mobile P2P (mP2P)

M-Pesa has shown that mP2P may be a big success. However, M-Pesa evolved in an environment in which access to banking services is limited. It remains to be seen whether mP2P can be equally successful in the developed world.

For the moment, there seems to be strong push into this area. New companies are expanding fast and have built a dedicated client base. The US upstart Venmo, in particular, is in a strong position. It has been taken over by PayPal, a company with a proven track record in the world of e-payments. In the past, PayPal has successfully implemented a wallet for e-payments, turning the email address into a kind of bank account number. PayPal does not only have a large customer base of consumers but also a large merchant base. PayPal has proven itself capable of adjusting its systems to the requirements of mobile commerce. With the rise of the smartphone and the increasing implementation of NFC, it seems likely that PayPal will also be able to make the shift to the "real" POS, converting the mobile phone number into a kind of bank account number.

mP2P is also likely to profit from the installation of real-time bank transfers. Such systems, like FasterPay in the UK or Express Elixir and BlueCash in Poland (Górka, 2015), allows bank account owners to send funds in "real time" to other accounts.[12] If widely implemented, such systems would allow providers to cease using expensive funding methods such as credit cards. On the one hand, real-time credit transfers can be seen as direct competition to mP2P offered by PSPs like Venmo. If a real-time bank transfer can be initiated via a mobile banking app, why use an intermediary such as Venmo? However, given ease of use and additional services such as buyer protection for PayPal users, mP2P providers may actually benefit from real-time credit transfers.

However, there are also problems that have to be overcome. First, security is an issue. Lately there have been complaints about systems like Venmo because of weaknesses in its security. Such problems have to be taken seriously, but ultimately it should be possible to fix them. However, in the long run, another issue may prove to be more serious: the unproven business case. Unless funded via credit card, Venmo payments are free, at the moment. The crucial question is whether users could be made to pay in the future. For now, market observers are doubtful. Thus, such mP2P systems need to find other revenue sources such as advertising, or they need to switch to a more traditional model that distinguishes merchants and consumers and provides merchant services against a fee.

7.6   Mobile operators on the side-lines?

Mobile operators have been experimenting for almost twenty years with m-payments. They have rolled out pilots, have formed (and disbanded) alliances, have partnered with banks and have lobbied regulators. All in all, a huge amount of money and management attention has gone into this area. But the results have been limited. To be sure, there have been some successes. Billing for ring tones, etc., has been a huge success. In countries with malfunctioning banking systems, mobile operators have been able to implement successful m-payments schemes like M-Pesa that provide some basic banking services to the unbanked.[13]

But apart from that, there seems to be little to show for the effort. In the US, AT&T, T-Mobile, and Verizon formed a joint venture ("Softcard", formerly known as "ISIS" and then rebranded for obvious reasons) to implement a joint method of m-payments. However, in 2015, Softcard was sold to Google and the payment application was integrated into Google wallet. Exit the mobile operators.

In Germany, to take another example, mpass was launched in 2008 as a joint venture of O2 and Vodafone with Telekom later joining. However, success has been limited and, at the moment, only O2 and Wirecard Bank, the issuer of the accompanying credit card, are actively promoting the system. Undeterred, German operators have started a new project "NFC City Berlin".

In the UK, Everything Everywhere, Vodafone and O2 formed a joint venture to launch a mobile wallet. However, after complaints from competitors, the EU Commission launched an in-depth investigation which delayed the project.

In the end, one wonders why mobile operators want to be in payments. Payment is a service that requires users' trust. In this respect, telephone companies have consistently ranked at the end of the field in surveys carried out in Germany, Austria and Switzerland (see Table 7.1)

It would also help if the customer base were relatively stable. But mobile phone customers are notoriously fickle and frequently changing the provider. (Maybe churn is such a big problem that telcos hope to use payments to reduce churn?)

Payment requires risk management. While telcos also have to have some risk management in place, this is unlikely to be of the quality required for payments. Payments is increasingly becoming a compliance business. Do telcos want to get deeply involved in that? Finally, payments are not core business. The payment business is complicated, demands a lot of attention and may easily get you bad press. So, all in all, it is not clear why telcos keep on trying.

Maybe it would be best for mobile operators to concentrate on the niche (not a small one!) of digital goods charged to the customer account. This type of operator billing has functioned well and is predicted to do well in the future.

7.7 European policy

As the examples discussed above show, individual players can be highly successful when bringing m-payment schemes to the market. Using standardised infrastructure, they tailor their products to the needs of their clients and carry out changes and improvements of their products

Table 7.1 Survey results: which payment service providers do you trust on the Internet?

	Germany	Austria	Switzerland
Banks	61.3%	69.4%	56.5%
Established PSPs	56.7%	47.3%	49.8%
Payment card companies	36.8%	58.6%	63.5%
Providers of shopping platforms	43.3%	46.2%	39.6%
Telecommunication companies	20.8%	20.1%	17.7%
ISPs	10.0%	5.3%	16.0%
No preference	10.1%	6.3%	10.8%

Source: Klees *et al.* (2013, p. 60).

as they go along. Such an approach may take a long time to cover the entire market. But by moving fast and not having to co-ordinate with other market players the launch of the product can be carried out fairly quickly. This approach is exemplified by players such as M-Pesa, Square and Apple.

The approach favoured by European policy makers looks different. They want ex ante co-ordination to make sure that new products reach the entire European market. Important elements of the EU political approach can be found in a resolution of the European Parliament (EP) (European Parliament, 2012) which is based on the EU Commission's Green Paper on "an integrated European market for card, Internet and mobile payments" (European Commission, 2011). The EP wants mandated EU-wide acceptance:

> The European Parliament...is therefore of the opinion that all national card, mobile and internet payment schemes should join or turn themselves into a pan-European SEPA-compliant scheme, so that all card, mobile and internet payments would be accepted everywhere in the SEPA, and that a necessary period should be suggested by the Commission for this transition. (European Parliament, 2012, R6)

Moreover, it stresses the importance of standards and of a co-ordinated implementation effort (European Parliament, 2012, R18).[14] As far as the development of standards goes, the EP wants, of course, that a good governance model is used and that all stakeholders have a say. Therefore, the EP asks the EU Commission "to propose a better SEPA govern-ance,...and allowing the development of technical and security stand-ards to be organised separately in support of the implementation of the related legislation; calls for a more balanced representation of all stake-holders in the further development of common technical and security standards for payment schemes" (European Parliament, 2012, R28).

Obviously, in the area of payments, security is important, and accord-ingly the EP also has something to say about security standards. In particular, it wants a "common governing body setting the require-ments" (European Parliament, 2012, R54).

In order to comply with the demands of the EP (which are largely based on the Commission's own ideas), the EU Commission has devised "The 2015 Rolling Plan on ICT Standardisation" (European Commission, 2015). In this "Rolling Plan" the EU Commission calls for more stand-ardisation and interoperability:

The advent of an integrated system of mobile payments in the EU is hampered by the lack of cross-border standardised and inter-operable technical solutions. The absence of shared standards, standardisation gaps and the lack of interoperability between the various market players are delaying the mass market adoption of this innovative payment method. (European Commission, 2015, p. 56).

But so far, the EU Commission does not envision any concrete steps:

The European Commission doesn't plan yet to engage into specific legislation since it requires a more mature market. However, it will continue the co-operation and discussion with the institutional players and the ESOs, and will launch/support appropriate standardisation initiatives as soon as gaps and needs are identified. DG GROW will pursue its work on the mapping of the market for mobile payments. (European Commission, 2015, p. 56).

While favouring a co-ordinated approach, European policy makers have been suspicious of co-operation. Antitrust concerns have frequently led to investigations that cost market participants valuable time.

Already during the first m-payment wave, regulators were anxious to prevent any strong position in the emerging m-payment market. For instance, when the Spanish bank BBVA teamed up with Telefonica Moviles in 2000 to come up with a joint m-payment scheme (Movilpago), they were instantly scrutinised by the Spanish competition watchdog (see Krueger, 2001). Anti-trust authorities demanded that other banks and telcos were allowed to participate. Obviously, this slowed down the whole project, and then the m-payment wave burst and everything surrounding m-payments became much more difficult.

The same has happened in the recent past when "Project Oscar," a planned joint venture of Everything Everywhere, Orange and Vodafone, became subject to an "in-depth investigation" of the European Commission (European Commission, 2012a and 2012b). In the end, the joint venture was cleared, but the participants lost valuable time and have been pursuing other co-operations since (Meyer, 2012).

Anti-trust is not the only concern. Policy makers are also prescribing ever-more detailed security measures that PSPs have to implement. In the field of e-payments, the European Banking Authority (EBA) has published binding security guidelines (EBA, 2014). These measures are likely to find a legislative underpinning in the to-be-agreed Payment Services Directive 2 (PSD2). The European Central Bank (ECB) has proposed almost identical guidelines for m-payments (ECB, 2014). If enacted, these security guidelines could prove to be a heavy burden for new m-payment ventures.

7.8   Summing up

The future role in payments of the mobile phone is still uncertain. For sure, Internet access will be increasingly carried out via mobile devices. But it is not yet clear whether that requires completely new payment instruments. Equally, the mobile phone may play a more important role at the POS. Still, it is by no means certain that it will replace cards to a large extend.

As far as policy goes, it is certainly true that standards are important. However, the approach favoured by the European Commission to look for a co-operative solution ex ante ("with all stakeholders") is a blueprint for standstill. Current innovations are building on standards such as common payment protocols or NFC. Nevertheless, in the product space, covering the relationship between service providers and consumers or merchants, proprietary solutions seem to be much more successful. This is a market-based "trial-and-error approach" rather than an attempt to fix everything between dozens of parties at the drawing board. Unfortunately, the current European regulatory paradigm seems to be completely different.

Notes

1. See Eurosmart market figures 2004–1999 (http://www.eurosmart.com/images/doc/WorkingGroups/Mkt-technoWG/eurosmart-figures-archives.pdf)
2. See National Audit Office (2001).
3. Krueger (2001, p. 8) provides a (non-exhaustive) list of m-payments schemes existing in the year 2001. Almost all of these have disappeared.
4. The first wave had its boom and bust roughly in parallel with the dotcom boom and bust. See Krueger (2001).
5. More information on HCE can be found on the Android website (https://developer.android.com/guide/topics/connectivity/nfc/hce.html) and in Consult Hyperion (2014).
6. See press releases from Visa (2014) and MasterCard (2014a).
7. But to be honest, while writing these lines the (Germany-based) author of this article is still waiting for an opportunity to carry out a contactless card payment.
8. Google's operating system Android is a more open system than iOS. From the banks' points of view this is an advantage.
9. There is no necessary link between EMV and NFC, but is likely that the installation of new chip-enabled terminals will lead to a huge increase in NFC capabilities.

10. Terms of commercial agreements for Apple Pay also seem to be an issue in Apple's negotiations with Canadian banks. See Trichur and Wakabayashi (2015).
11. "Payment initiation service" means a service to initiate a payment order at the request of the payment service user with respect to a payment account held at another payment service provider; Art 4 (32) (version of 1 December 2014). See also PaySys Consultancy (2015).
12. Salmony (2015) discusses the potential of a pan-European P2P m-payment system.
13. It still remains somewhat of a mystery why policy makers in developed countries think that the developed world urgently needs an M-Pesa-type m-payment system.
14. However, at the same time, the EP also does not want the EU Commission to mandate standards: "given the fast growing but, at present, immature phase of market development for electronic and mobile payments, imposing mandatory standards in these key areas for the enhancement of the digital single market in Europe would entail the risk of negative effects for innovation, competition and market growth" (R21).

Bibliography

451 Research. 2015. "Apple Pay outperforming PayPal in mobile payments, according to new 451 Research survey", New York, April 21.

Apple Inc. 2014. "Apple announces Apple Pay", Press release. (https://www.apple.com/pr/library/2014/09/09Apple-Announces-Apple-Pay.html).

Consult Hyperion. 2014. "HCE and SIM Secure Element: It's not black and white", Discussion Paper, June 2014 (http://www.chyp.com/assets/uploads/Documents/2014/06/HCE_and_SIM_Secure_Element.pdf).

Eijkman, Frederik, Jake Kendall, and Ignacio Mas. 2010. "Bridges to cash: The retail end of M-PESA. The challenge of maintaining liquidity for M-PESA Agent Networks", *Savings and Development*, No. 2, 219–252.

European Banking Authority (EBA). 2014. "Final guidelines on the security of Internet payments", EBA/GL/2014/12, 19 December 2014.

European Central Bank (ECB). 2013. "Recommendations for the security of mobile payments", Draft document for public consultation, November 2013.

European Commission. 2011. "Green Paper. Towards an integrated European market for card, Internet and mobile payments", Brussels, 11.1.2012, COM(2011) 941 final. (http://eur-lex.europa.eu/legal-content/EN/TXT/PDF/?uri=CELEX:52011DC0941&from=EN)

European Commission. 2012a. "Commission opens in-depth investigation into the creation of a mobile commerce joint venture by UK mobile operators Telefónica, Vodafone and Everything Everywhere", Press release, Brussels, 13 April 2012.

European Commission. 2012b. "Commission clears the creation of a mobile commerce joint venture by UK mobile operators Telefónica, Vodafone and Everything Everywhere", Press release, Brussels, 5 September 2012.

European Commission. 2015. "The rolling plan for ICT standardisation. Directorate-General for Internal Market, Industry, Entrepreneurship and SMEs", published on 24 March 2015, (http://ec.europa.eu/newsroom/dae/document. cfm?doc_id=9137).

European Parliament. 2012. "Card, Internet and mobile payments. European Parliament resolution of 20 November 2012 on 'Towards an integrated European market for card, Internet and mobile payments'", (2012/2040(INI)).

Fiveash, Kelly. 2014. "Apple Pay is a tidy payday for Apple with 0.15% cut, sources say", *The Register*, 13 September 2014, (http://www.theregister. co.uk/2014/09/13/apple_to_get_15_cents_for_every_100_dollar_payment_on_ its_pay_service_says_ft/).

Górka, Jakub. 2015. "Instant payments from the Polish perspective", Meeting of the Payment Systems Market Expert Group, European Commission, Brussels, 28 April 2015.

Guynn, Jessica. 2013. "Square taps into the mobile payment business", *Los Angeles Times*, 1 February 2013, (http://www.latimes.com/business/la-fi-square-dorsey-20130201,0,5416478.story)

Hernandez, Will. 2014. "The overlooked mobile payment: direct carrier billing", *Mobile Payments Today*, July 1 (http://www.mobilepaymentstoday.com/articles/ the-overlooked-mobile-payment-direct-carrier-billing/).

Isaac, Mike. 2014. "Apple Pay Signals New Era at Cash Register", *New York Times Online*, Sept. 30, 2014. (http://www.nytimes.com/2014/10/01/technology/ apple-pay-signals-new-era-at-cash-register.html)

Judt, Ewald and Loredana Viola. 2013. "M-Payments – Status und Akzeptanzbarrieren", *ÖBA*, 9/13, pp. 642–648.

Klees, Maria, Malte Krueger and Aline Eckstein. 2013. "Der Internetzahlungsverkehr aus Sicht der Verbraucher in D-A-CH – Ergebnisse der Umfrage IZV11", Eine Studie des ECC über den Online-Payment-Markt in Deutschland, Österreich und der Schweiz aus Verbrauchersicht, Ausgewählte Studien des ECC Band 3.

Krueger, Malte. 2001. "The future of m-payments – Business options and policy issues", Background Paper No. 2, Electronic Payment Systems Observatory, Institute for Prospective Technological Studies, Sevilla, (http://www.h-ab.de/ fileadmin/dokumente/krueger/2001_M-Payments_ePSO%20Background%20 Paper%202.pdf).

MasterCard. 2014a. "MasterCard to use host card emulation (HCE) for NFC-based mobile payments", Press release, (http://newsroom.mastercard.com/ press-releases/mastercard-to-use-host-card-emulation-hce-for-nfc-based-mobile-payments/).

MasterCard. 2014b. "Partnership creates a 'one stop shop' for banks and mobile operators to speed development of NFC payments offering to their customers", Press release, 25 February 2014, (http://newsroom.mastercard.com/press-releases/deutsche-telekom-telefonica-deutschland-vodafone-and-mastercard-join-forces-to-simplify-mobile-payments/).

Meyer, David. 2012. "Vodafone, O2, T-Mobile and Orange win EU thumbs-up for mobile wallet scheme", www.zdnet.com, 5 September 2012, (http://www. zdnet.com/article/vodafone-o2-t-mobile-and-orange-win-eu-thumbs-up-for-mobile-wallet-scheme/#!).

National Audit Office. 2001. "The auction of radio spectrum for the third generation of mobile telephones. Report by the Comptroller and Auditor General", HC 233 Session 2001–2002: 19 October 2001.

Paypers. 2015. "Google launches Android Pay, mobile payments scene heats up", Friday 29 May 2015, (http://www.thepaypers.com/mobile-payments/google-launches-android-pay-mobile-payments-scene-heats-up/760078-16).

PaySys Consultancy. 2011. "M-Payments: The acquiring side", *PaySys SEPA Newsletter*, August 2011, (http://paysys.de//index.php?option=com_content& task=view&id=42&Itemid=73).

PaySys Consultancy. 2015. "Who are the new kids on the regulatory PSD II-block?", *PaySys Report 01/2015*, (http://paysys.de//index.php?option=com_c ontent&task=view&id=42&Itemid=73).

Safaricom Limited. 2015. "Annual Report 2014".

Salmony, Michael. 2015. "Pan-European peer-to-peer payment by mobile phone including considerations on technical and commercial implementation options", *Banking and Information Technology (BIT)*, forthcoming.

Seyedi, Sep. 2015. "War of the Wallets", Crunch Network, posted 10 February, (http://techcrunch.com/2015/02/10/war-of-the-wallets/).

Square. 2015. "Square secures funding from new and existing investors to expand its popular small business financing program", *Square News*, 12 May 2015, (https://squareup.com/news/capital-investment).

Trichur, Rita and Daisuke Wakabayashi. 2015. "Apple Pay plans to launch in Canada this fall", *The Wall Street Journal*, Updated 17 April 2015, (http://www. wsj.com/articles/apple-pay-plans-to-launch-in-canada-this-fall-1429280816).

Visa International. 2014. "Visa to enable secure cloud-based mobile payments", Press release from 19 February 2014, (http://investor.visa.com/news/news-details/2014/Visa-to-Enable-Secure-Cloud-Based-Mobile-Payments/default. aspx).

8
Decentralised Blockchained and Centralised Real-Time Payment Ledgers: Development Trends and Basic Requirements

Harry Leinonen

8.1 Introduction

The number of virtual currencies based on blockchain technology grows rapidly, counting more than 400 different schemes today (ECB, 2012, 2015; Raymaekers, 2015). Bitcoin (Bitcoin, 2015) is the largest and most widely known, but it has several competitors such as Ripple (Ripple, 2015), Litecoin (Litecoin, 2015) and Peercoin (Peercoin, 2015) to name a few, and a longer list can be found at Cryptocoincharts (Cryptocoincharts, 2015). The term virtual currencies can be used to cover a larger variety of different Internet payment systems, some of which are not based on blockchain technology, but traditional centralised real-time accounts. PayPal (PayPal, 2015) is probably the best known centralised world-wide Internet payment system. In this chapter the term virtual currency will only cover the subset of virtual currencies which is commonly referred to as cryptocurrencies, that is, those that are based on blockchain technology and decentralised account databases or files. These payment instruments will be compared to traditional payment systems based on centralised account databases. Virtual currencies and blockchain technology have often been greeted as the new technology revolution that will fundamentally change paying in the future (see for example Harvey, 2015), but there are also more critical voices (see for example Tymoigne, 2015). The European Banking Authority (EBA) has published an Opinion on virtual currencies presenting potential benefits but also several severe risks (EBA, 2014). The aim of this chapter is to analyse the common features and elements of payment instruments in general and how virtual currencies and traditional payment instruments differ from each other. It is also worth noting that virtual currencies are mainly compared to traditional payment instruments and not to traditional currencies because virtual currencies are regarded as a new way of paying. Virtual currencies provide, in most cases, also a new currency, but the blockchain technology is independent from currencies because a blockchain ledger can operate in any currency even with traditional currencies, book-entry securities, digital gold accounts, etc.

The basic elements of any electronic payment system are

- the accounting methodology,
- the settlement asset or media,
- the currency unit of account for monetary liabilities,
- the infrastructure for processing payment transactions and
- the private and public regulations and supervision of the system.

These basic elements will be found in some form in every payment system. The blockchain technology provides just a new accounting methodology, which could be used by different types of electronic payment systems. The virtual currencies as payment instruments consist of several simultaneous changes to all of these elements in comparison to traditional payment instruments. The settlement asset, the currency, the infrastructure and the regulatory/supervisory regime are all different in virtual currencies. However, utilising blockchain technology does not require changes to these other components. For example, blockchain technology could also be used with traditional currencies and for traditional deposit accounts (see Ripple, 2015) and their project with Commonwealth Bank of Australia and Chromaway (Chromaway, 2015) and their bitcoin-based project with Cuber/LHV Bank in Estonia). This chapter analyses how these elements are covered within virtual currencies, and it ends with the development of some alternatives and conclusions.

Please note that the term "virtual currency" has several meanings; it is used to describe a payment instrument for transferring funds, a specific currency as unit of account and a settlement asset containing funds of value. It seemed to be the simplest solution to use the term for all different meanings as the context clarifies in which sense the term has been used; therefore, the term is in most instances used without extra attributes specifying the exact alternative meaning. The author hopes that this chapter will be helpful in clarifying the different dimensions of virtual currencies and especially the related regulatory issues.

8.2   The accounting methodology

There are several descriptions and definitions of blockchain technology (see for example Segendorf, 2014; ECB, 2015) starting from the original proposal (Nakamoto, 2008). The basic idea of the blockchain technology is to introduce a method to make transfers within a decentralised ledger of accounts securely and reconciling the complete ledger at the same time. The secure reconciling implies that the overall total of funds booked on individual accounts in the different parts of the decentralised ledger is exactly the same after each fund transfer. The total of the funds cannot be changed via fund transfers as the methodology ensures that any debit from one account will always be matched by a similar credit to another account. This is standard accounting practice, but what blockchaining has introduced is that this process can be automated and secured by cryptography in a decentralised ledger environment. The total funds in the decentralised blockchained ledger can only be increased by issuing more funds by an issuer and reduced by de-issuing by the issuer. Note that Bitcoin and similar virtual currencies do not provide de-issuing capabilities as they lack redeemability, but this is a design choice for particular virtual currencies and not a fundamental feature of the blockchain technology.

It is important in blockchained systems to store the transaction log to enable verification of the chain of transactions in order to avoid so-called double spending that is paying twice with the same electronic funds. An electronic account registration could otherwise be too easy to just copy and reuse. The blockchaining assures that there is only one unbroken transaction chain for each account for which the transactions have been reconciled with corresponding sending/receiving accounts. This can in a simplified example be viewed as system in which every transaction to accounts receives a sequentially increasing transaction number and the blockchain transaction log ensures that there are no duplications or omissions in this sequencing. If somebody would copy an account and try to do an additional transaction, there would be a duplication of this transaction number, and the transaction log would discard any duplication of this transaction number. Maintaining an overall consistent transaction log and overall reconciling is therefore the essential feature of blockchain technology.

Virtual currencies are also called cryptocurrencies because the transfers from one account to another are secured by public key encryption, that is, all transfers between accounts are secured by the public and private keys linked to sending and receiving accounts. This is another essential feature in ensuring the correctness of transfers between two accounts.

Blockchain technology provides a decentralised ledger and secure transfer capability between the ledger accounts. The numeric amounts booked on blockchained ledger accounts can represent rights to any kind of assets in the same way as in traditional ledgers. These assets could for example be deposits, other receivables, bonds, shares, commodities, etc., depending on what has been issued into these specific ledger accounts. The ledgers need therefore to have an issuer or an issuer community, which maintains the totals of the security accounts. This function can be organised in different ways, which will be analysed in the section on infrastructural aspects. In case of real assets like bonds, shares and commodities, there is a need for a depository function, which assures that the amount issued into the ledger is backed by the same amount of real assets. The transfers in the blockchained ledger representing payments could as well be made in gold or mutual funds as in virtual currencies or traditional currencies. What is transferred will be discussed in the section on settlement media and assets.

The main legal difference between traditional ledgers and decentralised blockchained ledgers is that traditional ledgers are always connected to one legal entity in charge of maintaining the ledger. Traditionally, all accounts are legally in the books of a given service provider, which is in charge of booking transfers and reconciling the ledger. A central bank is in charge of the accounts in its ledger, and a specific commercial bank is in charge of the accounts in its ledger. In traditional payment fund ledgers, there is therefore a need for a specific interbank settlement ledger in traditional payments systems, when cross-entity transfers are made between ledgers of different service providers. The traditional payment systems consist of a large network of individual centralised account ledgers connected via an inter-ledger settlement function in order to enable transfers between different ledgers. In a decentralised blockchained ledger, the accounts can be held by different legal entities and the overall reconciliation function is just a technical feature. For example, in the case of Bitcoin individual customer accounts are kept by the customers or their custodians. In the same way, the accounts of securities could be kept by custodians in the same decentralised, blockchained ledger reconciling the totals of issued securities. This decentralisation of accounts within a ledger brings a new structure to account keeping. Basically, blockchain technology provides a possibility to "flatten" old accounting hierarchies in line with "Internet-flatness" in other areas. An illuminating example could be that of current security accounts kept for each type of securities, where there are today several layers of custodians and sub-custodians under the issuing central securities depository, each having their own ledgers and an inter-custodian system for reconciling these security accounts. With blockchain technology this structure could be replaced by one common ledger for each type of security operating either at custodian level or even individual beneficial owner level. For example, shares of a given listed company would be accounted for in the same distributed general ledger. Buys, sells and other transfers would be made directly across those decentralised accounts.

All electronic payments need to be recorded on accounts, the accounts and transfers need to be reconciled, and also a transaction listing is needed. The production costs of account keeping is the same at the base level in both decentralised and centralised systems because the bookings will require the same kind of updates to data registers. However, as all individual accounts need to be connected for transfers among any pair of individual accounts, the blockchain technology brings a lower-cost solution for connecting individual accounts, which have previously been solved via hierarchical settlement systems.

8.3   The settlement media or asset

The settlement asset or media in traditional account-based payment systems are redeemable liabilities of the payment service provider, basically deposits with banks or other repayable liabilities of electronic money institutions and payment institutions (in EU jurisdictions) or possibly other payment service providers (in other jurisdictions). These redeemable liabilities are denominated in a traditional currency, generally the domestic currency. In traditional systems these liabilities are issued by the service provider, which keeps the centralised ledger of liabilities issued. When transfers are made within the same centralised ledger, that is, for example between deposit accounts of the same bank, the settlement asset will remain the same. When an interbank transfer is made, the settlement asset will be changed from the sending bank's liability to the receiving bank's liability. Although the transferred value, for example EUR 100, has the same currency value on both accounts, the entity liable for the value has changed from the payer's service provider to the payee's service provider. The payer and payee have claims on different banks. The identity of the liable will only become of interest in case of service providers' defaults, which may put these customer funds at risk, especially, when these claims have not been guaranteed by deposit insurance or other type of insurance or ring-fencing of customer funds.

If traditional currency-based liabilities were to be used in blockchain ledger solutions, it would require identifying whose liabilities would be used as the common settlement asset, that is, on which balance sheet these are recorded. One neutral alternative could in this case be central bank liabilities. This would basically create a public, government-provided e-money type of solution, which could replace current cash usage by maintaining many common elements with cash, for example the issuer and the legal tender status. Note that in blockchain technology the account keeping is decentralised, but the settlement media becomes common and centralised, while in traditional accounting the accounts are centralised, but the settlement media is individualised in an environment with several service providers.

Currently other assets than service providers' liabilities in traditional currencies are seldom used for ordinary electronic payments. However, because most securities are in book-entry format, these kinds of funds could also easily be used as settlement assets in electronic payments. This alternative is presented because, when using blockchain technology, it would be as easy to use ledger accounts backed by securities or commodities as settlement media as well as any virtual currency. A settlement media backed by securities or commodities would follow the exchange rates of that particular security or commodity or any constructed basket of securities or commodities. The blockchain technology provides thereby a possibility to return to an efficient use of commodity-based settlement assets. One interesting alternative could be a mutual fund type of arrangement based on highly liquid money market assets, which would provide market-based returns to the holders of the mutual fund assets, perhaps even on a continuous basis.

Current virtual currencies, Bitcoins and the like, are based on a new type of settlement media, which can be seen as perpetual, never redeemable and zero-interest bearing electronic bearer-bonds with a nominal value stated in a non-traditional currency. The virtual currency balances at nominal value are generally issued to the users by an undefined community of issuers, the so-called miners, based on the actual exchange rate at the point of issue. There is no liability to redeem the funds at any future point in time or to pay any interest on the funds by the issuers. There is neither any requirement for accepting virtual currencies as payments by merchants nor for settling private liabilities.

The decentralised blockchained book-entry system will record all owner-ships and transfers directly on the accounts of the owners and maintain an overall transaction database.

A large share of, especially, Bitcoins seems to be held as speculative investments because only a small share is used for daily payment operations (Raymaekers, 2015). These can be considered as highly speculative investments because there are no interest-based revenues. Speculative investments in non- or low-revenue securities will automatically end at some point, when investors need to cover their funding costs or they will find higher yields in more revenue-generating investments. Speculative bubbles have always burst at least eventually due to these reasons. It is easy to establish new virtual currencies and for traditional payment instruments to move to blockchain technology, which would imply that supply limitations currently resulting in "bubbling" prices will probably not exist in virtual currency types of investments or at least only for a rather short period.

Another comparison to paper-based instruments could be travellers' cheques issued by some private entity without any redeemability or any acceptance guarantees at any point in time. Customers and merchants would just be convinced that they can transfer the travellers' cheque at good value and as payment to some other person. However, traveller's cheques are generally issued in traditional currencies in order to be accepted in countries that are travelling destinations at good value and guaranteed repayment.

Cash currency (notes and coins) also provides no interest, but due to its legal tender position, it will always be accepted for payments by public authorities and by private persons and companies to the extent established in national legal tender requirements. These mandatory legal tender acceptance requirements vary across jurisdictions, from all kinds of private payments to some limited categories of payments like settling private liabilities. Cash is also redeemable because it can be changed to other settlement media, by citizens mostly to bank deposits. Banks are always able to return cash to central banks and change cash to central bank deposits. When cash in circulation decreases, central banks face a de-issuing process, which was momentarily rather large, for example, during the change-over process to euro (see cash statistics of ECB at http://sdw.ecb.europa.eu/browse.do?node=2745). Even in the future when cash usage will be substituted in large volumes by modern payment instruments, it will result in cash de-issuing. The legal tender requirement is a major difference between current virtual currencies and the cash type of fiat currency.

As the use and efficiency of blockchain technology is independent of the selected settlement asset, it will be interesting to observe the future market developments. Will the payers and payees at large be interested in using payment instruments as proposed by current virtual currency schemes, which do not generate any interest, do not contain any redeemability possibilities and come with unclear acceptance prospects? Will the competition among service providers bring other types of blockchain-based solutions on the market with improved customer settlement asset features and a more stable and reliable media of payment? One example of this kind of development is the Cuber/LHV Bank blockchain-based payment system in Estonia, which is based on redeemable funds in euros (see Cuber, 2015).

8.4   The currency unit of account for monetary liabilities

Generally a common currency has been introduced in most countries in order to establish a unit of account, a common measure for monetary transactions, for pricing goods and services and for payment purposes. The recent trend in the number of traditional currencies has been a decreasing one, due to common currency unions and some countries opting to use a foreign currency instead of creating their own. Some domestic currencies are also directly and strongly pegged to another foreign currency, which results basically in a national value variant of the underlying reference currency. Although the general economic outlook is today rather cloudy, the sustainable political reasoning behind common currency unions, for example the euro area, has been promoting growth and the expansion of common markets, both money and traditional markets, resulting in increased competition and improved employment of capital and other resources (see for example European Commission, 2008). Regarding payments, a single common payment area such as SEPA implies more efficient payment processing with lower transaction costs when the need for currency exchange disappears and the payment infrastructure is common and harmonised (ECB, 2013).

Although virtual currencies have been called currencies, probably mostly for marketing purposes, they lack some important elements of the traditional currencies. Firstly, virtual currencies are not legal tender, which can always be used for settling private liabilities, tax and other government payments. Secondly, merchant prices are primarily stated in traditional domestic currencies, and merchants convert these prices to virtual currencies by using actual exchange rates plus probably an allowance for exchange rate fluctuations and exchange costs.

The reason being that most merchants need to convert received virtual currencies to traditional currencies, in order for merchants to be able to pay their bills, salaries, etc. It would also be problematic and impractical to state prices in many different virtual currencies and update the price information constantly based on rapid intraday fluctuations. Thirdly, traditional currencies have a large secondary money market for different kinds of liabilities in traditional currencies. Although there exist some lending and borrowing based on some virtual currencies, virtual currencies operate more as book-entry securities with a limited amount of issued units. Thereby, virtual currencies cannot be considered to be fully fledged currencies, but more as non-redeemable payment assets with an individual exchange rate and value-determining function.

As virtual currencies are mainly used in Internet or in physical shops with Internet connections, the most probable pricing solution will be that basic prices are stated in a traditional currency and the prices in specific virtual currencies are stated upon customer requests based on the actual exchange rate during the moment of payment. The exchange rates of virtual currencies tend to be more volatile than traditional currencies, which will imply a considerable merchant currency exchange risk, when most of merchants' costs are dependent on traditional currencies. As virtual currencies operate without central banks or other entities with a goal of stabilising the value of the currency, the volatility of virtual currencies can be expected to be high even in the future. For example, the exchange rate fluctuations of Bitcoin have been very high over the years (Ali and Barrdear, 2014; Polasik *et al.*, 2015).

Virtual currencies resemble book-entry bonds as assets in that ownership rights giving title to the assets are recorded on accounts identifying the asset and owner. However, the exchange rates of traditional bonds depend mainly on the interest paid on the bonds in comparison to the general interest level and the trust in the issuers' possibilities for repayment at the due date, that is, the credit risk associated with the asset. Virtual currencies as assets carry no interest, and there is no due-date for repayment and no issuer to guarantee repayment. There is therefore a large credit risk for the investors, which will be materialised at least in the situation when a specific virtual currency will be abandoned by the users and replaced by a more advanced or for other reasons more preferred payment instrument. The interest in buying and accepting virtual currencies will therefore depend on the competition from other payment instruments, which will develop over the years, both regarding cost efficiency and asset value. All payment instruments will, at some point in time, be replaced by more efficient ones in the same way as the developments currently facing cheques and cash. Bonds with investment features like those of virtual currencies would probably be very difficult to place on traditional bond markets.

Virtual currencies resemble book-entry-based bonds also from their issuing policies. Virtual currencies have established different issuing policies, which determine the overall issued amount of particular virtual currencies; see for details in Table 8.1 on issuing policies.

A limited issuing policy is important because over-issuing is a guaranteed path towards a rapid fall in asset value. Virtual currencies therefore have some technical features in their algorithms, which control the issuing, both totals and yearly growth. In traditional bond issuing, the issuing limitations are controlled manually.

Virtual currency systems contain generally a technical maximum for the number of issued coins and a geometrically decreasing pattern for issuing of new coins. Table 8.1 shows the characteristics of some virtual currencies, which show clear differences in the total number of coins. Peercoin seems to follow a different issuing pattern compared to the other virtual currencies in the example. As pointed out already by early quantity-based monetary theorists (Fisher, 1911; Pigou, 1917), the use and value of money is also dependent on the circulation speed. In the 19th- and 20th-century cash environment, the circulation of cash was rather stable as different physical logistical limitations did set the circulation pattern. However, the Internet environment lacks circulation speed limitations as payments can be processed in microseconds. The low volume of Bitcoin transactions compared to issued Bitcoins points towards a possibility of a strongly fluctuating circulation speed over

Table 8.1 Examples of issuing policies by virtual currencies

Virtual currency	Issuing method	Growth pattern	Absolute maximum
Bitcoin	Algorithmic	Geometric	21 million coins
Litecoin	Algorithmic	Geometric	84 million coins
Namecoin	Algorithmic	Geometric	21 million coins
Dogecoin	Algorithmic	Geometric	100 billion coins
Peercoin	2 algorithms	1% infl. target	no technical limit

Source: Author's analysis.

time, if balances held for speculative purposes start to be used actively for payments.

In traditional currencies, the total volume of currency-based liabilities depends mostly on banking-sector developments. Banks can create more currency, euros and dollars held by customers, by providing credits to their customers, which will at the same time create more bank deposits to be used for payments (McLeay *et al.*, 2014). This has no direct relationship with the amount of "base money", that is, of physical currency printed by the central bank or the deposits maintained on central bank accounts. The amount of borrowing and lending, that is, demand and supply of money, is determined more by the general interest rate level and interest margins on traditional money markets. This kind of secondary market of money creation could and seems to grow also within virtual currencies. In the Bitcoin users community there seems to be an increasing supply of Bitcoin lending. Currently most Bitcoin safe-keeping providers can be categorised as custodians. However, some custodians could evolve to virtual currency deposit takers, which would reinvest the received Bitcoins and provide interest on deposited virtual currency funds (the difference between custodians and deposit takers is analysed more in detail in the section on infrastructures). The larger this secondary market of virtual currencies will become, the larger its impact will be on virtual currency exchange rates and the use of virtual currencies. The development could follow the pattern of traditional currencies, where the issued "real" Bitcoins would become base money and function as the liquidity needed for the secondary market of Bitcoin claims.

As there are a large number of virtual currencies on the market, these will compete for the total virtual currency demand. Technical developments, design issues, pricing policies, public and private regulations and supervision will most probably affect customers' interest in different virtual currencies and also in advanced traditional efficient payment instruments based on blockchain technology. The demand for a specific virtual currency can thereby change radically and rapidly, especially as there seems to be large speculative investments in virtual currencies.

The future will show how volatile exchange rates of virtual currencies will become without any institution acting as a stabiliser and without any real assets used for backing the virtual asset value, in addition to the lack of a repayment feature similar to traditional bonds. How important is it to establish an own currency for the employment of blockchain-based payment instruments, or could these operate also using some of the existing traditional currencies or using more trustworthy real asset backing?

8.5   The infrastructure of processing payment transactions

Traditional payment infrastructures have been of so-called three-party or four-party types and based on redeemable liabilities in traditional currencies as outlined in Figure 8.1 cases a) and b).

In a three-party infrastructure, for example PayPal, the payers and payees have accounts with the same payment service provider, which keeps an updated account database of each of its customers. It also keeps a transaction list of all transactions, but these listing are public only to the customers regarding their own transactions. The main problem with the three-party schemes is the need for payers and payees to use the same service provider, which limits user connectivity and results in monopoly structures or requires users to employ several parallel service providers in order to solve the connectivity problem and be able to make payments to any payee and receive payments from any payer. On the other hand, PayPal provides today global connectivity.

The traditional payment services provided by banks are operated in a four-party setup, in which the payers and payees can maintain accounts with different service providers and an interbank clearing and settlement system facilitate interbank transfer possibilities. The clearing and settlement systems together with common transaction processing standards will provide connectivity among all customers of all service providers in the common payment area established by the common clearing and settlement function. The SEPA region (Single Euro Payment Area) in Europe is an example of a large common cross-border connectivity area. However, in most cases clearing and settlement systems operate

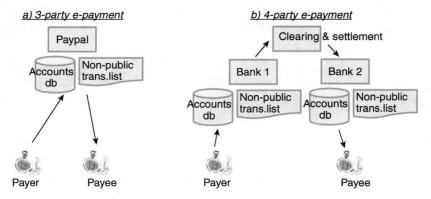

Figure 8.1   Traditional e-payment infrastructures

efficiently only on national levels. A basic problem in the current global Internet environment has therefore been to provide global connectivity for traditional payments. The international card schemes, mainly MasterCard and Visa, have been successful in providing global connectivity for card payments. However, in card payments payee services and payees are generally limited to merchants, and card payments cannot be used, for example, for consumer-to-consumer payments.

In these traditional e-payment systems, each service provider keeps accounts and transaction lists for each of its customers. The account information in traditional payment systems is not public, and service providers maintain strict access controls. Only customers themselves can access the account information and initiate payments. However, because payers must due to regulatory requirements (which are analysed in next section) know payees and each transaction must also contain payer information, payers and payees are generally known to each other. In these traditional setups the service users have a claim on the service provider in traditional currencies, which they need to redeem based on customer requests. Customers need to trust that the service providers can redeem the funds in the future. This is ensured via service provider regulation, supervision of service providers and in addition for consumer customers via deposit guarantee schemes (these elements will be analysed more in detail in next section).

Payment transactions could also be settled by using securities (bonds, mutual funds, owner certificates or shares) processed in a securities settlement system. This kind of infrastructure is sketched in Figure 8.2.

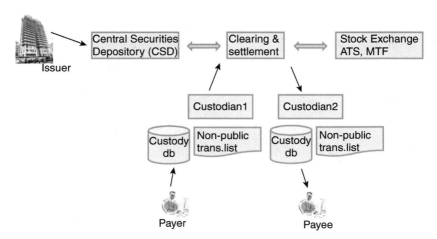

Figure 8.2   A payment infrastructure based on settlement of securities

Book-entry securities are issued by an issuer, which is liable for interest and dividend payments, repayments for bonds and different kinds of corporate actions in case of shares. The credit risk and other risks associated with the issuer will affect the value of individual securities. Different funds consisting of a portfolio of securities distribute the risks of individual securities, resulting in a less volatile exchange rate compared to individual securities. Book-entry securities are issued within a CSD (Central Securities Depository), which manages and reconciles the issued totals of securities, as these are for safe-keeping distributed to custodians. Customers will select one or several custodians to manage their investment portfolios. CSDs can also operate in three- or four-party mode as described above. However, there is a clear trend towards increasing links between CSDs resulting in four-party setups. This is also a requirement for CSDs operating in the EU based on the EU Regulation on Central Securities Depositories (EU 909/2014).

The value of each individual security is determined on the market based on trading using different trading platforms, that is, exchanges, alternative trading systems (ATSs) or multilateral trading facilities (MTFs). As these operate in real time supporting high-frequency trading, users can rapidly change the content of their portfolios. This provides also the possibility to use securities in the future as payment instruments, especially in infrastructures with immediate delivery. The payers would make payments out of their portfolios, and the payees would receive payments in securities converted by the trading platforms according to their portfolio requirements. Traditional payment systems are limited to the deposit type of redeemable liabilities of the service providers. Securities settlement-based systems can broaden the assets available for settling payments, especially when blockchain technology is employed.

The infrastructure of securities settlement-based infrastructure was described above as it resembles on many elements in the infrastructure of virtual currencies as can be seen from Figure 8.3.

Figure 8.3 uses Bitcoin as a general example of virtual currencies because several of them are basically copies of the Bitcoin structure. The issuers of virtual currencies are called miners (originally a comparison with mining gold). In Bitcoin and alike the issuing is performed based on solving a crypto-algorithmic challenge and which is used to provide a degressive issuing growth ending a maximum amount of issued coins (see for details ECB, 2012). There are also other possible solutions for establishing a given set of numbered coins and desired growth over years, which would require less computer power than that of Bitcoin. The miners have an important task in the infrastructure when they

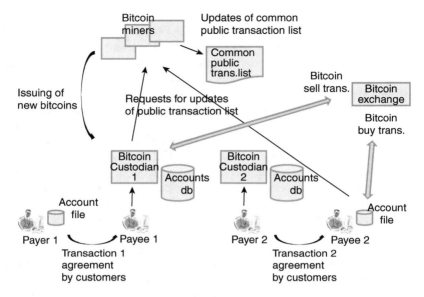

Figure 8.3   The payment infrastructure of virtual currencies

reconcile the total amount of Bitcoins in circulation by updating a common transaction list and ensuring that no Bitcoin balance is used twice, the so-called double spending control. Thereby, compared to the securities settlement infrastructure, the miners perform a combination of some of the tasks of issuers and CSDs. The payees need to make a request to the miners to include the Bitcoins they have received in the public transaction list in order to ensure that they get title to the funds and are able to use the received Bitcoins. If there were a double spending situation, the miners would accept the transaction presented first and discard any additional later transactions.

The Bitcoin balances can be kept by the users themselves or by Bitcoin custodians. It is highly important that the access to the Bitcoin account balances are strongly protected, as otherwise it will be easy for e-criminals to steal the Bitcoins from the current owners with a very small probability to be identified and prosecuted. E-criminals could for example use Trojan horse-type malware, which will register the private keys used by the owners for later abuse by the e-criminal. The Bitcoin account addresses are based on pseudonyms and will not reveal the identity of their users as such. An e-criminal would use a given pseudonym only once or for a short period, before withdrawing in cash the stolen Bitcoins at a Bitcoin automat or use a non-traceable Bitcoin exchange transaction for removing any trace to the final destination of the funds. The users must also protect their Bitcoin files and associated passwords physically because, if these are destroyed, they cannot be recreated in the Bitcoin setup. Although the public transaction lists would make it possible to calculate specific account balances, the current Bitcoin structure will not allow recreating destroyed transaction balances due to customer identification problems.

The pseudonyms in use can protect customer identity to some extent, but because some payees and payers will be able based on their bilateral transactions and relationships to learn each other's pseudonyms, these will not provide complete anonymity. Because the transaction list is public, it will be possible to find out all transactions made by one pseudonym. This provides additional possibilities to analyse payment patterns of known and unknown pseudonyms. In order to hide customer identities more thoroughly, the customers themselves and custodian employed by them can disguise transactions behind a layer of other and even one-time-only pseudonyms.

Because most consumers lack the ICT knowledge for maintaining secure Bitcoin storage, they will need a custodian-type service provider for safekeeping their funds. Users would at least need to have very safe back-up systems for technical defaults, safe access controls against e-criminals and secure storage for their private encryption keys. It is then highly important that these custodians employ strong access controls so that only the rightful owners can access these custodian accounts. As the number of Bitcoin users has increased, also the custodian services for Bitcoins have increased.

There seems also to be a trend towards deposit taking service providers in virtual currencies, which are ready to provide account maintenance services to users, against a reduction of custodian charges or even positive interest given that customers agree to keep the funds untouched for a longer period, for example 12 months. Depositing customers provide the right to reinvest these finds, which means that the service provider can reinvest these funds, for example, for 12 months without a liquidity risk. This kind of service is very close to what is consider deposit taking of traditional currencies. However, there is currently generally no deposit insurance or reserves, which would guarantee deposited funds against different kinds of credit risks.

When customers use custodians or deposit takers, the infrastructure of virtual currencies starts to become very similar to infrastructures of traditional securities settlement and payment systems. The blockchain technology is then just employed among service providers and produces a secured, decentralised settlement layer for real-time payments among these account service providers. This has been seen as an important development in order to provide real-time payments in a large payment area (Leinonen *et al.*, 2002). This kind of developments would probably both increase the technical security and user interface convenience in virtual currencies.

Virtual currency exchanges are specialised in trading specific virtual currencies to and from traditional currencies. This is mostly done using traditional card payments or credit transfers for the cash leg. These virtual currency exchanges have exactly the same tasks for determining the exchange rates for virtual currencies against traditional currencies as traditional securities exchanges have for different kinds of securities.

Although it is often stated that Bitcoin users would be able to make transactions directly between them without any third parties, this is not true. They need to rely on the miners regarding confirmation and acceptance of transactions to secure their funds. Most consumers would also use Bitcoin custodians or deposit takers to safeguard their assets, which can be compared with the securities custodians or banks. The blockchain technology differs partly from the traditional account keeping methodology, but basically the same elements are found in both technologies, and the users need to have trust in the infrastructural service providers.

Although it is often stated that Bitcoin users would be able to make transactions without costs, this is not true either. Miners will have costs in maintaining the public transaction list and confirming transactions as well as in mining for Bitcoins in order to issue more coins. The technical crypto-algorithmic structure of Bitcoin has been considered to be highly resource consuming compared to solutions used by other virtual currencies, for example Litecoin and Ripple. The computer resources needed by Bitcoin miners will grow exponentially over the years when the network of Bitcoin addresses grows (Ali and Barrdear, 2014). The miners are also charging for their services, currently 0.0005 Bitcoins (which equals EUR 0.10 at an exchange rate of 200 for Bitcoins) for each confirmed transaction. The charges of miners need to grow in the future, when the computing resource need grows and the revenues from Bitcoin issuing decrease due to fewer newly issued Bitcoins. The Bitcoin custodians charge for their custody services, for example, in the case of Easywallet 1% monthly interest plus 0.9% per transaction with a limited safekeeping guarantee for the users (see Easywallet, 2015). The virtual currency exchanges will also charge trading fees in the same way as traditional exchanges. The fees of virtual currency exchanges vary between 0.1% and 0.6%, with some smaller free exchanges (Bitcoin-exchange-costs, 2015). These figures point to rather high customer charges for using Bitcoins, even higher than for low-cost traditional e-payments. This might be due to the high level of speculative investments in Bitcoins, the rather low level of real payment use and limited service provider competition.

Comparing the true social costs (real total production costs without internal cost transfers among infrastructural entities) of traditional and virtual currency payments will be difficult as it has proved to me very difficult already within traditional payments (Schmiedel *et al.*, 2012; Norges Bank, 2014). The true social costs are non-transparent and difficult to extract from service providers' and users' cost accounting systems. However, as the future points towards immediate processing of all e-payment transactions somewhere in the "Internet cloud", this implies the same relative cost tag for employed resources for similar accounting services, and it will be difficult to find any major cost differences between these technologies. For example, custodians will have the same custodian system costs irrespective of the assets maintained on custody accounts. Miners' services resemble those of CSDs and issuers. The overall costs will also depend on the regulatory requirements and the establishment of a level playing field between new and traditional payment instruments from a regulatory point of view.

The transaction confirmation process maintained by virtual currencies is rather slow. Bitcoin transactions are processed at minimum with a delay of 10 minutes, but this can be prolonged during rush hours to 60 minutes, while Ripple can confirm transactions in some seconds and Litecoin in 1–2 minutes. This makes current virtual currencies difficult to use for payments at points of sale requiring fast cashier services. Paying with virtual currencies using payers' own data files will require that payers carry with them laptops, tablets, etc., capable of running the virtual currency user software. This will limit the payment situations in which virtual currencies can be used conveniently. Traditional payments can be rapid, global and rather low cost as shown by cash withdrawal services at ATMs and online card purchases. It is thereby completely feasible for traditional payment service providers to establish service with world-wide connectivity and with delivery speed in some seconds already using traditional accounting methodology.

Another increasingly important service of the payment infrastructure is its possibility to transmit remittance information associated with the payment for the use of the payees and payers. For example, payees need to reconcile their receivables based on received payments, which requires some reference info for linking payments and corresponding invoices. The initial virtual currency designs lack this kind of transfer possibilities of remittance information.

Global Internet services point towards increased direct payment user connections and a flat organisational structure, which can be used to establish simplified global infrastructures for basic payments. These developments are to a large extent dependent on competition and other regulatory issues which will be discussed in the next section.

8.6   Private and public regulation and supervision

Payment systems are governed by private and public regulations and supervision. Service providers agree generally among themselves on technical operational rules and standards facilitating payment processing, for example the EPC (European Payments Council, 2015) in the EU, NACHA (NACHA, 2015) in the US and SWIFT (SWIFT, 2015) for international transfers. Private players may also agree on supervisory functions and different kinds of statistics in order to ensure that participating parties follow agreed-upon rules. Public regulations are implemented via legal measures with the objective to ensure that payment systems operate according to the needs of consumers and other citizens and that the systems are beneficial or at least not detrimental from a general social point of view. Public supervisory bodies and procedures are created in order to ensure that available payment services are operated according to regulations. Current payment systems are thereby governed by a combination of private and public regulations and supervision. Because all payment systems constitute a network of numerous counterparties, regulations are needed in order for the systems to operate in a reliable and expected way. History has clearly proved that payment and banking systems need to be regulated and supervised in order to achieve a necessary level of both stability and efficiency. History has also shown that it is difficult to find the best balanced level of regulation and supervision as concerns about over-regulation are voiced during "good" times and concerns about under-regulation become topical in times of crisis. However, the purpose of regulations is to benefit the society and economy as a whole.

Typical private regulations in both the case of virtual currencies and traditional payment services have been transaction processing standards, although some have been set by authorities in the SEPA-area. The Bitcoin open source applications and corresponding standards have been developed by private interested parties.

It is important to avoid regulatory arbitrage across systems and instruments, which would imply that for different payment instruments, service providers or users would be regulated differently concerning the same type of issues. This requires that current regulations and supervisory processes should be automatically implemented on any new payment instruments, service providers or users on the market. Regarding virtual currencies, authorities have found it partly difficult to decide on the correct policy stance because virtual currencies differ on several points from traditional payment systems and there have been difficulties in determining how to define virtual currencies. On the other hand, it should not be possible for new or current service providers to circumvent regulations and supervision just by employing a new form of account technology. Efficient regulations should be independent of technical details. Although the service providers in the virtual currency environment are identified by new terms, they provide similar types of services, which are common for any kind of payment system.

A functional definition of virtual currencies is needed as the basis for regulatory policies. Based on the previous analysis, a functional definition would be that these are electronically recorded financial assets resembling bearer-bonds that are traded on exchanges with a nominal value stated in a virtual currency and which are developed to be used also as electronic payment instruments. If virtual currencies are defined in this way, current regulations should be extended to virtual currencies along the following policy lines:

1. Every issuer of the first instance of a virtual currency, basically every miner, needs to be identified, and these issuers need to inform the investors and users of virtual currencies of the basic features of the underlying bearer bond-type of assets, for example non-interest bearing, perpetual non-redeemable liability and acceptability limitations and uncertainties regarding the voluntary basis of infrastructural setup. These financial assets need to be issued within a CSD or a network of CSDs.
2. As miners also maintain specialised CSD services and settlement facilities for the transfer operations for these bearer bonds, the miners should operate based on CSD licenses in line with those for other book-entry securities.
3. The virtual currency exchanges maintain specialised trading platforms for one or several virtual currencies, for which they would need a trading platform license in the same way as other comparable trading platforms.

4. When a service provider offers safekeeping services for securities without these funds becoming a part of the service providers' balance sheet, it constitutes custodian services, which require a corresponding license.

5. When a service provider receives virtual currencies from the general public in deposit mode and it becomes a liability on the service providers' balance sheet and the service provider may reinvest these funds, the reception of virtual currencies become comparable to deposit taking, which requires a banking license. There should not be any regulatory difference if the funds received are based on traditional currencies or new virtual currencies.

The objective of these licensing requirements and related supervisory arrangements is to ensure that users' rights are honoured and that the infrastructure has a long-term solid basis and that users' potential losses are minimised, for example, due to insufficient security and access controls, criminal abuse of funds, bad management, manipulation of exchange rates, discrimination of user groups, etc.

Consumers' assets need to be protected at an acceptable level regarding both custody and deposit type balances. Custodians and deposit takers need to be able to refund their customers for different types of losses due to errors, mistakes, etc., in custody and deposit services. In the current Bitcoin setup, but probably also in most of the other virtual currency setups, users will lose their funds in the case of physical destruction of funds or if passwords are forgotten. As it is technically possible to recreate such balances using the public transaction list, it could be seen as a basic requirement for virtual currencies to provide recreation facilities in order to increase consumer protection.

Ensuring sufficient competition is important in regulated industries in order to ensure efficient services. Individual virtual currencies compete as payment services both with other virtual currencies and traditional payment instruments. However, the charges of the mining services show cartel-type constructions, which are inconsistent with current competition legislation. The miners, for example, in the Bitcoin community charge 0.0005 Bitcoins for confirming Bitcoin transactions. As all miners maintain the same charge, this seems to be cartel-type price-fixing among service providers, which limits competition. It would be important from a competition point of view to find a charging solution open for competition. Currently miners receive considerable revenues based on issuing new Bitcoins, for which they can keep the total issuing price. However, as the number of issued Bitcoins comes closer to the total to be issued (current situation is about 67% of the overall total), this revenue stream will disappear, and miners will need to rely completely on transaction charges. This will increase the transparency of Bitcoin costs, and increased cost-transparency would be important already now. It will also imply changes to the business model of Bitcoin (Ali and Barrdear, 2014).

The payment and financial industry in general has during the past decades been required to implement anti-money laundering, tax-evasion restraining, counter-terrorism funding and know-your-client procedures. All of these are in the interest of the society and citizens. Without these requirements, taxation would become more skewed due to increased tax evasion and terrorism, and criminality would increase, which would have a negative impact on the general public. E-criminals are less interested in payment instruments which are based on traceable transactions. Therefore, regulations require that the payers and payees in traditional payment systems are identified in line with know-your-customer demands, which reduce, for example, different kinds of money-related robberies. Europol has identified major risks related to criminal usage of anonymous or pseudonymous virtual currency transfers (Europol, 2015, pp. 30–31). From the society's point of view it would be important to extend this requirement also to virtual currencies, which are currently based on unidentified pseudonyms. Current payment solutions have been criticised for revealing too much information about their users. One balanced alternative could be that all payment accounts, traditional and virtual currency-based, would need to be registered by authorities. Payments made with such instruments would just reveal a plain pseudonym or register identifier, which authorities could use when tracking criminal payments, etc. This could be compared to the register plates on cars, which are essential in reducing car thefts, hit-and-run accidents, etc. This kind of solution would maintain sufficient anonymity, but provide also sufficient traceability with very limited impact on daily transaction processing. This could be enforced by forbidding citizens, especially merchants, from making virtual currency transactions with non-registered counterparties.

This kind of regulatory policy would be in contradiction with many of the political ideas behind current virtual currencies. The general stance in regulations has been that all service providers need to follow the same minimum regulatory requirements in order to ensure safe and trustworthy services. This can be compared to other transportation services, for example flights and sea vessels, that all service providers need to fulfil the same minimum safety and other requirements. Most industries, including healthcare, food production, etc., are regulated, and all service providers follow common industry rules. The basic question regarding virtual currencies is therefore to what extent they should follow the common regulations for the payment industry.

8.7 Development alternatives

Payment developments have generally been very slow, that is, customers have been rather reluctant to move to new payment instruments. One important reason is most probably the employed hidden price mechanisms characteristic both for traditional and modern payment instruments (Leinonen, 2008, pp. 136–146). Customers cannot observe cost differences and are therefore happy to continue the use of costly instruments such as cheques and high-value notes. All new payment instruments including virtual currencies face the same problem of non-transparent pricing.

Blockchain technology is just a new type of accounting methodology, which can be used by all kinds of service providers and payment systems. As pointed out in the section on infrastructures, applying blockchain technology to inter-custodian or inter-bank transfers would result in an efficient settlement mechanism, which could be used both in virtual currency and traditional systems.

Virtual currencies solutions lack connectivity among each other and advanced remittance information features. However, they provide world-wide reach based on common standards for almost immediate payments, which provide them with a competitive edge over traditional credit transfers operating basically on the regional level. In order for traditional payments, basically credit transfers, to match the international services of virtual currencies, banks need to introduce instant credit transfers on a global basis. This may sound like a very challenging task, but banks have already back in 1990s implemented automated teller machine services, which provide instant cash withdrawals world-wide in real time 24/7, that is, most debit card customers can withdraw cash in real time from their bank accounts anywhere in the world. A world-wide instant credit transfers solution could be based on IBAN-account numbers, ISO 20022 transaction formats and a blockchain settlement system operating in a payment network, for example SWIFT. Basically all of these building blocks are already in place within the SWIFT community, but it operates at slower speed and higher overhead due to legacy burdens.

Regulators will be in a central role in deciding on regulations to govern new payment solutions in order to find a balanced policy stance among different alternatives from a social point of view. Regulators' decisions can both promote and bar new and efficient developments. It is essential in order to balance the risks that all payment services are governed by the same kind of regulation and supervision. As future payment systems and virtual currencies are already now truly global systems, the regulators and supervisors will need to cooperate strongly and coordinate their actions globally. Internet has provided global markets and connections for which citizens need global payment solutions. Regulators and supervisors need to ensure that these solutions are stable, trustworthy and efficient also in cross-border contexts when different transaction parties and service providers operate in different jurisdictions.

8.8 Conclusions

Virtual currencies and traditional payment instruments consist of the same basic elements. In order to gain and maintain the long-term trust of their users, all payment instruments need to be based on trustworthy and efficient solutions for these basic elements: accounting methodology, settlement asset, currency, infrastructure and regulatory setup.

Based on the analysis in this chapter, blockchain technology has the potential to provide a secure, decentralised payment and settlement network operating in real time 24/7, which is important in the future dominant digital Internet- and cloud-based payment environment. However, virtual currencies (as non-interest bearing perpetual bearer bonds without real asset backing) seem to be a rather weak settlement media with major exchange rate risks and credit risks to their users. Users will probably have more trust in payment instruments based on backing in real securities or with legal tender support. There seems to be a rather clear trend towards a reduced number of traditional currencies, and it is difficult to foresee why the single global digital Internet market would benefit from a large number of competing virtual currencies. The infrastructural parties in virtual currency-based and traditional payment systems are basically the same, although the accounting method is different, which implies that current service providers should have a good competition possibility if/when they employ efficiently the same modern technology as virtual currencies. Regulators will face two major challenges: firstly, how to extend current regulation policies to the infrastructures and processes of virtual currencies, while still maintaining a level playing field among new and old service providers, and secondly, how to achieve global regulatory coordination for open global payment systems and instruments. Payment services will at some point shift to

24/7 real-time services, and blockchain technology may have a specific role in such developments.

Bibliography

Ali, R. and Barrdear, J. 2014. "The economics of digital currencies", *Quarterly Bulletin*, Bank of England, 2014 Q3.

Bitcoin. 2015. www.bitcoin.org as per 15 June 2015.

Bitcoin-exchange-costs. 2015. https://en.bitcoin.it/wiki/Comparison_of_real-time_trading_exchanges as per 15 June 2015.

Chromaway. 2015. www.chromaway.com as per 15 June 2015.

Cryptocoincharts. 2015. www.cryptocoincharts.info/coins/info as per 15 June 2015.

Cuber. 2015. www.cuber.ee as per 15 June 2015.

Easywallet. 2015. www.easywallet.org as per 15 June 2015.

European Banking Authority (EBA). 2014. Opinion on virtual currencies. 4 July 2014.

European Central Bank (ECB). 2012. Virtual currencies, October 2012.

European Central Bank (ECB). 2013. Second SEPA migration report, October 2013.

European Central Bank (ECB). 2015. Virtual currency schemes – a further analysis, February 2015.

European Commission. 2008. EMU@10: Successes and challenges after ten years of Economic and Monetary Union, 2/2008.

European Payments Council (EPC), 2015. www.europeanpaymentscouncil.eu as per 22 June 2015.

Europol. 2015. Exploring tomorrow's organized crime, European Police Office, 2015.

Harvey, C.R. 2015. "Don't judge Bitcoin by its early inevitable problems", *Wall Street Journal*, 1 March 2015, http://www.wsj.com/articles/do-cryptocurrencies-such-as-bitcoin-have-a-future-1425269375 as per 22 June 2015.

Fisher, I. 1911. *The Purchasing Power of Money* (revised edn 1911). Macmillan, New York, 1922.

Leinonen, H. 2008. Payment Habits and trends in the changing e-landscape 2010+, *Bank of Finland Expository Studies* A:111, 2008.

Leinonen, H., Lumiala, V.-M. and Sarlin, R. 2002. "Settlement in modern network-based payment infrastructures – description and prototype of the E-Settlement model", *Bank of Finland Discussion Proposal Series*, No. 23.

Litecoin. 2015. www.litecoin.org as per 15 June 2015.

McLeay, M., Radia, A. and Thomas, R. 2014. "Money creation in the modern economy", *Quarterly Bulletin*, Bank of England, 2014 Q1.

NACHA. 2015. www.nacha.org as per 15 June 2015.

Nakamoto, S. 2008. "Bitcoin: A peer-to-peer electronic cash system", *Consulted*, Vol. 1, No. 2012, 28.

Norges Bank. 2014. Costs in Norwegian payment systems. *Papers*, No. 5.

PayPal. 2015. www.paypal.com as per 15 June 2015.

Peercoin. 2015. www.peercoin.net as per 15 June 2015.

Pigou, A.C. 1917. "The value of money", *The Quarterly Journal of Economics*, Vol. 32, No. 1 (Nov., 1917), pp. 38–65

Polasik, M., Piotrowska, A., Wisniewski, T., Kotkowski, R. and Lightfoot, G. 2015. "Price fluctuations and the use of Bitcoin: An empirical inquiry." Paper presented at ECB's and Bank of Finland's joint conference on retail payments in June 2015.

Raymaekers, W. 2015. "Cryptocurrency Bitcoin: Disruption, challenges and opportunities", *Journal of Payments Strategy & Systems*, Vol. 9, No. 1, pp. 30–40.

Ripple. 2015. www.ripple.com as per 15 June 2015.

Schmiedel, H., Kostova, G. and Ruttenberg, W. 2012. "The social and private costs of retail payment instruments – A European perspective." *ECB Occasional Paper Series*, No. 137/September 2012.

Segendorf, B. 2014. "What is Bitcoin?" *Sveriges Riksbank Economic Review*, Vol. 2014, No. 2, pp. 71–87.

SWIFT. 2015. www.swift.com as per 22 June 2015.

Tymoigne, E. 2015. "As a currency, Bitcoin violates all the rules of finance", *Wall Street Journal*, 1 March 2015, http://www.wsj.com/articles/do-cryptocurrencies-such-as-bitcoin-have-a-future-1425269375 as per 22 June 2015.

Index